ABORIGINAL ISSUES TODAY
A legal and business guide

edited by
Stephen B. Smart, LL.B.
Michael Coyle, LL.B.

Self-Counsel Press
(a division of)
International Self-Counsel Press Ltd.
Canada U.S.A.

Printed in Canada
First edition: January 1997

Canadian Cataloguing in Publication Data
Main entry under title:
    Aboriginal issues today
    Includes index

    (Self-counsel series)
    ISBN 1-55180-035-7

        1. Native peoples — Canada — Legal status, laws, etc.*
    I. Smart, Stephen B. (Stephen Beverley), 1944- II. Coyle, Michael, 1960-
    III. Series.
    KE7709.2.A26 1996   342.71'0872   C96-910717-X
    KF205.Z9A26 1996

The excerpt from Secrets from the Center of the World, by Joy Harjo and Stephen
Strom, published by the University of Arizona Press (1989), is used by permission of
the University of Arizona Press.

Graphics in "First Nations and Taxation" used by permission of the Indian
Taxation Advisory Board.

Excerpts from The North, Michael S. Whittington, ed., reproduced with the
permission of the Minister of Public Works and Government Services Canada, 1996.
Source: Privy Council Office.

Map on pp. 242 and 243 is a portion of "Comprehensive Land Claims in Canada"
(revised June 1992) and is reproduced with the permission of the Minister of Supply
and Services Canada, 1996. Source: Indian and Northern Affairs Canada.

Self-Counsel Press
(a division of)
International Self-Counsel Press Ltd.

Head and Editorial Office	U.S. Address
1481 Charlotte Road	1704 N. State Street
North Vancouver, BC V7J 1H1	Bellingham, WA 98225

NOTICE TO READERS

CONTENTS

FIGURES

FOREWORD

by Justice Harry S. LaForme

All landscapes have a history, much the same
as people exist within cultures, even tribes.
There are distinct voices, languages that be-
long to particular areas. There are voices inside rocks, shallow washes, shifting skies;
they are not silent. And there is movement,
not always the violent motion of earthquake
associated with the earth's motion or the
steady unseen swirl through the heavens, but
other motion, subtle unseen, like breathing.
A motion, a sound, that if you allow your
inner workings to stop long enough, moves
into places inside you that mirror a similar
landscape; you too can see it, feel it, hear it,
know it.

Joy Harjo and Stephen Strom,
Secrets of the World

"Aboriginal issues and the law." When I was first informed
that a book about this was in the works and was to be a
practical guide to Aboriginal law and business, it inspired me
to hearken back over my professional career, indeed, over my
life. I was curious as to whether history had provided sufficient material for such a book and, if so, whether the public
was either interested in, or in need of, one. My immediate
thought was, "How could this be, since the area of study of
Aboriginal law just recently started?" or so it seemed and felt
to me. I had to ask myself, "Could we have possibly moved
so far, so quickly, that we are now capable of writing books
on this subject?"

My first incursion into the arena of Aboriginal issues was as the executive director of the Association of Iroquois and Allied Indians. At that time, Aboriginal issues were referred to as "Native rights." The term "First Nations" was, if anything, nothing more than a thought someone might have had but dared not articulate. Indians had membership in bands which were then, and continue to be, defined by the Indian Act. Every aspect of an Indian's life was literally governed and regulated by that 17th-century paternalistic composition of British colonial legislation. For example, the Indian Act, S.C. 1884, c. 27, stated that —

> Every Indian or other person who engages in or assists in celebrating the Indian festival known as the "Potlatch" or in the Indian dance known as the "Tamanawas" is guilty of a misdemeanour, and shall be liable to imprisonment for a term of not more than six nor less than two months in any gaol or other place of confinement.

Indians were designated as either status or non-status, a designation which continues to some extent to this day; the present day Indian Act also continues to distinguish between "persons" and "Indians." "Eskimos" were just then being properly identified as "Inuit," and "Métis" was an historical term used to describe the exploits of Louis Riel. "Self-government," as it related to Aboriginal people, wasn't a commonly used term and "sovereignty" was an expression reserved, even then, for Québec.

It was 1970 and Indians were organizing from coast to coast to stop the Liberal government of Pierre Elliott Trudeau from implementing its Indian assimilation policy known as the White Paper. Many will no doubt recall that the White Paper was a federal Liberal government initiative formulated and authored by Minister of Indian Affairs, Jean Chrétien.

Aboriginal issues in the seventies were mostly political; there were very few legal issues. That is to say, few of the issues were the subject of litigation or, for that matter, of education and academics. The few instances of litigation that *did* occur (*Drybones* and *Lavell*, for example) signalled that Indians were adamant in their desire to remain unique in Canada, with a separate status and had no desire to fully assimilate into mainstream Canadian society. Such cases have influenced many recent and current court challenges.

For the most part, however, issues were hammered away at in the boardrooms of Ottawa and in the chambers of band councils, not in the courts. Aboriginal people didn't go to law school, nor was the subject of Aboriginal people addressed in any meaningful way in classrooms. Indeed, in 1973, there were only five Aboriginal lawyers in Canada. The issues were dealt with through the mutual exchange of rhetoric and constant political posturing.

Johnny Yesno, host of the CBC radio program "Our Native Land" at the time, was inspired to say that, "if an airplane were to fall from the sky, it was a sure bet that on board would be an Indian with an attaché case either going to or coming from a conference." This climate and approach were brought about in part by the attention to Aboriginal issues the American Indian Movement (AIM), a radical Indian paramilitary group, had aroused in the United States (after a shoot-out with the FBI in South Dakota) and, to a lesser degree, in Canada (some may recall Anicinabe Park in Kenora). AIM's approach demonstrated the potential for violent confrontation over Aboriginal issues, and, I believe, significantly contributed to Canadian governments' willingness to negotiate the concerns of Aboriginal people. However, that approach began to change in the mid to late seventies.

Two events occurred in 1973 which, in my view, changed dramatically the scope of Aboriginal issues in Canada and the approach taken toward their resolution. First, Professor Roger Carter, then Dean of the Faculty of Law at the University of Saskatchewan, established the Program of Legal Studies for

Native People (Native Law Program). Second, there was the Supreme Court of Canada's decision in *Calder v. Attorney General of British Columbia*. The combined effect of these two events, I'm convinced, contributed enormously to the alteration of the future course of Canada and recent history as we know it.

At the time Professor Carter began the Native Law Program, as well as there being only five Aboriginal lawyers in the entire country, there were virtually no legal texts and only limited publications on Aboriginal issues in Canada. Professor Douglas Sanders of the Native Law Program's summer program had written several articles and produced a textbook exclusively on Aboriginal issues for the Native Law Program. Justice Kenneth Lysyk had, to a lesser extent, written on the subject, and Justice Peter Cumming and Neil H. Mickenberg had published *Native Rights in Canada*.

For the most part, these academics were considered to be the experts in the field of Aboriginal law and their writings and publications made up virtually the entirety of the national library on Canadian Aboriginal legal issues. The law that we as law students studied consisted mainly of the Canadian case of *St. Catharine's Milling* and U.S. cases such as *Worcester v. Georgia* and *Johnson v. McIntosh*. These cases, together with an array of cases testing the limits of provincial jurisdiction over Indians and reserves under section 88 of the Indian Act were, for the most part, the extent of the legal authority that existed at the time.

As a result of Professor Carter's program, Aboriginal people were finally being encouraged to attend law school, and many did. Today, Aboriginal law graduates number in the hundreds. Many practise in the area of Aboriginal rights, while many others teach Aboriginal law courses in law schools across the country. Virtually all of these graduates write on Aboriginal issues and all have contributed to the reshaping of Canadian contemporary history.

Aboriginal land claims, as we now know and approach them, emerged to the greatest extent from the decision in *Calder*. In this case, the Supreme Court of Canada addressed the issue of whether or not Aboriginal people in Canada had any legally enforceable Aboriginal title to land. Three of the justices said yes, three said no, and the last dismissed the claim on a legal technicality. While the net effect of the decision in *Calder* was that there was no majority decision of the court, it nonetheless profoundly influenced the attitude of the federal government. The federal government took the view that Aboriginal people did indeed have some form of legal interest in land and determined that the most appropriate approach to resolving this issue was through negotiation with Aboriginal people.

Since 1973, a veritable industry has grown out of the federal government's recognition of Aboriginal land claims and the coincident need to resolve the historical and legal wrongs such claims represent. Land claims require negotiation which in turn require specialists, particularly persons versed in law. Much creative thought, vast sums of money, and volumes of literature have spun out of the pursuit to resolve Aboriginal land claims. Unfortunately, the issue and attempted resolution of land claims have also resulted in continuous conflict and, regrettably, all-too-frequent tragedy. Can any of us ever forget Oka?

The next significant chapter in the evolution of the awakening to Aboriginal issues in Canada came with "repatriation" of Canada's Constitution in 1982. "Repatriate" was the term Prime Minister Trudeau and his government commonly used to describe the process Canada had undertaken to amend the British North America Act, incorporate into it a charter of rights and freedoms, and remove Great Britain's jurisdiction over Canada's constitution.

Treaty rights, Aboriginal self-government, and land claims took on an entirely new gloss. No longer were these issues merely topics for gratuitous negotiation or subjects simply for academic discussion and study. The dam had been broken. Aboriginal people, as well as the vast majority of Canadians, were realizing that Aboriginal people occupied a unique place in Canadian history and in current society. Their grievances and aspirations could no longer be ignored; they had to be addressed and proper vehicles to do so needed to be found. Some matters achieved recognition and attention through the courts while others pursued a course of perilous confrontation (as at Gustafsen Lake, B.C.) and outright violence (as at Oka, Québec, and, more recently, at Camp Ipperwash, Ontario).

I am truly amazed when I look back over the past 25 years to see how advanced and complex Aboriginal issues and their study have become. Literature examining every aspect of land claims and related subjects has been and continues to be produced, while the varied approaches to Aboriginal issues, together with their successes and failures, have been recorded.

The question of whether the actions of professionals over the past 25 years have directly affected the lives of Aboriginal people is open to debate. Certainly, many Aboriginal and non-Aboriginal people would say nothing has changed for the better. Others, such as myself, would argue that the last 25 years have merely laid the foundation for Aboriginal prerogative and self-determination. Still others would argue that the implementation of the White Paper policy continues and is now merely being pursued in a more subtle fashion. Further, they would contend that the law, the professionals, and some Aboriginal people themselves are leading the parade toward the ultimate assimilation of Aboriginal people.

I am of the cautious opinion that now the foundation for Aboriginal self-determination exists, and everyone can and should get on with the task of building on the foundation.

This book, in my view, illustrates much of the content and many of the components of that foundation.

Twenty short years ago, my library on Aboriginal issues barely filled up half of a shelf in my bookcase. Today I'm constantly looking for more space in that bookcase for my latest acquisition. The past two and one-half decades have been thrilling and heart-stopping in their content and the pace at which Aboriginal issues have become such a necessary component of Canadian society. Any university law school not teaching Aboriginal issues cannot boast of being one of the best law schools. Law firms that do not have a lawyer capable of addressing Aboriginal issues must surely realize they are missing out on one of the most dynamic, challenging, and satisfying areas of law now practised in this country. Finally, anyone unaware of Aboriginal issues and their evolution cannot say they know either the true history of Canada or the legitimate aspirations and desires of Aboriginal people. They are missing an indisputably vital piece of Canadian history and will be blind to the exciting future as it unfolds.

The vast majority of the literature that documents and comments on the evolution of Aboriginal issues over the past several decades has been legal and academic in nature. This book brings to the reader a commentary and explanation of these issues in a language and style understandable to all. Aboriginal concerns are not the exclusive domain of Aboriginal people or the professionals and academics who work and study in this area. They are matters that have an impact on all Canadians and should, therefore, be matters that all Canadians have the opportunity to know and understand. This book gives them that opportunity.

I mentioned earlier that in 1973 there were only five people who were academics and considered experts by most of us interested in pursuing Aboriginal law issues. While each remains a founder of what we now call Aboriginal law, as well as a leading expert in the field, it can no longer be said to be their exclusive domain. I personally know well each of the contributing authors to this book and have tremendous respect for all of them. Moreover, I've had the distinct privilege of working in a professional capacity with most of them. They are now also considered to be among the leading experts on Aboriginal issues and each has contributed significantly to the body of work and development of Aboriginal issues in Canada. It is an area that is fascinating and complex as well as poignant and tragic. Yet it remains a part of Canada that is least understood and quite often barely tolerated by non-Aboriginal people. And, yes, there is most definitely a need for this book.

While there is still a great distance to be travelled down the road of Aboriginal rights in this country, this book will take us a long way down that road, especially to the first junction — namely, understanding.

PREFACE

The last 25 years have been a watershed in the evolution and recognition of Aboriginal rights in Canadian society, business life, and law. The map of Canada has been significantly redrawn with extensive land claims settlements in Yukon and British Columbia and new political boundaries in the Northwest Territories. Contemporary treaties now cover vast areas of northern Québec while other agreements have implemented creative solutions to self-government issues in various regions. Very important, Canada amended its constitution in 1982 to protect Aboriginal and treaty rights.

These developments have not come easily and, in many instances, the changes have been responses to confrontations. Nor have the changes been well understood by the public. Canadians, for a number of reasons, have not completed the process of finding a satisfactory overall resolution to the issue of the appropriate place for Aboriginal persons and First Nations in Canadian political, legal, and economic life.

Aboriginal people in Canada come from diverse cultural backgrounds and live in widely different circumstances. Each Aboriginal community in Canada has its unique set of challenges and problems. Of the approximately 1.25 million Aboriginal people living in Canada, about 50% are status Indians, meaning that the federal government recognizes certain rights and entitlements under the Indian Act. Many of these status Indians live on the patchwork of 608 Indian reserves across this country. There are also approximately 600,000 non-status Indians and Métis who live off reserve and whose Aboriginal rights have, to date, largely been ignored. Finally, there are the Inuit of the Northwest Territories, Yukon, Labrador, and northern Québec who do not fall within the Indian Act but who have their own Aboriginal and treaty rights.

Aboriginal issues often seem extremely complicated. To date, an understanding of these issues has been restricted to a fairly small group of experts. This book explores these difficult issues so that they may be more accessible and understood. We hope that whether you are a Mi'kmaq in eastern Canada, a neighbor of a Cree or Ojibwa community in central Canada or on the prairies, or an employee with a resource development company in British Columbia, you will gain new insights from this publication.

We felt that this book should be written equally by Aboriginal and non-Aboriginal persons. All contributors are passionate in their commitment to finding solutions to the outstanding problems. Our contributors include chiefs of First Nations, Aboriginal law professors, mediators, and lawyers either working hard with governments to develop solutions or advancing claims on behalf of First Nations in the courts or as negotiators. We hope this book will provide readers, whether chiefs, band council members, municipal officials, government employees, or interested individuals, with a clearer understanding of the background to Aboriginal issues in contemporary Canada so that Canada might be a much better place for *all* of us.

Finally, the reader must appreciate that this book relates to the laws as developed in the Euro-Canadian legal system. It deals with Canadian law, not Aboriginal law developed by Aboriginal peoples. It is an undoubted truth that since the arrival of European settlers to Canadian shores, successive Canadian governments and courts have done little to incorporate or recognize the laws and practices of Aboriginal societies within the rest of Canadian law and society. That activity and a book on Aboriginal law from that perspective remain for another day.

To all those who have worked and contributed to this book we offer a most heartfelt *Miigwech*.

Stephen B. Smart
Michael Coyle

INTRODUCTION: AN OVERVIEW OF THE ABORIGINAL PERSPECTIVE*

by Kevin Bell

Aboriginal Issues Today outlines the laws that affect Aboriginal peoples in Canada. Because law is an important component of human relationships, this book provides a perspective of the place that has been made for the original inhabitants of this country. More important, some ideas are offered in the following chapters on how that relationship can be improved for all, allowing Aboriginal peoples to more fully participate in all aspects of Canadian society including greater participation in its benefits.

The subject of Aboriginal peoples' relationship with Canada is arising with increasing regularity within public debate. Despite Canadians' increased scrutiny of the subject, no other subject is as plagued with misunderstanding, creating an environment ripe for misjudgment, injustice, and distortion. Misunderstanding is not the only problem hindering Aboriginal peoples and other Canadians from obtaining a more mutually beneficial relationship: some of the problems stem from the current state of the law.

a. EUROPEAN SOCIETY AT FIRST CONTACT

To appreciate the current state of Canadian law affecting Aboriginal peoples, it is important to understand what was occurring within and between European nations at the time they first encountered Aboriginal peoples. Europe, consistent with its developing market economy, was interested then in exploiting the abundant resources — including minerals, furs,

---

* *The views expressed in this introduction are those of the author and should not be attributed to anyone else or any organization.*

1

and timber — of the new world. At the same time, increasing contact with peoples from around the world, including contact with peoples from very different societies, stimulated new thought about the nature of society. European theories about society almost invariably reflected the view that European societies represented an apex in some immutable progression in social structures. Society was seen to progress because solutions to problems of living and working together had been invented that were innately better than their predecessors, or, in 19th century Social Darwinist terms, were "fitter." The "current society" then was considered superior to previous societies.

For example, the transition from hunting and gathering economies to agriculturally based economies was explained by some as arising from discovery of the secrets of crop reproduction and the discovery of the economic advantages of agriculture. Societies whose economies were based on agriculture were considered fitter than those based on hunting and gathering. Likewise, the institutions of European society were explained as arising as a result of the invention of new institutions; less efficient institutions were discarded for ones which worked better — and better inventions resulted in innately superior societies.

This is an oversimplification of diverse and developing social theories over several centuries of European thought. Even so, the outline is very important to an understanding of the law affecting Aboriginal-Canadian relations today because it is one that still affects the way Canadians think.

It is also helpful, in understanding Canadian law affecting Aboriginal peoples, to understand certain basic principles about the connection between laws and the societies within which they arise. Laws are intimately linked to the wider society within which they are found, and generally promote that society's goals. Historically, a major European focus in the Americas was resource exploitation. Thus laws were developed to facilitate world resource exploitation. For example, the doctrine of discovery conferred rights in "unoccupied" lands to the first discoverer, so one of the major issues Europeans had to contend with was what to do with the original inhabitants of the newly discovered lands to be settled. Social theories of the superiority of European societies provided a ready solution to the inconsistency between international legal conventions and the European desire to develop the world's resources. The Aboriginal nations were not considered to be organized or "civilized" societies, so the Americas were not considered occupied, and the European nations were free, according to law, to exploit their wealth. These laws, created to allow settlement of lands already occupied by other peoples, are the same laws which influence legal relationships between non-Aboriginal Canadians and the Aboriginal peoples within Canada today. It is not surprising then, that those legal principles sometimes provide unstable ground on which to build a more workable and equitable partnership between Aboriginal and non-Aboriginal Canadians.

Laws that were developed to facilitate exploitation of lands occupied by Aboriginal people still influence current law. For example, in the late 19th century, when Canadian courts first articulated the nature of Aboriginal interests in land, judges decided that these interests were a mere and insubstantial personal right to use land. So, when Aboriginal peoples wished to sell their land, their rights disappeared prior to the conclusion of any land sale and collection of proceeds. Of course, in property law involving non-Aboriginal interests, it would be considered bizarre and disruptive to any rational system of property if the legal interests in property disappeared at the moment the property was placed on the market for sale.

One result of this different treatment is that if there is a fundamental breach in a property agreement of purchase and sale, the owner of "non-Aboriginal property" can retain his or her property. On the other hand, if there is a fundamental breach of an agreement concerning Aboriginal interests in land, the land is lost to the Aboriginal owners. The most effective remedy of return of the land is denied Aboriginal peoples. Today, the different treatment is justified on grounds of protecting the integrity of non-Aboriginal property rights. And, of course, the different treatment is supported by relying on early European social theories that Aboriginal use of land was insubstantial and therefore less worthy of legal protection than non-Aboriginal use of land.

Recently the Supreme Court of Canada decided that a financially sophisticated stock broker, knowledgeable about a tax shelter about which he received advice from an accountant, was owed a fiduciary duty by the accountant. (A fiduciary duty is a special legal duty to act in the best interest of another person and arises when the fiduciary has power to affect the legal interests of another vulnerable person.)

In another recent case involving Aboriginal rights in land, however, the Supreme Court decided that Canada owed no fiduciary duty to a First Nation in taking a surrender of reserve land from the First Nation. Yet it is well known that federal officials had, until relatively recently, a profound influence, and in many cases absolute influence, over First Nations' decisions on land surrenders.

The contrast between the two cases is startling and such apparently significant different treatment causes deep consternation for Aboriginal peoples. I suggest those laws that have been influenced by the principle that Aboriginal land interests are not as worthy of protection as non-Aboriginal property interests should be reexamined. Aboriginal perspectives regarding the sacredness of land and its importance to cultural survival in an environment where Aboriginal lands have been severely diminished and where it is difficult or in many cases impossible to increase them, should also be considered in judicial determinations.

b. ABORIGINAL SOCIETY AT FIRST CONTACT

When Europeans first came to the Americas they found Aboriginal societies that were diverse, culturally rich, complex, and that had endured for millennia. There were about 50 Aboriginal languages spoken in Canada. The Aboriginal peoples had constructed effective social and cultural solutions to those challenges that face all peoples in living and working together.

At the time of contact with Europeans, the population in Canada has been estimated at between 500 000 and 2 million. Most of the societies were based on hunting and gathering, consistent with a northerly clime, although the Iroquois in what is now southern Ontario, whose population is estimated to have been as much as 60 000, were farmers. Other peoples depended to a lesser extent on farming and managed and manipulated uncultivated plants such as wild rice. The peoples of the Northwest Coast probably had the densest population of any non-agricultural society anywhere in the world, estimated as being as high as 200 000 people, made possible by the rich and diverse food and other resources on the coast. Archeological evidence indicates that the Americas had long been populated to the extent of carrying capacity for the economies employed.

With the exception of those of the northwest coast, the Aboriginal societies in Canada were based on egalitarianism in which individuals did not have coercive power or control over other members of the society. The social control institutions were distinct from European institutions serving similar purposes. The sedentary societies of the west coast, consistent with their population densities, were hierarchal.

Up to 93% of the Aboriginal population in the Americas was decimated in the 16th century, usually in advance of actual contact, by the spread of European disease for which there was little immunity.

Initial relationships in the 16th and 17th centuries between Europeans and the Aboriginal peoples of Canada were based on trade. The success of the European fur trade depended on good relations with the Aboriginal peoples. For example, while the French typically asserted sovereignty over their Aboriginal trading partners, in practice, the French acknowledged the Iroquois rights to their territories and the Iroquois power to grant lands and hunting rights to French settlers. For their part, Aboriginal peoples became increasingly reliant on European trade and protection and found themselves increasingly overshadowed by European military power.

The Royal Proclamation of 1763 reserved a vast territory beyond the colonies to the exclusive use of the Aboriginal Nations and provided that Aboriginal lands could only be alienated through agreement with the Crown. Shortly after, when the English gained greater military power over Aboriginal peoples, the relationship shifted fundamentally, from one in which the English were primarily concerned with peace to one in which the primary goal was the acquisition of land from Aboriginal peoples.

c. EUROPEAN-ABORIGINAL RELATIONS IN THE 19TH CENTURY

During the 19th century, the territories of Aboriginal peoples within much of Canada were taken in huge land cession treaties in exchange for relatively small reserves, promises of hunting and fishing and other rights, and other promises. Many Aboriginal peoples whose ancestors entered into these treaties dispute the accuracy of these written treaty terms. Instead of giving up their lands to the Europeans, Aboriginal peoples maintain that the agreements involved sharing their lands with the Europeans, not ceding them.

In the 19th century, Aboriginal societies were considered inferior and, consistent with liberal thought, it was felt that Aboriginal people should be "assisted" in becoming civilized and converted to Christianity. Assimilation, or at least the removal of independence, was the goal, which was the second stage in acquiring Aboriginal lands and resources (the first being the creation of alliances and partnerships by necessity in acquiring access to furs). The methods used included the removal of Aboriginal individual and government powers, indoctrination and systematic destruction of Aboriginal cultures through missionary activity and residential schools with access permitted only to inferior educations, control over individual mobility and band and individual finances, the creation of policies that made farming impossible, and the imposition of legal sanctions against practising Aboriginal spirituality, meeting and organizing, and the pursuit of legal redress for breach of legal rights. For Aboriginal peoples, there was no law, to a large extent, until statutory amendments in 1951. Most Canadians, when they first learn this fact, find it hard to believe — it seems so inconsistent with the principles Canadians assume to have prevailed for all.

Some defend Canada's historical policy toward Aboriginal peoples on the basis that the motivations underlying treatment were well intentioned and were more morally enlightened than what prevailed in the rest of the world at the time. Whether or not that is the case, there is a danger that anecdotes about well-intentioned people can create false ideas that Aboriginal people somehow "benefited" by having their governmental and individual power removed, wealth stripped away, and access to legal remedies denied.

Likewise, some commentators point to the fact that the English and Canadian governments acquired Aboriginal land and resources not by the sword, for the most part, but through a more humane process of treaty making. A debate as to whether Canadians should feel proud or guilty about this does not contribute a great deal to a discussion about Aboriginal issues today. Instead, an understanding of historical relationships is more helpful in that it provides some understanding of the relationship today.

7

d. TREATY MAKING IN THE 18TH AND 19TH CENTURIES

The process of treaty making in Canada, whether motivated by altruistic notions or not, was a practical and efficient process from the non-Aboriginal perspective because at first it provided access to a lucrative fur trade and later it was an efficient process in acquiring Aboriginal land and resources. Treaty making was certainly more efficient than acquisition by conquest. Acquisition by agreement as a process of first choice was part of British colonial policy. The English and Canadian governments acquired everything that could be acquired by war, but with less effort and risk, by entering into the large land surrender treaties of the 18th and early 19th centuries which covered much of Canada. The English and non-Aboriginal Canadians essentially acquired all the land and resources that built one of the wealthiest nations in the world, in exchange for allowing the Aboriginal peoples to shelter and feed themselves, which removed at the time the burden of supporting the Aboriginal populations. When properly understood, the benefits promised to the Aboriginal peoples under the written European and non-Aboriginal Canadian versions of the treaties were really benefits also to the non-Aboriginal signatories. And the process of treaty making probably resulted in Aboriginal attitudes more conducive to cooperation then what would have resulted after warfare.

The marginalized state of Aboriginal peoples can in no small way be traced to the effects of forced cultural change and the resulting disintegration of individual and governmental power. The effects are etched deeply in the lives of all Aboriginal peoples in Canada today. The fact that many Aboriginal people have survived and have been able to lead productive lives and to look to the future with hope in the face of overwhelming challenges is a testament to the strength and substance of surviving Aboriginal values.

Nonetheless, the injury is deep. When compared with the general Canadian population, the Aboriginal life expectancy at birth is lower, the mortality rate higher, the suicide rate higher, education level and enrollment rates are lower, the ratio of children in care higher, the percentage of "adequate housing" is dismally lower, the adequacy of water delivery and sewage disposal is lower, unemployment is significantly higher, average individual income is significantly lower, family violence...drug abuse...despair....But there is much hope too. The statistics indicate significant improvements over the last three decades. And the elders still show the path to a good life.

e. HISTORIC TREATIES AND ABORIGINAL TITLE TODAY

Current debate arises about Aboriginal peoples' access to hunting and fishing resources promised in treaty or arising under the doctrine of Aboriginal title. Interest groups that compete with Aboriginal people for hunting and fishing resources complain that a priority access violates one of the fundamental values of Canadian society: equality under the law. Aboriginal peoples, though, view priority access as a development which gives some meaning and content, albeit very late, to treaty promises to hunt and fish.

According to the written versions of the large land surrender treaties, the Aboriginal peoples received reserves, hunting and fishing rights, and other relatively small consideration while the English or Canadians got everything else. Any arguments that Aboriginal peoples had equal opportunity to the wealth of the country ignore the facts that they were prevented from accessing that wealth by law, policy, and practice. Although Aboriginal peoples paid dearly through treaty to maintain their hunting and fishing rights, in many cases the rights were ignored and treaty promises broken.

Shortly after treaty promises were made respecting Aboriginal peoples' rights to hunt and fish, a lucrative non-Aboriginal commercial fishery developed in parts of Canada. The result was that when the fish were plentiful and more valuable, and when the treaty ink was barely dry, the fishing resource was denied to Aboriginal peoples. Now, when the inland fishing resource is greatly depleted, the courts have begun to give some meaning to treaty rights to fish, but the jealous reaction of competitors has been swift and hard.

It is curious that some commentators complain that the current treaties being negotiated based on Aboriginal title claims grant greater access to resources then what Aboriginal peoples are entitled under the doctrine of Aboriginal title. At the same time, these commentators fail to recognize that non-Aboriginal Canadians have had access to all the Crown resources for the last century, and will continue to have access to the grand majority of those resources, even though they have no legal entitlement. If it is considered beneficial, as a matter of policy, for one segment of Canadian society to have access to resources, then why is access to those same resources by other Canadians considered justifiable only if there is constitutional entitlement? Real efforts to promote equal opportunity by policy makers and business are welcomed by Aboriginal peoples and coincide with their own aspirations.

Aboriginal peoples realize the importance of economic development for survival as a distinct people. Although there are special legal and other barriers to economic development that Aboriginal peoples must overcome, beyond lacking a capital pool and investment capacity, creative solutions are being devised and if there is sufficient will, the barriers can all be overcome. There is increasing motivation within Canadian business to assist in overcoming barriers as Canadians begin to understand that the welfare of Aboriginal peoples can have an effect on the welfare of all Canadians. This growing understanding could represent a fundamental shift in thinking from one in which the removal of resources from Aboriginal peoples was considered of benefit to Canada, to one in which Canadians perceive benefit in sharing wealth or allowing Aboriginal peoples to generate additional wealth, obtaining a more equitable partnership in Canada.

Aboriginal peoples in many cases agreed historically to share their land and resources with the newcomers through treaty, but the result cannot be characterized as sharing. If the relationship had been more equitable, Aboriginal people would have shared in the great wealth of Canada and by so doing would have been easily able to pay for the government services now rendered and, like the rest of Canada, would have money left over for economic development. Instead, Aboriginal peoples have been denied access to the economy generated from their own lands and resources, and as a result have paid astronomically more than what other Canadians pay for their government services. This does not mean that there aren't legitimate concerns on both sides of the debate to be addressed, but in order to have a meaningful dialogue, the Aboriginal perspective must be considered.

A debate has recently arisen in which some propose that the problems that plague Aboriginal peoples arise because governments have afforded "special" treatment to Aboriginal peoples which has led to their marginalization and separation from the rest of Canada. The solution proposed to the problems is that Aboriginal peoples should cease to be treated differently from other Canadians. I think that these arguments represent a third and final stage in attempts to assimilate Aboriginal peoples. It is clear from history that it is not special treatment that has kept Aboriginal peoples separate from Canadians, but attempts over the last two centuries to assimilate them. Assimilation attempts have prevented Aboriginal societies from participating with other Canadians in the economy, and have distinguished Aboriginal peoples from other Canadians by removing from them powers that the rest of Canadians take for granted as necessary in exercising responsibilities and determining their own destinies.

Use of the word "assimilate" is somewhat inaccurate in the context of the 19th and 20th century because it implies that attempts were made to incorporate Aboriginal peoples as full members of non-Aboriginal society. That was not the case as Aboriginal peoples were prevented from participating in Canadian society in many ways. The goal was to ensure Aboriginal powerlessness, facilitating access to Aboriginal resources, not to make them equal partners. The result was separation and marginalization.

In light of the above, addressing Aboriginal peoples' separation from Canadian society by assimilation is really advocating pursuing the very policy that has actually created the separation we see today. The policies of the 19th and 20th century have created today's problems of dependency and poverty. Assimilation solutions which are currently being advocated will promote and continue separation, not ensure greater participation.

Some Canadians think that the institutions of Canadian society must be adopted by Aboriginal peoples, a position said to be supported by principles of equality and the practicality of uniformity. It is basic in western thought that institutions of society, if they are to work well, must fit well with the entire society and culture. Institutions formulated in one culture will usually not work well in another culture, particularly if forced on another culture that has significant differences. To foist inappropriate institutions on an Aboriginal people is to ensure that the society will not work well, creating problems for the people in it. It will not foster greater positive interaction and participation. It will lead to the same predictable results obtained over the last two centuries by application of the same policies. While uniformity can promote efficiency and practicality, it is clear that institutions inappropriate for a particular sociocultural setting create the greatest inefficiency. Principles of equality demand that people in different circumstances must sometimes be treated differently.

Assimilation is not the answer. Aboriginal peoples will resist it. It will prevent greater Aboriginal participation in and contribution to Canadian society. Attempts at assimilation are cruel to those who linger in cultural limbo and many now realize that it results in a lose-lose situation since the marginalized state of one segment of society affects us all. Continued marginalization caused by attempts to assimilate is hardly compatible with the idea that Aboriginal peoples are welcomed partners in Canada. There are, happily, other options.

When Aboriginal peoples achieve self-government, they will acquire the power necessary to heal. Exercising control over one's own destiny is fundamental to being a whole person. The institutions Aboriginal peoples build will be responsive to their traditional values and also to the world around them. With power comes responsibility and Aboriginal people will by necessity interact with the surrounding society to a greater extent than now, but on terms of their own choice, and will forge a more meaningful and equitable partnership with the rest of Canada.

Aboriginal peoples understand the importance of history, and how history can shed light on the current relationship of Aboriginal peoples and non-Aboriginal Canadians. Although recounting history may cause discomfort to some, it gives no comfort to Aboriginal peoples. Ultimately, the purpose is not to cause discomfort but to create understanding of the present so that the future can be wrought better. The following chapters provide insight to the present relationship and suggest paths to the future.

1

ABORIGINAL AND TREATY RIGHTS IN CANADA

by Tony Mandamin

Aboriginal and treaty rights are unique rights held by the Aboriginal peoples of Canada. Aboriginal rights were recognized and exercised as an integral aspect of the fabric of pre-contact Aboriginal societies. These rights were acknowledged and respected in the treaties made between Aboriginal peoples and Europeans. However, as time progressed, Aboriginal and treaty rights were given lesser importance and were largely disregarded or forgotten by Canadians. The legal recognition of Aboriginal and treaty rights in Canadian law, through court decisions and legislation, was a gradual process.

In 1982, Canada's constitution was amended to constitutionally recognize these unique rights of Aboriginal peoples. Section 35(1) of the Constitution Act, 1982, provides:

> The existing aboriginal and treaty rights of the aboriginal peoples of Canada are hereby recognized and affirmed.

Aboriginal and treaty rights were not created by the 1982 constitutional amendment. These unique rights originate in the traditional rights Aboriginal peoples exercised before the coming of the Europeans and in the solemn treaty agreements made between these two peoples.

This chapter reviews the process by which Aboriginal and treaty rights became recognized in Canadian law. It first examines how the common law came to recognize the existence of Aboriginal rights and then reviews the history of treaty making and court recognition of treaty rights. Finally, it discusses modern-day court decisions that have profound impact on how Aboriginal rights are considered today, and the significance of the 1982 constitutional recognition of Aboriginal and treaty rights.

a. ABORIGINAL RIGHTS

The Oxford English Dictionary defines "aboriginal" as "dwelling in any country before the arrival of later European colonists." The Constitution Act, 1982, defines Aboriginal peoples as including the Indian, Inuit, and Métis peoples of Canada. Aboriginal rights are the rights of Indian, Inuit, and Métis that originated in the rights exercised by Aboriginal societies before contact with the Europeans.

Aboriginal peoples lived in North America in organized societies long before the coming of the European colonists. Aboriginal societies were diverse and varied, each with their own culture, language, traditions, and social organization. Aboriginal rights were a fundamental aspect of the distinctive culture of Aboriginal societies, and the rights enjoyed by the members of the Aboriginal societies, individually or collectively, encompassed a wide range of subjects.

Aboriginal peoples' occupation of traditional territories provides the basis for their right to Aboriginal title. Aboriginal societies' historical capacity to select their leadership is the basis for the contemporary non-Indian Act capacity of First Nations to select chiefs and counsels by "custom." As well, family relationships and obligations within Aboriginal societies give rise to recognition of traditional Indian marriages and Inuit custom adoptions in Canadian law. Probably the most well known Aboriginal right is the right of members of Aboriginal societies to pursue their livelihood of hunting and fishing.

b. RECOGNITION OF ABORIGINAL RIGHTS

1. Aboriginal rights and the common law

The recognition of Aboriginal rights in Canadian law is rooted in the evolution of the common law, which is part of Canada's legal heritage. The common law now contains the principles laid down by the courts over the course of several hundred years. The genesis of the common law recognition of Aboriginal rights is a 1611 English court decision in *Calvin's Case*. Considering the validity of non-English laws of other countries, the court concluded that, "If a King come to a Christian kingdom by conquest,...he may at his pleasure alter and change the laws of that kingdom; but until he doth make an alteration of those laws the ancient laws of that kingdom remain."

2. *Calvin's Case* and American Indian rights

The legal concept that the laws of a country continued after English sovereignty was introduced to that country was applied to North America's Aboriginal people in a trilogy of court decisions about American Indian rights in the early 1800s. Chief Justice Marshall of the U.S. Supreme Court applied the legal principle first stated in *Calvin's Case* to the Indian Nations. The European nations, in Marshall's view, acknowledged that Indians, as the original inhabitants, had a legal interest in traditional lands and enjoyed traditional rights derived from their own social organization.

In the first of the cases, the 1823 case of *Johnson v. McIntosh*, Marshall wrote that the Aboriginal peoples —

> were admitted to be the rightful occupants of the soil, with a legal as well as just claim to retain possession of it, and to use it according to their own discretion; but their rights to complete sovereignty, as independent nations, were necessarily diminished.

16

In the second case, *Cherokee Nation v. Georgia*, Marshall sought to reconcile the reality of American domination with the existence of the Cherokee Nation by describing the Cherokee Nation as a "domestic sovereign nation." Although again acknowledging the Indians' right to occupy the land until they voluntarily extinguished it, Marshall was reluctant to describe the Indian Nations in the United States as foreign nations.

Nations have laws and their members have rights based on those laws. Marshall examined how Indian people have Aboriginal rights that originated in the original laws of Aboriginal Nations more closely in *Worcester v. Georgia*. He wrote:

> The Indian nations had always considered as distinct, independent, political entities, retaining their own natural rights, as the undisputed possessors of the land since time immemorial....The words "treaty" and "nation" are words of our own language, selected in our diplomatic and legislative proceedings, by ourselves, having each a definite and well understood meaning. We have applied them to Indians as we have applied them to other nations of the earth.

3. Recognition by Canadian courts

Marshall's decisions established the validity of traditional laws and rights of Indian Nations in the United States. In Canada, the recognition of Aboriginal rights by the courts took a different route. Instead of the comprehensive legal approach recognizing sovereignty of Indian Nations used by Marshall, Canadian courts went on a case-by-case basis, focusing on specific aspects of Aboriginal rights.

The first Canadian court case considering an Aboriginal right was the 1867 case of *Connelly v. Woolrich and Johnson*, which examined the validity of a marriage made by Indian custom. A North West Company clerk married a Cree woman according to the custom of her tribe, and they lived as a married couple for 28 years, having six children. When the clerk retired from the fur trade, he returned to Lower Canada and shortly after that parted from his Indian wife and children. He then married another woman in a Catholic wedding and started a second family. When the clerk died, he left in his will his entire estate to his second wife. His son from his first marriage sought a share of the estate based on a community of property between a husband and wife. The court recognized the Cree custom marriage as a legal marriage and awarded part of the estate to the son of the Indian marriage.

A much later case recognizing Aboriginal family rights involved Inuit custom adoptions. In the 1960s, the Northwest Territories had introduced an adoption ordinance imposing many requirements that were difficult or impossible to meet in the distant regions of the Territories, such as requirements for marriage certificates and other official and procedural certificates. In an adoption hearing for an Inuit child named Katie who had been adopted according to Inuit custom, Judge Sissons of the Territorial Court declared Katie's adoption by Inuit custom valid.

While marriage and adoption rights based on Aboriginal custom were readily recognized, the Canadian courts took much longer to recognize Aboriginal rights such as Aboriginal title, hunting, and fishing rights.

The pivotal case on Aboriginal rights was the 1972 case of *Calder v. The Attorney General of British Columbia*. The Nisga'a of British Columbia's Upper Nass Valley — where no treaty had ever been made — had long maintained that they had Aboriginal title to their traditional lands. The government of British Columbia denied the claim and eventually the Nisga'a began an action in court for a declaration that they held Aboriginal title. The case came before the Supreme Court of Canada, which needed to decide whether Aboriginal title existed in Canadian law and, if so, if it still existed or if it had been extinguished by land legislation enacted over the years by the government.

Justice Hall, speaking for three of the seven judges, found that Aboriginal title existed and did not depend on treaty, executive order, or legislation. Justice Judson, speaking for three of the other judges, similarly concluded that Aboriginal title was recognized by Canadian law.

In 1972, well over 100 years after Confederation, the Supreme Court concluded that Aboriginal title was recognized by Canadian law. However, it divided on whether the provincial government's land legislation extinguished Aboriginal title (see section **d.** below).

Aboriginal fishing rights for food and ceremonial purposes were recognized in the important 1990 Supreme Court of Canada decision in *R. v. Sparrow*. Sparrow was a member of the Musqueam First Nation in British Columbia. The federal fishery regulations for net size had been changed and Sparrow was charged for using a net of unauthorized size. His defence was that he had an Aboriginal right to fish, as the Musqueam had resided and fished in the area for centuries for food and ceremonial purposes. The court decided that the Musqueam Indians had an Aboriginal right to fish for food and ceremonial purposes.

Other courts have also found there is an Aboriginal right to hunt for food. For example, the British Columbia Court of Appeal in *R. v. Alphonse* found that a Shuswap Indian hunting deer on traditional hunting grounds had an Aboriginal right to hunt for food.

c. TREATY RIGHTS

1. Treaty making

An Indian treaty is usually understood to be an agreement between the Indians and the government. However, Aboriginal peoples were accustomed to making treaties among themselves before the Europeans arrived. The Iroquois Confederacy, for example, was formed at least a century before contact with the Europeans by a sacred agreement between five, and later six, Iroquois Nations. Treaty making was an accepted process for the Europeans as well. Accordingly, treaties became a common way to define relationships between Indians and Europeans. These treaties served various purposes, including peace making, relinquishing rights to land in exchange for compensation and guarantee of rights, and providing for social and economic adjustment such as education, relief in times of famine, and medical and agricultural aid. Although specific rights were promised or confirmed in treaties in the earliest days of Canada's history, the legal recognition of treaty rights developed more gradually in the courts and in legislation.

2. The courts' treatment of treaty rights

Initially, Indian treaties were characterized as mere agreements between the government and the Indians, a personal obligation, in some instances, by a governor representing the government. However, this limited interpretation of Indian treaties changed in the 1964 case of *R. v. White and Bob* when the Supreme Court of Canada decided that Indian treaties gave rights with legal effect and that interpretation of Indian treaties should uphold the honor of the Crown. In the 1981 case of *Taylor and Williams*, the Court again emphasized the honor of the Crown, stating that any "appearance of 'sharp dealing'" by the Crown would not be tolerated. As well, any ambiguous words in a treaty were not to be interpreted to the Indians' disadvantage if another interpretation was possible, and any evidence of how the parties to the treaty understood the words could be used to reduce ambiguity.

3. Peace and friendship treaties

Early Indian treaties tried to establish peaceful relations between the Crown and the Indians. In 1752, the Mi'kmaq in Nova Scotia signed a treaty with the English governor of

Nova Scotia. According to the treaty, the Mi'kmaq would ratify earlier peace treaties and end their hostilities. The Indians promised to try to persuade other tribes to also enter treaty. If they did not, both the Crown and the Mi'kmaq would join to oppose the hostile Indian tribes. The Mi'kmaq were guaranteed their right to pursue hunting and fishing as usual. As well, annual renewals of friendship by the Indians were to be reciprocated by the English with the giving of gifts. The Indians promised to help shipwreck victims and the English promised that Indians could bring their disputes with the English to the English courts.

The Supreme Court of Canada considered the validity of this treaty in the 1985 Nova Scotia case of *R. v. Simon*. An Indian who had been charged with illegal possession of a rifle and ammunition in an area where firearms and ammunition were prohibited during closed season raised his treaty right to hunt as a defence. The court found that the Mi'kmaq chiefs and the English colonial government had the capacity to make a treaty. It also found that the treaty hunting right, existing before the treaty as an Aboriginal right of the Mi'kmaq, was a legal right that could be raised as a defence to the charge in 1985.

A second pre-Confederation treaty confirmed the right of the Huron to continue with traditional ceremonies in a Québec provincial park. When Huron Indians camped in the park in 1987, the question was raised whether they could camp without permits required by the provincial park.

In 1760, the Huron, allies of the French in the struggle between the English and French, agreed with the English to end the hostilities between them. The treaty text was very brief, providing for a stop to the hostilities, safe conduct for the Huron's return to their home territory, and a right to continue to practise their customs. There was also a provision for trade between the English and the Huron.

The Court decided that the parties had the capacity to enter into a treaty and that the treaty guaranteed the Huron the right to practise their religion and customs on the parkland without permits.

4. Treaties made under the Royal Proclamation of 1763

In 1763, the British consolidated their rule of North America by issuing a Royal Proclamation. The proclamation declared, in part, that if the Indians were willing to part with their lands, surrender to the Crown must be agreed to at an assembly convened for that purpose. The proclamation had a significant impact on the treaty-making process between the Indians and the Crown. Previously, many treaties were primarily peace and friendship treaties; now surrender of Indian lands became a predominant component of Indian treaties. The map in Figure #1 shows the general areas covered by treaties from the 1850s to the 1920s.

The earliest treaties following the Royal Proclamation involved sale of land by the Indians to the colonial governments. However, the terms of the treaties began to extend to other subjects. In the 1862 Manitoulin Island treaty, the terms included surrendering land, paying money, establishing Indian reserves, and assuring fishing rights. Some 12 years earlier, in British Columbia, James Douglas, the chief agent of the Hudson's Bay Company at Fort Victoria, made similar treaties with the Indians on Vancouver Island, confirming lands reserved for the Indians and promising that their hunting and fishing rights would continue.

While the record of the treaties was usually set down in writing, the treaty, being the actual agreement between the Indians and the Crown, could include oral agreements made during the treaty negotiations. In an 1818 treaty, the written text did not mention hunting and fishing rights. However, the minutes of the treaty negotiations included references to hunting and fishing:

FIGURE #1
MAP OF "HISTORIC INDIAN TREATIES"

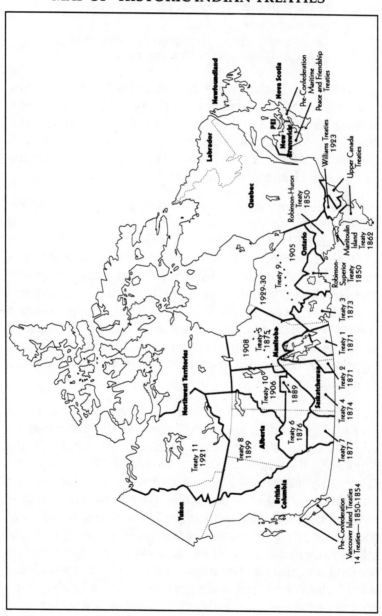

The Indians: "Father. We hope that we shall not be prevented from the right of Fishing, the use of the Waters, & Hunting where we can find game...."

Government reply: "The Rivers are open to all & you have an equal right to fish & hunt on them."

When two Indians were charged in 1977 with harvesting bullfrogs, they raised a defence of treaty right to hunting and fishing, as reflected in the minutes of the 1818 treaty negotiations. The court concluded that this oral agreement, though outside the terms of the treaty, was part of the treaty made between the Indians and the Crown.

The treaty-making process became more formal and extensive by the middle of the 1800s. The Robinson-Huron and the Robinson-Superior Treaties of 1850 covering lands north of lakes Huron and Superior in northern Ontario were forerunners for the numbered treaties on the western prairies. In these treaties, negotiated before public assemblies of Indians, the Indians gave up their claim to traditional lands in return for the establishment of Indian reserves, the payment of annual annuities, and the continuation of hunting and fishing rights over their traditional territory. The numbered treaties followed this pattern.

The content of the treaties evolved as they progressed westward, as Indian leadership, aware of the prior treaties, negotiated the best terms they could for their people. Treaty 6, covering the central portions of Saskatchewan and Alberta, is a good example of the numbered treaties. In return for the surrender of 313 400 square kilometres of land, Treaty 6 provided for the establishment of Indian reserves, treaty payments, economic assistance for the transition to agriculture, education, medical aid, and the right to pursue a livelihood of hunting and fishing. The treaty also stated that the Indians would observe the law and maintain peace and good order among themselves, and between themselves and others.

5. Modern-day treaties

The treaty-making process continues in present times, since large areas of Canada are not covered by historical treaties. The Crown and the Indians continue to negotiate agreements for the release of Aboriginal title in return for treaty guarantees. These agreements address compensation for surrender of Aboriginal title, resource use, hunting and fishing, Indian reserves, and self-government.

The first of the modern-day treaties was the 1975 James Bay and Northern Québec Agreements between the Crown and the Cree and Inuit of northern Québec. Similar agreements settling Aboriginal comprehensive land claims include the Inuvialuit Agreement of the western Arctic, the Yukon Agreement, and the Nunavut Final Agreement of the eastern Arctic. The negotiation of similar agreements continues in the Mackenzie region of the Northwest Territories and in British Columbia.

These modern-day agreements are recognized as treaties in section 35(3) of the Constitution Act, 1982:

> For greater certainty, in subsection (1) "treaty rights" includes rights that now exist by way of land claims agreements or may be so acquired.

d. ABORIGINAL AND TREATY HUNTING AND FISHING RIGHTS

1. Do treaty rights prevail over provincial legislation?

The legal recognition of Aboriginal and treaty hunting rights has been an involved process. Because, according to the Constitution Act, 1867, Indians are within federal jurisdiction, Indian treaty hunting rights have been considered beyond provincial wildlife legislation. According to section 88 of the Indian Act, provincial laws of general application — laws that are applied to everyone, such as traffic laws — can apply to Indians unless inconsistent with the terms of any Indian treaty or federal Indian legislation, or of a regulation or bylaw made under the Indian Act. Accordingly, if an Indian is charged under provincial game legislation, the courts consider whether there is an Indian treaty giving the Indian a right to hunt. An Indian treaty right will prevail over provincial game legislation.

For example, in *R. v. White and Bob*, the Supreme Court of Canada concluded that an agreement between Governor Douglas and the Indians granting the Indians the right to hunt was an Indian treaty within the meaning of section 88. Similarly, the Ontario Court of Appeal decided in *R. v. Taylor and Williams* that the oral agreement on fishing and hunting between the Indians and colonial authorities was part of the treaty agreement that gave the Indians the right to harvest bullfrogs. In *R. v. Simon*, the Supreme Court of Canada found that Aboriginal hunting was a right confirmed by the 1752 Mi'kmaq treaty.

2. The Natural Resources Transfer Agreements

In the prairie provinces of Manitoba, Saskatchewan, and Alberta, the situation of treaty rights was different. In each of the three provinces, treaties were signed between the Crown and the Indians. The lands in the prairie provinces, formed out of a federal territory, continued to be federal Crown lands, although each province had its own provincial government. In 1930, the federal government transferred the federal Crown lands to the prairie provincial governments, putting them in the same position as other provinces in Confederation. Section 12 of the Natural Resources Transfer Agreements (NRTA) states that provincial legislation applies to the Indians, although Indians also had the right to hunt, trap, and fish for food year round on any unoccupied Crown land or land they had a right to access.

Federal, provincial, and British legislation constitutionalized the NRTA. In the 1932 case in which an Indian was charged with deer hunting shortly after the passage of the NRTA, the Alberta Court of Appeal associated section 12 with the Indian treaties, if not with prior Aboriginal rights. The trial judge stated:

> The intention was that in hunting for sport or for commerce the Indian like the white man should be subject to laws which make for the preservation of game but in hunting wild animals for the food necessary to his life, the Indian should be placed in a very different position from the white man who generally speaking does not hunt for food and was by the proviso to section 12 reassured of the continued enjoyment of a right which he has enjoyed from time immemorial.

However, Indian hunting rights in the prairies were considered to emanate from the NRTA instead of the treaties. While section 88 of the Indian Act and section 12 of the NRTA provided a basis for legal recognition that treaty rights overrode provincial game legislation, the situation was different with federal legislation.

The issue first arose in 1968, when an Indian in the Northwest Territories was charged with hunting a duck out of season. The Indian was a member of an Indian band that signed Treaty 11 with the Crown in 1927, a treaty including a guarantee of hunting rights for the Indians. However, the Indian was charged under the federal Migratory Birds Convention Act, an act passed according to an international convention between Canada, the United States, and Mexico protecting migratory birds. In convicting the Indian despite the treaty defence, the court concluded that although the federal government had made a treaty promise to the Indians, it had breached the promise by its legislation. However, the federal government's power to enact legislation breaching a treaty promise was unquestioned.

The same outcome arose under the NRTA in the prairie provinces. A Manitoba Indian was charged with hunting ducks out of season under the same federal Migratory Birds Convention Act. The Supreme Court of Canada concluded that section 12 of the NRTA could not be raised in defence because the NRTA's constitutional guarantee of the right to hunt and fish for food bound only the provincial government and not the federal government. Later, an Indian was charged under federal fisheries legislation with possessing fish not caught under a licence, with the same result.

The effect of section 12 on Indian hunting and treaty rights in the prairie provinces has been the subject of many court cases. In *R. v. Horseman*, the Supreme Court of Canada decided that section 12 extinguished the treaty right to hunt commercially in exchange for extension of the right to hunt for food throughout the entire province. Recently, in *R. v. Badger*, the Supreme Court decided that the right of Indians to hunt food on lands not in use was based on the original treaty right. The treaty right had been modified by the enactment of the NRTA but not extinguished.

In *R. v. Badger*, the Supreme Court elaborated further on the nature of an Indian treaty. An Indian treaty was the actual agreement made between the Crown and the Indians. The written treaty text did not necessarily record the full extent of the treaty, and Indian elders' understanding was also to be used in interpreting the treaty. The nature of the treaty was sacred, involving the honor of the Crown, and it was to always be assumed that the Crown intended to fulfil its promises.

3. Do Aboriginal rights prevail against competent legislation?

Legal recognition of Aboriginal hunting and fishing rights lagged behind recognition of treaty hunting and fishing rights. While section 88 of the Indian Act and section 12 of the NRTA were interpreted as the basis for recognizing Indian treaty hunting rights, Aboriginal rights were not recognized in any equivalent legislation.

Indeed, Aboriginal rights were not recognized as having legal effect before the 1972 decision in *Calder v. The Attorney General of British Columbia*. When the Supreme Court of Canada recognized Aboriginal title in *Calder*, the question remained of whether Aboriginal rights could prevail against competent legislation ("competent" means valid in the sense that it has to be legislation that can apply to the Aboriginal or treaty right: legislation attempting to define Aboriginal or treaty rights is not competent to affect these rights).

In *R. v. Derrickson*, a 1976 British Columbia Aboriginal fishing case, the Supreme Court of Canada stated that because the regulations of the Fisheries Act were validly enacted, the Aboriginal right to fish in the particular area was subject to the regulations of the act. Before 1982, federal fisheries legislation prevailed over Aboriginal fishing rights if such rights existed. In 1982, the situation changed with the constitutional protection that section 35(1) of the Constitution Act, 1982, gave Aboriginal and treaty rights.

Aboriginal fishing rights were recognized in the 1990 Supreme Court of Canada decision in *Sparrow*; the British Columbia Court of Appeal held that a B.C. Shuswap Indian had an Aboriginal right to hunt for food in his or her people's traditional hunting grounds; and Aboriginal hunting rights have also been recognized for Inuit people and for Métis people in Manitoba. Although Aboriginal and treaty rights are recognized in Canadian law, whether these rights prevailed against federal or provincial legislation was still a question. The answer turns on the interpretation of section 35(1) of the Constitution Act, 1982, and the application of the *Sparrow* decision.

When that section recognized existing Aboriginal and treaty rights, the question remained, What is the meaning of this provision? This question was first addressed in 1990 by the Supreme Court of Canada in *R. v. Sparrow*. The court dealt with three issues: What is meant by the word "existing"?

29

What is the effect of recognition and affirmation? Finally, what happens if the constitutional provision is infringed?

The Supreme Court decided that the word "existing" means "unextinguished." An Aboriginal right could be extinguished before 1982 if legislation clearly was intended to extinguish the Aboriginal right. A treaty right could be extinguished with the consent of the Indian's party to the treaty. The onus of proof of extinguishment was on the party alleging extinguishment. Unless extinguishment was proven absolutely, the Aboriginal right continued to be an "existing" right.

The next question was the effect of the constitutional recognition and affirmation. The Crown found that the words "recognition and affirmation" embodied the fiduciary, or trust, relationship between Aboriginal peoples and the Crown. However, recognized and affirmed rights were not absolute: federal legislative powers still included the right to legislate Indians according to section 91(24) of the Constitution Act, 1867. However, before the enactment of section 35(1), federal and competent provincial legislation could infringe on Aboriginal rights. With the passage of section 35(1), the Crown must now justify any legislation infringing on Aboriginal or treaty rights.

The justification test requires that the legislation have a valid legislative objective and satisfy the special trust relationship between the government and the Aboriginal peoples. If, in questions of resource management, such as of fisheries, basic conservation requirements are met, priority should be given to Aboriginal peoples for the exercise of their rights. In *Sparrow*, the Supreme Court concluded that, under the constitution, top priority must be given to Musqueam food fishing rights so long as valid conservation measures had been met. Where unjustified legislation infringed on Aboriginal rights, then, the Constitution being the supreme law of the land, the offending legislation would not restrict the exercise of the Aboriginal right.

In *Sparrow*, the Supreme Court of Canada decided that the Musqueam had an Aboriginal right to fish for food and ceremonial purposes. It decided the meaning and effect of the section 35(1) recognition and affirmation of Aboriginal rights. Finally, it decided that the evidence at trial did not properly address the question of justification of the legislation and directed a new trial on that issue. However, the retrial of *Sparrow* never occurred. Because the Supreme Court had provided a guideline to approach section 35(1) issues about Aboriginal rights, the federal government and the Aboriginal peoples are exploring ways of reaching a common understanding on the exercise of Aboriginal fishing rights.

The constitutional acknowledgment of Aboriginal and treaty rights was the result of a long struggle for recognition of Aboriginal peoples' rights. Section 35(1) of the Constitution Act, 1982, is a basis for interpretation of Aboriginal and treaty rights by the courts. More important, it confirms that the relationship between governments and Aboriginal peoples is one that must be based on respect. The constitutional recognition of Aboriginal and treaty rights marks the beginning of a new era for Aboriginal peoples, one in which Aboriginal peoples, governments, and the Canadian people seek a common understanding and appreciation of the rights of Aboriginal peoples.

2

ABORIGINAL LAND RIGHTS

by Stephen Aronson

One of the most controversial subjects between Aboriginal peoples and successive Canadian governments and corporations is Aboriginal land rights. In a sense, the continuing history of Canada is the story of competition and conflict over land and resources between these groups. These conflicts frequently lead to litigation or to blockades or other even more aggressive confrontations, as in Kanesatake (Oka), Ipperwash, or Gustafsen Lake.

The ways in which successive British colonial and Canadian governments have dealt with Aboriginal land rights and the recognition of these rights in the law of Canada — recognition through legislation, treaty, or common law (the law developed by judicial decisions) — are explored in this chapter.

a. ABORIGINAL TITLE — WHAT IS IT?

Aboriginal peoples, organized in their own societies, occupied, governed, and used the lands, waters, and resources of Canada before European colonization. This simple fact is the basis of all Aboriginal land rights and many of the claims against Canadian governments, both federal and provincial. "Aboriginal title," "Indian title," "Indian interest," and "Aboriginal land rights" are terms expressing this fact.

Aboriginal land rights are unique rights, or to use an expression frequently found in court decisions on this subject, *sui generis*. Aboriginal land rights are not comparable to concepts of Canadian property and real estate law. Part of the uniqueness flows from the spiritual and cultural relationship that Aboriginal peoples have with the land, part flows from the general Aboriginal and Canadian principles that Aboriginal land rights are not transferable or saleable except to the Crown, and yet another part flows from the particular geographic environment in which a specific Aboriginal people resides. Aboriginal land rights include, but are not restricted to, self-government, language, and culture, as well as hunting, fishing, and the use of natural resources.

b. EARLY HISTORY AND THE ROYAL PROCLAMATION OF 1763

The first European settlements in the Maritime provinces and Québec were primarily French. The French did not attempt to settle the entire region, so the issue of Aboriginal land rights was not significant. There were, however, many conflicts between the French and British over the eastern portion of North America in the late 17th and 18th centuries. These conflicts were largely brought to an end by the Seven Years' War, in which France gave up to Britain territories that included Québec and the Maritimes (Acadia). Both the French and British were allied to various Indian tribes for trade and military purposes during these conflicts. These alliances of peace and friendship were often confirmed in compacts or treaties.

At the conclusion of the war, the British Crown issued the Royal Proclamation of 1763, perhaps Canada's earliest and longest lasting constitutional document. The main objective of the Royal Proclamation was to create systems of government in the areas formerly occupied by France. The special provisions for the protection of the territories of the Aboriginal peoples were designed to alleviate their concerns, about their land rights.

The Royal Proclamation set out the boundaries of the territories to be reserved for First Nation hunting grounds and from which European settlement and trade, except under licence, were to be excluded.

In Canada, "Indian hunting grounds" included, roughly, a corridor of land between what were then the northern limits of the territory of Québec and Rupert's Land (see section c. below) and an ambiguous area that extended westerly and northwesterly into territory which had not been much explored by the British. This lack of certainty over boundaries contributed to the claims by Aboriginal peoples west of the Rocky Mountains and to the corresponding denials by the governments of British Columbia and Canada of the existence of Aboriginal land rights in those areas.

The Royal Proclamation is a major reason for the land cession treaties. The proclamation recognized that the Aboriginal peoples had land rights. It also established that only the Crown could purchase Aboriginal lands. The proclamation's strict regulations for the acquisition of Aboriginal lands established the foundation for the relationship between the British Crown and the Aboriginal title holders. This relationship was assumed by the Canadian Crown at Confederation. (Under the Indian Act, a First Nation may not directly transfer reserve lands to a third party but must first transfer them to the federal government. A First Nation, by a community vote, must consent to the Crown receiving its interest in the particular reserve land through a process known as a surrender. The requirement that the surrender be made to the Crown, and not to the third party wanting the land, is found in the Royal Proclamation. This surrender process is required even when the land is to be leased, rather than sold, to a third party.)

c. RUPERT'S LAND ACT

One of the first steps taken by Canada following Confederation was to expand its land and resource base. The advancement of settlement and the construction of a transcontinental railway to assist in that settlement stimulated the desire for more land. The lands required were known as Rupert's Land and the North-Western Territory — the lands of the Hudson's Bay Company.

According to the Constitution Act, 1867, Rupert's Land was transferable to Canada. An important condition of the transfer obligated the federal government to make adequate provisions to protect the First Nations and resolve their claims to compensation for land required for settlement.

This obligation compelled the federal government to begin the negotiation of the "numbered treaties" (see Figure #1 in chapter 1). Some portions of the Hudson's Bay Company territory, an area never clearly defined, are lands in northern Ontario and Québec. By entering into treaties, the federal government believed it had met the obligation to deal with the Aboriginal peoples who were the landholders in Rupert's Land.

d. THE TREATIES

The 18th-century treaties with First Nations in the Maritimes are virtually all peace and friendship agreements which do not include any surrender of lands. In some treaties, for example the Treaty of 1752, Aboriginal hunting and fishing rights are confirmed. There are also many pre-Confederation land cession treaties that opened southern Ontario and Vancouver Island to European settlement. Large tracts of lands near lakes Huron and Superior were surrendered under the Robinson-Huron and Robinson-Superior treaties in the mid-1850s. These treaties became the model for the numbered treaties.

Many of these treaties contain impressive terms and today our political and legal systems are forced to deal with the different understandings held by the parties to the treaties. Historical treaty documents were never drafted by the Aboriginal occupiers of the land, and often the Aboriginal view was that they were not surrendering or giving up all rights to ownership of the land but that they were sharing the land with the new settlers.

Treaties 1 and 2 (1871) were concluded only one year after Rupert's Land and the North-Western Territory were admitted into the new Dominion of Canada. Within five years — lightning speed by today's standards of land claims settlements — Treaties 3 (1873), 4 (1874), 5 (1875), 6 (1876), and 7 (1877) cleared the way for Euro-Canadian settlement between Lake Superior and the Rocky Mountains. Treaty 8 (1899) allowed miners to travel freely between Edmonton and Yukon goldfields. Treaty 9 (1905) permitted more railway construction into northern Ontario. Treaty 10 (1906) followed on Canada's addition of new provinces in Saskatchewan and Alberta (1905). Finally, the negotiation of Treaty 11 (1921) allowed developers freer access to the oil deposits at Fort Norman in the Northwest Territories.[1]

The numbered treaties confirmed the Aboriginal peoples' hunting and fishing rights. They also provided for reserve lands and a formula to calculate the amount of reserve lands to be set aside for First Nations. Special provisions — for the Crown to provide education, medical services, annual treaty payments, agricultural implements, animals, and twine and ammunition for hunting and fishing — vary from one treaty to another. The Crown has not always honored these treaty obligations and many outstanding claims result from broken treaty promises. Often, insufficient quantities of land were set aside as reserves under the treaties. There have been some settlements of treaty land entitlement in Saskatchewan, and negotiations continue in Alberta and Manitoba.

e. ST. CATHARINE'S MILLING AND LUMBER COMPANY V. THE QUEEN

While the treaty-making process proceeded at a rapid pace, the federal, Québec, and Ontario governments were involved in disputes over the ownership of the land and resources in those provinces. Several Privy Council (Canada's then ultimate appeal court) decisions clarified the respective rights and jurisdiction of the federal and provincial governments of the lands covered by a treaty.[2]

The most important of these decisions, *St. Catharine's Milling and Lumber Company v. The Queen*, came after the 1873 signing of Treaty 3 in Ontario. Both the province and Canada granted timber leases to a portion of the territory sold by that treaty to the St. Catharine's Milling and Lumber Company. The federal government argued that section 91(24) of the Constitution Act, 1867, gave it not only legislative authority but also ownership of lands reserved for Indians and subsequently sold by treaty. Based on this view, the federal government had made grants in territory that had been sold by treaty to private parties. Ontario, on the other hand, took the position that the lands sold in Treaty 3 were owned by the province under section 109 of the Constitution Act, 1867, and therefore that the province could make land grants in treaty areas.

The resulting federal-provincial litigation turned on the question of the effect of the treaty sale. The Privy Council held that on the signing of the treaty, the underlying provincial title to the lands was finalized.

In effect, the courts concluded that section 91(24) of the Constitution Act, 1867, was a grant of legislative authority to parliament to regulate Indian reserve lands; it was not a grant of the ownership of lands within provinces which are sold by treaty. However, the federal government had the exclusive authority to take a surrender of the Aboriginal title.

According to *St. Catharine's Milling*, the surrender of lands by Aboriginal peoples removes their ownership interest in these lands in favor of the province. It is this Aboriginal interest which is at the centre of comprehensive land claims, as Aboriginal land rights may still exist in areas that are not covered by land cession treaties.

According to the early court decisions interpreting Treaty 3, the federal government is obliged to pay compensation to

First Nations under a land treaty. Therefore, although the province may be the ultimate beneficiary of a treaty land cession, it has no responsibility to contribute any of the compensation, nor can the federal government now legally require any reimbursement from the province. In some of the more recent treaties in Ontario and Québec, however, the provinces contribute substantially to the compensation payable.

While these early court decisions characterized the Aboriginal interest in land as usufructuary, the First Nations ("the rude redmen of the north," according to one trial judge) were not represented before the courts in any of these cases. Early litigation was primarily about federal and provincial rights and obligations resulting from Aboriginal title cessions, not federal or provincial obligations or responsibilities to First Nations and other Aboriginal peoples.

f. THE ONTARIO AND QUÉBEC BOUNDARIES EXTENSION ACTS

The result of the early Privy Council decisions caused the federal government to enter into a series of agreements in Ontario to remedy the problems of land grants and title to Indian reserves. The federal government adopted the position, at least in Ontario and Québec, that no new treaties would be made unless the province agreed, and also agreed to pay any incurred costs.

Since the federal government did not benefit from signing treaties, it took the position that any associated costs should be paid by the provinces. This was perhaps the first sign that the federal government was intent on shifting its responsibilities toward Aboriginal peoples to the provinces.

In Ontario, the first of these agreements (in 1891) required the concurrence of the provincial government to any future treaties and provincial representation on any commission established to negotiate a treaty. The federal policy of requiring Ontario to pay compensation for the surrender of First Nation lands was included in the agreement to extend the provincial boundary. Subsequently, Ontario was an active participant in the negotiations and settlement of Treaty 9 and the Williams treaties of 1923. A similar agreement in Québec extended that province's boundary on the same terms and conditions and was an important factor leading to the James Bay land claims settlements.

g. DEVELOPMENT OF FEDERAL POLICY ON ABORIGINAL LAND RIGHTS

Aboriginal peoples continued to press claims to Aboriginal rights, particularly in British Columbia, where only a small portion of the province is covered by treaty. It would be impossible to describe the numerous boards, commissions, and inquiries that governments used to look into Aboriginal land rights — their reports and recommendations form a significant part of the holdings of the public archives of Canada!

In response to the number of grievances and claims by First Nations and other Aboriginal peoples then being put forward, the federal parliament made shocking amendments to the Indian Act in 1927. These amendments made it an offence, punishable by fine or jail, for any person (including a lawyer) to receive or raise any money from Indians to advance a land claim without the consent of the Superintendent General of Indian Affairs.

The major post-war study undertaken by the federal government, the Hawthorn Report in 1967, acknowledged the policy of the British and Canadian governments to purchase the Indian interest in lands by treaties. Aboriginal land rights were viewed more as historical claims to hunting and fishing rights than as a set of much broader continuing rights.

The Hawthorn Report and a major internal government review of federal Aboriginal policy led to a draft policy document on Indian Affairs known as the 1969 White Paper. The proposed policy did not recognize any Aboriginal rights but, rather, suggested the integration of Indians and their lands into the dominant Canadian society. Until the decision in *Calder* in 1973, there was no change to the federal policy, which did not recognize Aboriginal land rights.

The importance of the relationship between Aboriginal title and treaties cannot be overstated. During periods when government policy did not recognize the validity of Aboriginal title, governments failed to make treaties with First Nations. This was the case in much of British Columbia and Québec. During much of the 20th century, successive federal and provincial governments simply declined to deal with the land rights and claims of Aboriginal peoples in areas that were not subject to treaty.

In the 1973 case of *Calder v. Attorney General of British Columbia*, the Supreme Court of Canada rendered its decision on the Nisga'a claim of Aboriginal title to the Nass Valley in northwestern British Columbia. Three of the judges were of the opinion that Aboriginal title could be extinguished implicitly by legislation or land grants — that a claim to Aboriginal land rights has been superseded by Euro-Canadian law. Three other judges took the position that express legislation was required to extinguish Aboriginal title. The case was unfortunately decided on a technical point, namely that the Nisga'a had failed to obtain the consent of the provincial Crown to the action, a prerequisite to beginning the legal proceeding.

Justice Judson expressed the view that in *Calder*, native people were asserting their right "to continue to live on their land as their forefathers had lived." He further stated, "This right has never been lawfully extinguished." This conclusion has come to be seen as a watershed in the recognition of Aboriginal land rights.

Despite the long-standing view of successive governments, six of the seven members of the Supreme Court finally recognized the existence of Aboriginal title. The *Calder* decision concluded that Aboriginal land rights exist at common law and that legislation is not the only legal means of recognition. Immediately after the decision, Prime Minister Pierre Trudeau told a group representing the Union of British Columbia Indian Chiefs, "Perhaps you have more legal rights than we thought you had when we did the White Paper."

With this nudge from the Supreme Court, a federal review of the 1969 White Paper policy was conducted and the federal government adopted its current policy of negotiating and settling Aboriginal title claims by entering into new land cession treaties. The highest court in the land had made it clear that Aboriginal peoples in this country did in fact, under certain circumstances, have unresolved legal rights and title to certain lands.

The *Calder* decision led to the first comprehensive claims policy of the federal government and negotiations with the Nisga'a. These negotiations, after more than 20 years, have just recently led to a comprehensive settlement of the claim including, among other important things, 2 000 square kilometres of land and the subsurface rights to resources for the Nisga'a.

h. ABORIGINAL LAND RIGHTS IN CONFLICT WITH EURO-CANADIAN GOVERNMENTS: THE NORTHWEST TERRITORIES AND QUÉBEC

Several significant resource development projects in the early 1970s brought Aboriginal land rights into conflict with Euro-Canadian governments. Oil had been discovered in the Mackenzie Valley in the western Northwest Territories, and a private consortium of pipeline companies proposed that a pipeline be constructed to carry the oil to southern markets. In northern Québec, a major hydro-electric project had begun.

In *Re Paulette's Application to File a Caveat*, the claimants, representing 16 First Nations in the Mackenzie Valley, sought to file a document asserting an interest, based on Aboriginal land rights, in over one million square kilometres of territory. If successful, the caveat would have made it difficult for the federal government to issue the interests in Crown land needed by the pipeline companies. The Registrar of Land Titles referred to the courts the issue of whether a caveat could be filed. The question before the court was whether Aboriginal title is an interest in land for the purposes of the federal Land Titles Act. If this Aboriginal title was an interest in land, a caveat could be filed.

The Northwest Territories Supreme Court agreed, in 1973, that the applicants did have Aboriginal rights to the lands claimed, which was a sufficient interest in land to allow a caveat to be filed. The court expressed doubt that Treaties 8 and 11 had surrendered the Aboriginal title to much of these lands. A number of legal proceedings related to this application were also before the courts. To resolve the dispute, the federal and territorial governments, together with the Aboriginal peoples occupying these lands, began to negotiate a comprehensive land claims settlement.

At the same time, in a different part of Canada, the Cree, Naskapi, and Inuit of northern Québec were trying to prevent the development of the James Bay hydro-electric project. This multi-billion dollar plan would significantly alter the geography of the area with the diversion of rivers, construction of massive dams, and flooding in over one million square kilometres of their traditional territories. The Cree of James Bay sought an injunction to stop the project.

The James Bay Cree established that they and their ancestors had used and occupied the territory since time immemorial. In 1973, after a year of hearings, the Québec Superior Court granted the injunction; work on the project stopped. The major reason for granting the injunction was Québec's obligation under the 1912 Québec Boundaries Extension Act to settle Aboriginal claims in the territory. The Québec Court of Appeal eventually overturned the trial decision in 1974, but only after the representatives of the Cree, Inuit, and federal and provincial governments had signed an agreement — the James Bay and Northern Québec Agreement — in principle to settle the Aboriginal claims.

i. THE LAW OF ABORIGINAL TITLE — LANDMARK DECISIONS

Court decisions in the Northwest Territories, British Columbia, and, as with the James Bay Agreement, Québec, confirm that Aboriginal land rights exist. Four decisions in particular have affected the law of Aboriginal title — *Baker Lake, Guerin, Sparrow,* and *Delgamuukw.*

1. *Baker Lake*

In 1978, the Inuit of Baker Lake, a hamlet in the eastern Northwest Territories, applied for an injunction to prevent the federal government from issuing prospecting permits and mining leases over 78 000 square kilometres of land. In *Hamlet of Baker Lake v. Minister of Indian Affairs and Northern Development,* the Inuit asserted that they had Aboriginal land rights to the area, having used and occupied the area for thousands of years. They argued that mineral exploration and development would interfere with the caribou hunt. The federal government argued that the Aboriginal land rights of the Inuit had been extinguished by Canadian legislation.

The Federal Court, referring to the *Calder* decision, agreed that Aboriginal title exists at common law. Once established, these rights could be extinguished only by a surrender from the Inuit to the Crown or by specific legislation that clearly intends to extinguish that title.

The decision in *Baker Lake* also sets out the facts a claimant must establish to prove Aboriginal title at common law:

(a) the claimants and their ancestors were members of an organized society;

(b) the organized society occupied the specific territory over which they assert the Aboriginal title;

(c) the occupation was to the exclusion of other organized societies; and

(d) the occupation was an established fact at the time the Crown asserted sovereignty.

An Aboriginal claimant's assertion of Aboriginal land rights must be examined in the context of history, anthropology, and the facts of the particular claim. The test for Aboriginal land rights established in *Baker Lake* has been applied in a number of other judicial decisions.

There are situations, as in *Baker Lake*, in which more than one Aboriginal group asserts Aboriginal land rights over the same lands or the same Aboriginal rights. This is because there are no artificial boundaries between the lands used by neighboring Aboriginal groups and resources may have been shared. Natural boundaries, such as river or lake systems or mountains, commonly marked traditional territory. Generally, the overlaps are at the borders of the traditional territories of these neighboring Aboriginal groups.

2. *Guerin*

The federal Crown has the legal title to most Indian Act reserves. The Aboriginal interest in these reserves is the same as in lands still subject to Aboriginal land rights. In *Guerin v. The Queen*, the courts examined the relationship between Canada and a First Nation leasing reserve land according to the Indian Act.

In *Guerin*, the Musqueam First Nation in North Vancouver had surrendered a portion of its reserve lands to the Crown so that the lands could be leased for use as the Shaughnessy Golf Club. The First Nation discovered some years later that the rental arrangements made were not in its best interest, as the rental rates charged by the Crown to the golf club were below market value. The Musqueam claimed that there was a fiduciary, or trust-like, relationship between the Crown and the First Nation. They also alleged that the Crown had breached this fiduciary obligation to the First Nation in dealing with the land. The courts decided that the land had been leased as a golf course at less than fair market value and that the Department of Indian Affairs had not carried out the requirements of the First Nation Council.

In this 1985 decision, the Supreme Court of Canada agreed that the Crown and First Nations had a fiduciary relationship arising on the surrender of reserve lands. This relationship is based on the historical relationship between the Crown and Aboriginal peoples, confirmed in the Royal Proclamation of 1763. Once a land surrender is approved by the First Nation, the Crown, as fiduciary for the First Nation, must deal with the land for the benefit of the First Nation. The Crown, once it has control of the land, has the discretion to determine what is in the best interests of the First Nation.

The Supreme Court confirmed damages of $10 million to the Musqueam First Nation as a result of the Crown's breach of its fiduciary obligation in the leasing of the reserve lands. Many First Nations that have received less than fair market value from the Crown for surrendered lands have since filed claims for compensation from the Crown. Other First Nations have surrendered lands to the Crown for sale; the lands have not been sold by the Crown, leaving these First Nations without compensation. These lands are treated as provincial Crown lands because the surrender, under Canadian laws, gave full ownership to the province. The principles set out in the *Guerin* decision are frequently relied on to support claims for the return of these lands.

Guerin is concerned only with the surrender of reserve lands under the Indian Act. Most commonly, the transfer of interests in reserve land to the Crown is followed by a transfer of that same interest to a third party — whether a cottager or a shopping centre developer. However, the fiduciary principles established in *Guerin* apply to all lands surrendered to the Crown, whether they are reserve lands or lands on which Aboriginal title still exists.

3. *Sparrow*

The Constitution Act, 1982, is the supreme law of Canada. Section 35(1) recognizes and affirms the "existing aboriginal and treaty rights of the aboriginal peoples of Canada." In *Sparrow*, the Supreme Court of Canada was asked to decide if a member of the Musqueam First Nation had an existing Aboriginal right to fish for food purposes. It decided that a federal fishing regulation requiring the use of a certain size net does not extinguish an Aboriginal right to fish: this right continues to exist even though there is an otherwise valid regulation. According to the Supreme Court, the constitution must be interpreted to give existing Aboriginal rights precedence over government policy and legislation.

In *R. v. Van der Peet*, decided on August 21, 1996, the Supreme Court stated that the test to determine if a claimed right is aboriginal, starts with a determination of whether the particular custom, practice, or tradition is integral or essential to the distinctive culture of the Aboriginal group claiming the right.

Aboriginal rights are not absolute, however. Before the Constitution Act, 1982, Aboriginal rights could be extinguished. To establish that Aboriginal rights were extinguished before 1982, the courts require a sale or surrender of the right, legislation that clearly extinguishes an Aboriginal right, or legislation that can only be interpreted as extinguishing the right. Therefore, existing Aboriginal or treaty rights are rights that have not been extinguished by surrender or legislation before 1982.

After 1982, section 35(1) of the Constitution provides a significant degree of protection to existing Aboriginal and treaty rights. It is no longer possible to extinguish Aboriginal land rights without the consent of the particular Aboriginal peoples having an interest in those lands. It may not even be possible to extinguish Aboriginal land rights by legislation without Aboriginal consent, even if compensation is paid. However, it may be possible to regulate Aboriginal land rights in consultation with the affected Aboriginal communities.

The *Sparrow* decision requires that the Aboriginal land claimant establish a pre-1982 existing Aboriginal or treaty right. Once the right is established, the Aboriginal group must establish that the particular legislation or activity interferes with or limits the exercise of the rights in question.

The Supreme Court created a two-fold test to determine if the legislative interference or limit is justified. The court must consider the purpose of the legislation and the honor of the Crown in dealing with Aboriginal peoples.

There may be a valid objective for the law in question, such as conservation of a natural resource or public safety. It is not, however, sufficient to suggest merely that the limit is in the public interest. If a valid legislative objective is found, the analysis continues with the second part of the test. In this part, the special trust relationship between the Crown and Aboriginal peoples is considered to determine if the interfering legislation or action is justified.

Where there is competition for a natural resource subject to an existing Aboriginal right, the law in question may need to be amended to give Aboriginal people priority access to the resource. For example, in *Sparrow*, the Supreme Court ruled that existing British Columbia fishing regulations could not be enforced against any Aboriginal group in British Columbia exercising its Aboriginal right to fish for personal consumption or ceremonial purposes.

To consider another example, the federal government may wish to construct and maintain a temporary fire road for six months across lands subject to Aboriginal title. Assume that the road interferes with a particular use and occupation

— the use of a spiritual site. If the consent of the Aboriginal group cannot be obtained, can the government expropriate the lands? Once the Aboriginal group has established a right to use and occupy the lands and has also established that the road interferes with that right, the justification test must be applied to determine if the expropriation is valid.

The justification test may require the answer to questions such as, What is the purpose of the legislation authorizing the road? Could the purpose be achieved by other means, by using a different route, or by using non-Aboriginal lands? Was the smallest amount of land taken? Was compensation offered? Were reasonable efforts made to negotiate the use of the land with the Aboriginal group? Were any efforts made to protect the spiritual site from damage? The inquiry into whether the interference is justified, and therefore valid, will consider the specific circumstances of the Aboriginal land rights and of the interference. The reasoning in the *Sparrow* decision has been applied in many other cases, particularly those involving hunting and fishing rights.

4. *Delgamuukw*

One of the most important decisions affecting the law of Aboriginal title is *Delgamuukw v. British Columbia*, involving all of the issues reviewed in this chapter. The claimants in *Delgamuukw* are hereditary chiefs of Gitksan and Wet'su-wet'en tribal Houses. These two distinct cultural groups have used and occupied 59 000 square kilometres of lands in the Skeena and Bulkley river systems around Hazelton, Morice-town, and Smithers in British Columbia. The two Aboriginal peoples have been neighbors in the territory for thousands of years and although they speak different languages, they have over time adopted similar customs.

In 1983, the 51 hereditary chiefs began a legal action against the province in the British Columbia Supreme Court for a declaration of ownership and jurisdiction over the lands that they had used and occupied since time immemorial. The province added the federal government as a party to the action. The chiefs argued that their ownership of the lands claimed included "...the right to use, harvest, manage, conserve, and transfer the lands and material resources." At trial, the claim was interpreted to be a claim to Aboriginal title to the lands. The trial took about one year to complete, at a cost to all parties of more than $20 million.

The British Columbia Supreme Court found that colonial legislation passed before 1871, when British Columbia joined Confederation, had extinguished all Aboriginal land rights except those continuing to exist on Indian reserves and adjacent lands. The legislation, according to the court, clearly intended to extinguish Aboriginal land rights, although it did not refer to those rights.

This finding made it unnecessary to consider applying the *Sparrow* justification test, since the court concluded that there were no existing Aboriginal land rights in 1982. The province had title to the land and the right to dispose of those lands without the burden of Aboriginal title. Despite this finding, the trial court found that the province has a fiduciary obligation to permit vacant Crown land to be used for Aboriginal purposes so long as the land remains vacant.

Finally, the court accepted the four elements of Aboriginal title set out in *Baker Lake*. However, the court decided that Aboriginal land rights were restricted to "...what their ancestors obtained from the lands and waters for their Aboriginal life." The plaintiffs' claim that fur trapping for trade purposes is an Aboriginal right was considered by the court to be an activity that arose after Europeans arrived. The court therefore concluded that it was not a protected Aboriginal right.

The appeal by the hereditary chiefs to five judges of the British Columbia Court of Appeal in 1993 resulted in four separate opinions. The majority acknowledged that Canadian common law recognizes Aboriginal land rights and that these rights are recognized by section 35(1) of the Constitution Act,

1982. Several members of the Court of Appeal took the position that the Aboriginal land rights of the Gitksan and Wet'suwet'en peoples had not been extinguished by legislation permitting the government to make land grants for settlement. That legislation, passed before British Columbia joined Confederation, did not express a clear intent to extinguish Aboriginal land rights in the territory. After 1871, only the federal parliament had the authority to deal with Aboriginal land rights according to section 91(24) of the Constitution Act, 1867. Because parliament had not passed legislation extinguishing the claimants' land rights, the majority of the court concluded that the First Nations in *Delgamuukw* continue to have Aboriginal land rights in the territory.

However, the precise nature of these rights was not determined in *Delgamuukw*, although the rights are unique and a burden on the title of the provincial Crown. These rights can also co-exist with the rights and interests of other parties. The *Delgamuukw* decision has been appealed to the Supreme Court of Canada and a decision in this important case is expected soon.

j. THE CURRENT SITUATION

Land treaties cover almost all of Ontario, the Prairie provinces, and portions of British Columbia. Modern treaties have been concluded in Yukon, the Northwest Territories, and in northern Québec, although many questions about these treaties remain outstanding. First Nations in treaty areas across the country continue to pursue and negotiate claims for issues arising from these treaties — issues that First Nations claim were either not dealt with or were dealt with inadequately under the treaties. Treaty issues are dealt with more fully in chapter 1, and a description of existing land claims negotiations can be found in chapter 3.

In some areas not covered by treaty, the federal government has acknowledged that Aboriginal land rights may still exist — in parts of Yukon, Northwest Territories, British Columbia, Québec, and Labrador, for example. However, the federal government has, in general, relied on two arguments to reject Aboriginal title claims in eastern Canada. Because of the longer history of colonization and development in that region, the federal government takes the position that treaties and colonial legislation permitting the granting of land to settlers have extinguished any Aboriginal title.

The second argument often used to reject Aboriginal land rights is that the Aboriginal peoples in eastern Canada no longer use or occupy settled lands in a traditional manner. Several First Nations in eastern Canada have challenged the validity of these arguments. Many have never signed a land treaty (including some First Nations in Ontario), and many do not accept the argument that land registry systems leave the governments without any legal obligation to honor Aboriginal land rights. Importantly, the Supreme Court of Canada, in a recent case involving the Teme-Augama First Nation in northern Ontario, noted that even where Aboriginal title to lands has been technically extinguished, the honor of the Crown may require the government to negotiate a just settlement of outstanding land issues.

In light of this, it is clear that Aboriginal peoples and enlightened federal and provincial governments need to continue the dialogue and negotiation of land rights. Aboriginal peoples will also continue to seek court decisions recognizing their land rights in Canadian law. A resolution of these issues will require creativity and good faith on the part of all participants, not only by the lawyers and judges but also by politicians and a public aware of the history and law described in this chapter.

Although Canadian courts have grappled with the question of Aboriginal land rights for well over a hundred years, there is still considerable uncertainty about the application of these rights in present-day Canada. While recent decisions of of the Supreme Court of Canada and the entrenchment of Aboriginal rights in the Canadian constitution make it clear that these rights must be honored by Canadian governments, key issues about their scope remain outstanding.

Finally, it is important to remember that Canadian court decisions to date have almost always been decided by non-Aboriginal judges unversed in the Aboriginal approach to land use. Our respective cultures and legal traditions do not share a common view of land. Living in harmony with land and resources is a major theme of Aboriginal cultures. The exploitation of lands and resources is a major theme in the economy and law of Canada. The resolution of land claims brings these two different perspectives together; such resolutions are being made in the hope that they will benefit all.

ENDNOTES

[1] George Brown and Ron Maguire, *Indian Treaties in Historical Perspective*, (Ottawa: Research Branch (DIAND), 1979).

[2] *St. Catharine's Milling and Lumber Company v. The Queen (1889), 14 App. Cas. 46; A.G. Canada v. A.G. Ontario*, [1897] A.C. 199; *Ontario Mining Co. v. Seybold*, [1903] A.C. 73; *Dominion of Canada v. Ontario*, [1910] A.C. 637.

3

LAND CLAIMS NEGOTIATIONS IN CANADA

by Michael Coyle

On March 22, 1996, the Canadian public learned that the government of British Columbia, the federal government, and the Nisga'a Tribal Council had signed an agreement-in-principle that calls for the transfer of $190 million and some 2 000 square kilometres of land to the Nisga'a people. If it is ratified, the agreement will form the basis of the first modern-day treaty in British Columbia. Why would the governments agree to make such a commitment? On what basis were the amounts of money and land determined? Why did the negotiations take 20 years to complete? How were the rights of non-Aboriginal people factored into the negotiations?

As of the fall of 1996, the federal government was involved in roughly 100 land claims negotiations with First Nations across the country. Another 260 claims were being reviewed by the federal government to determine whether negotiations should begin. Most of the provinces were also involved in land claims negotiations, either together with the federal government or on their own. The government of Ontario alone has received at least 40 land claims from First Nations in the province. Yet little information is readily available to the public about what actually goes on in land claims negotiations. With so many land claims being negotiated, and federal settlement payments last year in excess of $60 million, the Canadian public has an understandable interest — as do members of First Nation communities — in learning about the basis and nature of land claims negotiations in Canada today.

a. WHAT IS A LAND CLAIM?

1. Aboriginal peoples' land rights

Setting aside for the moment legal and bureaucratic distinctions, at the heart of every land claims negotiation in Canada today is a claim by an Aboriginal community that a government in Canada has violated or failed to address that community's legal rights to its land. The land rights of Aboriginal peoples in Canada can generally be broken down into two categories.

First, an Aboriginal community may have rights based on Aboriginal title to their traditional lands. Canadian law has recognized the importance of these kinds of Aboriginal land rights since at least 1763, when a royal proclamation guaranteed that Aboriginal peoples' traditional lands would not be interfered with unless the Crown first received the consent of the Aboriginal people involved. The legal basis of Aboriginal title is described in detail in chapter 2, but it is worth noting that the concept that anyone — non-Aboriginal or Aboriginal — can acquire legal property rights from the lengthy uninterrupted possession of land has been recognized by the English common law since at least the Middle Ages. The federal government negotiates claims based on Aboriginal title through a process known as the Comprehensive Claims Policy.

The second broad category of land claims includes cases where the federal or provincial government, or both, allegedly violated a specific legal obligation to an Aboriginal community, whether set out in a treaty, statute, or the common law. Such a claim might be based on an illegal expropriation of Aboriginal lands, failure to implement promises made in a treaty or any other agreement, fraud committed by government or an agent acting on its behalf, breach of trust, or any other violation of Canadian law. Claims of this kind generally fit into the federal claims process known as the Specific Claims Policy.

2. Land claims and Canadian legal principles

Before examining Canada's land claims policies further, certain key points are worth noting. First, contrary to what some Canadians may believe, land claims negotiations are not an attempt to address some generalized sense of dissatisfaction on the part of an Aboriginal community with their lot in contemporary Canadian society. Nor do claims negotiations involve applying vague moral standards to reassess in hindsight the treatment of Aboriginal people by Canadian governments. Instead, Canada's land claims policies require a basis in Canadian legal principles before the government of Canada will enter into negotiations.

The relationship of land claims and Canadian legal principles is significant. In a sense, it means Aboriginal communities are negotiating on Euro-Canadian turf. The cultural, spiritual, and social views held by Aboriginal communities about their relationship to their land do not figure largely in the formulation of federal and provincial land claims policies. First Nations negotiating or litigating land claims in Canada must accept this limitation.

On the other hand, because claims being negotiated are claims based on Canadian law, it is difficult for members of the public to argue that Aboriginal people are receiving preferential treatment by the mere fact of having their land claims resolved. To the extent that claims may be based on special laws applying only to Aboriginal people (such as the Indian Act, certain provisions of the Royal Proclamation of 1763, or the provisions of Indian treaties) these laws already form part of the constitutional and legal framework on which this country has been built. Those Canadians, of whom there may be a significant number, who believe that resolving land claims is unfair because it constitutes "special treatment" of Aboriginal people should look to amending the Canadian Constitution, renegotiating the treaties, and rewriting Canadian laws before criticizing the policy of negotiating land claims.

3. The role of provincial governments

Canada's constitution, statutes, and common law also determine whether the local provincial government may have a role to play in a land claims negotiation. Depending on the historical facts, an agency of the provincial government may have violated or failed to recognize a First Nation's legal rights or may have participated with the federal government in an illegal taking of Aboriginal land. Canada's constitution gives jurisdiction over most public lands in a province to the provincial rather than the federal government, and public lands may be affected by a land claim. Finally, in many cases the only available public lands that might be contributed to an acceptable modern settlement of the claim will be owned by the provincial Crown.

For these reasons, most provincial governments are prepared to participate in land claims negotiations to resolve potential provincial liabilities and to clear up uncertainties about land title. Although each participating province has its own policy or approach to claims negotiations, in general the provinces also negotiate based on their understanding of their legal rights and obligations in a claim. In some provinces, such as British Columbia, promoting fairness and economic certainty are also key stated goals of their claims policy.

It is important to recognize that each province's negotiation criteria may well differ from the federal government's. Finding a settlement satisfying both the federal and provincial policies as well as the Aboriginal community's principles and aspirations is often one of the major challenges in land claims negotiations involving the province.

b. THE ADVANTAGES OF NEGOTIATION

1. Costs

There are many reasons why negotiating a land claim may be preferable to trying to resolve the issues in court. Taking any but the simplest Aboriginal case to the Supreme Court of Canada can cost $500 000 or more for the First Nation alone. And the Supreme Court is where the case will end up if the issues are at all contentious. Rarely will an Aboriginal community have the necessary resources. Assuming a First Nation does have the resources, the litigation will be a lengthy process that can take a decade to complete.

In the meantime, until there is a final decision by the courts, the uncertainty created by an Aboriginal land claim may discourage investment in the area, hinder economic and resource development, possibly lower local property values, and heighten tensions between the Aboriginal community and its neighbors. This hidden cost of not resolving land claims is difficult to measure but is very real, as residents of the Temagami area in Ontario or municipalities in the region of Six Nations will readily attest.

Uncertainty over land titles in a significant portion of the province may also have a negative effect on the interest rates at which the province is able to borrow money. One prominent chartered accounting firm recently estimated the financial cost of the uncertainty over land claims in British Columbia alone at more than one billion dollars.

Failure to negotiate land claims settlements in a timely way can also lead to dangerous confrontations, as Canadians know all too well. The human price of such confrontations can be tragic, leaving antagonism and bitterness between the Aboriginal community and its neighbors.

And the financial cost of physical confrontation can far exceed what it would have cost all sides to achieve a negotiated settlement. It has been reported that to address the Oka crisis, for example, the federal and provincial governments spent more than $150 million — without settling the claim itself, which is still outstanding.

2. "Tailor-made" settlements

Negotiation also offers the advantage of allowing the parties to develop their own tailor-made settlement of the issues. If lands illegally taken from a First Nation are now occupied by other members of the public, substitute Crown lands might be found that can meet the community's needs and rectify the original injustice. If the Aboriginal community and its neighbors share a need to use resources that are the subject of a claim, it may be possible to establish a creative regime in which the resources will be co-managed. This was the approach taken, for example, in the 1994 settlement of the Mississauga Northern Boundary Claim. That settlement led to the co-management of a significant portion of the Blind River in Ontario, meeting the First Nation's interests in the watershed while ensuring water quality and water level controls acceptable to the province and the town of Blind River.

The courts, on the other hand, are limited in the remedies they can provide and are reluctant to prescribe complicated orders that will be difficult for them to monitor and enforce. Nor does the court process permit broad community input (either Aboriginal or non-Aboriginal) into the development of a claim settlement. Possible as part of the negotiation process, community input should increase the likelihood of achieving an enduring settlement that will be respected both by the Aboriginal community and its non-Aboriginal neighbors.

3. Canada's legal obligations

There is a final and perhaps more fundamental reason for governments in Canada to be open to the negotiation of land claims. Canada is a country that prides itself on its reputed adherence to the rule of law. Its citizens expect their governments to comply with their legal obligations. If an individual is entitled, for example, to Canada Pension Plan payments, Canadians would be astonished if the government had a policy of regularly refusing to make the payments it owes. Presumably Aboriginal people are entitled to the same standard. There is ample evidence that Crown governments have repeatedly violated specific commitments and legal obligations to Aboriginal communities in historical dealings. This is not a statement of personal opinion: it is the conclusion of the Supreme Court of Canada in *Sparrow*, of the Canadian Human Rights Commission, and of government legal departments. Given that legacy, it does not seem unreasonable that governments should be willing to make some effort to fulfil their legal obligations to Aboriginal people through negotiation.

c. WHEN IS NEGOTIATION NOT THE BEST OPTION?

While there are many advantages to negotiating claims, negotiation will not always be the preferred option. In some cases the issues in dispute may be too important or too controversial in law for a negotiated settlement to be likely or preferable. In other cases the parties have reached an impasse in negotiations (some of the reasons for this are described later in the chapter) and believe negotiation is no longer a viable path to settlement. In still other cases, the amount of money at stake may exceed the annual budget allocations of the federal government (now $37.5 million annually for all specific claims settlements in Canada).

The Six Nations of the Grand River, for example, began legal proceedings in 1995 for a Crown accounting of all Six Nations moneys and lands the Crown has dealt with since 1784. The Six Nations' original territory ran from the Grand River's source to its mouth, extending six miles in each direction from the river — a total area of hundreds of thousands of acres. The potential financial implications of this single claim are enormous and certainly larger than the usual Ontario "share" of the specific claims budget. Perhaps it is not surprising that this claim has found its way to court.

In some cases, then, negotiations (or at least the usual negotiation processes) may not always seem a viable option for the parties. Still, negotiation of land claims can produce significant results. In the seven years leading up to the spring of 1996, for example, the negotiation of 43 treaty land settlements in the Prairies have resulted in the transfer of 277 000 acres of provincial land and the payment of $627 million to First Nations. The track record in eastern Canada does not begin to approach the Prairie experience, for reasons which remain the subject of debate. But the 100 land claims discussions now proceeding in Canada are testimony to the parties' belief in the potential of negotiation.

d. THE NEGOTIATION PROCESS

Since the actual negotiations on a land claim are almost always conducted behind closed doors, one might well wonder just who is at the table, what they discuss, and how it can take up to 20 years to complete the discussions.

A typical claims negotiation meeting involving a First Nation will be held in the government's council chambers or the First Nation's community hall. Around the table will be representatives of the federal government, the provincial government if it is involved, and the First Nation. The chief and several councillors and elders from the First Nation will likely be at the table. They will also have a lawyer whose role in large part is to ensure that the First Nation does not unwittingly compromise its legal rights.

Each government will have a spokesperson, its chief negotiator, who will have a mandate from senior government officials (perhaps from a deputy minister or, in large claims, from a minister or from cabinet). With the chief negotiator will be one or two assistant negotiators and a government lawyer. If a neutral third party is facilitating the negotiation, as is the case in most tripartite claims negotiations in Ontario, a chairperson whose role is to assist the parties to work through their agenda and to keep a neutral record of agreements reached will be at one end of the table.

Members of the First Nation community may also be in the room. Normally, neither the news media nor representatives of public interest groups will be present at the negotiations which, after all, are designed to resolve a specific legal dispute between the Aboriginal community and the Crown. (The role of the public in settlement negotiations is an issue to which we return later in this chapter.)

In a "typical" claims negotiation, the parties have been meeting once every month for several years. In many cases, as in the Nisga'a negotiation and the average current negotiation in Ontario, the claim was filed with the government more than ten years ago. What has happened since the claim was filed and what are they discussing?

1. Criteria for acceptance of the claim

If the federal government is involved in the negotiation, it is because it has accepted the claim as a comprehensive claim, a specific claim, or a "claim of another kind."

(a) Comprehensive claims

Comprehensive claims deal with situations where an Aboriginal group asserts that it continues to have Aboriginal title to some or all of its traditional lands. This type of claim is particularly important in areas of the country where treaties were not signed at the time of European settlement, as in most of British Columbia and in significant portions of the Northwest Territories, Yukon, Québec, and Labrador. As outlined in chapter 2, the concept of Aboriginal title has been recognized in Canadian courts since at least the Supreme Court of Canada's 1973 *Calder* decision.

The federal Comprehensive Claims Policy was announced in 1973 as a response to the *Calder* decision. If the parties at the table are negotiating a comprehensive claim, the Aboriginal group has filed a statement of claim that includes the following points:

(a) The Aboriginal group is, and was, an organized society.

(b) The organized society has occupied the specific territory over which it asserts Aboriginal title since time immemorial. The traditional use and occupancy of the territory must have been sufficient to be an established fact at the time of assertion of sovereignty by European nations.

(c) The occupation of the territory by the Aboriginal group was largely to the exclusion of other organized societies.

(d) The Aboriginal group can demonstrate some continuing current use and occupancy of the land for traditional purposes.

(e) The group's Aboriginal title and rights to resource use have not been dealt with by treaty.

(f) Aboriginal title has not been eliminated by other lawful means.

(b) Specific claims

If the parties at the table are negotiating what the federal government considers to be a specific claim (as is the case for most negotiations involving the Prairie provinces and Ontario, where the vast majority of the province is covered by treaties), the First Nation has submitted and documented a claim asserting that the federal government has —

(a) not fulfilled a treaty or agreement between Indians and the Crown,

(b) breached an obligation arising out of the Indian Act or other statutes pertaining to Indians,

(c) breached an obligation arising out of government administration of Indian funds or other assets,

(d) illegally disposed of Indian land,

(e) failed to provide compensation for reserve lands taken or damaged by the federal government or any of its agencies under authority, or

(f) committed fraud in connection with the acquisition or disposition of Indian reserve land by employees or agents of the federal government.

The above criteria for accepting claims are paraphrased from the federal government's specific claims and comprehensive claims policies.

(c) "Claims of another kind"

The terms *specific claim* and *comprehensive claim* are not terms or concepts that have been used by the courts. Nor is it clear that the acceptance criteria under the two policies cover all situations in which a court would find the government to have violated or failed to address its legal obligations. It has been pointed out, for example, that neither federal claims policy refers to the fiduciary, or trust-like, obligation of the Crown toward Aboriginal peoples, a key underpinning of recent court judgments ruling on the relationship between the Crown and Aboriginal people. Also, while the law regarding land claims has evolved significantly over the past ten years, the Comprehensive Claims Policy has not changed since 1987, and the criteria listed above for the Specific Claims Policy have not changed since 1982. As a result, some commentators have suggested that federal land claims policy should be simplified, and should expressly reflect the current state of the law. While such a change has not yet occurred, the federal government has in recent years agreed to enter certain land claims negotiations — "claims of another kind"

— if a land claim appears to have legal merit but does not fit the strict parameters of either policy.

(d) Provincial governments' criteria for claims

We have seen that provincial governments are also often involved in land claims negotiations. If a provincial negotiator is at the table, he or she will be guided by that province's policy for accepting and negotiating claims. In general, although the provinces do not have published policy guides similar to the federal claims manuals, provinces participate in land claims negotiations on the basis that the interests of the province and its residents may be affected by the claim.

2. Research and legal review

To get a land claim to the negotiating table, the Aboriginal group must research in detail the facts giving rise to the claim. The federal government reviews that research and then does its own supplementary or "confirming" research to verify and complete the factual basis of the claim. (If a province is involved, the province also reviews, separately, the claim's historical and legal merits.) The federal Department of Justice then reviews the historical research to determine whether there is indeed legal merit to the claim. The Specific Claims Policy requires the department to ignore statutes of limitation (laws specifying a certain period of time after which rights cannot be enforced by legal action) during its review, for the purposes of negotiation, although the federal government reserves the right to use such defences if the claim goes to court.

At the end of this research process, which will typically take the parties between two and five years, if the federal government is prepared to enter into negotiations, it provides a formal acceptance letter, setting out the basis on which it is willing to do so. The letter will make clear that the government's decision to negotiate should not be interpreted as an admission that it is legally liable on the claim.

Usually, the Aboriginal group receives some federal funding to support its research on the claim and will, after the claim is formally accepted, annually negotiate loan or grant funding to support its participation in the negotiations. (The situation is somewhat different in British Columbia, where the B.C. Treaty Commission allocates negotiation support funding to Aboriginal claimants, primarily through loans.)

The federal approach to specific and comprehensive claims is explained in detail in the following publications, available from Indian and Northern Affairs Canada: *Federal Policy for the Settlement of Native Claims, Outstanding Business: A Native Claims Policy, Specific Claims,* and *Process Manual for Specific Claims: Draft.* These policy statements reflect the views of the federal government and are not necessarily accepted by First Nations or by provincial governments, each of which have their own written or unwritten claims policy. The federal government's claims processes are continually evolving and leave considerable scope for interpretation and creativity in resolving a claim if the parties choose to take advantage of this.

e. THE ISSUES BEING NEGOTIATED

Regardless of the type of claim bringing them to the negotiation table, there is always one central challenge for the parties to resolve: how to find practical ways in a modern context to fulfil historical obligations of the government. Comprehensive claims require the parties to collectively agree on a set of rights, compensation, and other benefits to be provided in exchange for the Aboriginal group's release of its claim to Aboriginal title over its traditional lands.

The challenge in a specific claim is generally to assess the monetary value of the losses suffered by the First Nation and, where lands have been wrongfully taken, to determine whether the original lands are available to be returned to the First Nation without unduly interfering with the rights or interests of other members of the public, or whether substitute lands should be given if original lands are no longer available.

1. Assessing compensation

Determining the appropriate amount of monetary compensation is a key component of most land claims settlements. Here it is important to note that the Comprehensive and Specific Claims policies call for different approaches. The Specific Claims Policy sets out 10 detailed criteria the federal negotiator must generally apply in offering monetary compensation. The stated purpose of these criteria is to establish a consistent set of guidelines for monetary compensation that restores the First Nation, insofar as money can, to the position the First Nation would have enjoyed had the federal government not breached its rights. The federal government's goal in the negotiations is to obtain, to the extent possible, empirical evidence of the First Nation's losses. The policy does not provide for compensation for cultural damage to the First Nation, for general suffering as a result of historic wrongs, or for losses the federal government believes were suffered by persons within the First Nation rather than by the First Nation as a collective.

The detailed criteria set out in the Specific Claims Policy are certainly not universally acceptable to many First Nations or their lawyers. It is probably fair to say that in specific claims, the acceptable range of total compensation will be heavily influenced by the parties' views of how Canadian legal principles would measure the government's potential liability. This is certainly the approach that must be considered by First Nations' lawyers and is presumably taken by provincial governments where their legal liability is also in question. In recent years, all parties have tended to favor using jointly chosen appraisers and loss-of-use consultants, according to jointly agreed terms of reference, to help reach agreement on an objective measure of the First Nation's losses and to avoid lengthy disputes between experts. In larger claims the parties may even have two jointly chosen professionals report separately to provide greater confidence in their results.

No criteria for determining compensation are included in the federal Comprehensive Claims Policy, although the policy states that compensation may be provided in a number of ways, including cash, resource revenue sharing, and even government bonds. In practice, recent history suggests that all parties will focus on forward-looking approaches, balancing the need to promote economic self-sufficiency for the Aboriginal claimants, the nature and size of the claim, fairness to all parties affected by the claims, and modern fiscal realities.

2. Including land in the settlement

Not surprisingly, a key component of most land claims negotiations is determining whether land will be provided to the First Nation in a final settlement. If the government has broken a legal obligation to set aside land for the First Nation, if the Crown has failed to enter a treaty with the First Nation, or if land has been illegally taken by the government, the federal government generally accedes to a First Nation request that a particular amount of available land be added to the First Nation's territory.

This might be achieved by the First Nation using settlement proceeds to purchase lands on the open market. Or if Crown land is available in the area, the settlement agreement may provide for the province to transfer selected Crown lands to Canada in trust for the First Nation. If the province is willing to consider transferring lands or recognizing land-related rights as part of a settlement, it will generally hold public consultations before finalizing the arrangement.

In comprehensive claims in particular, the recognition of specific land-related rights is also a key negotiation issue. Generally, these might include rights for sub-surface resources, waters in the claim area, forests, wildlife and fisheries, protecting cultural artifacts, rights of access, and rights of the Aboriginal group to manage and govern settlement lands.

3. Extinguishment of rights

A third key issue the parties must address is how to ensure that the claims settlement achieves finality. The federal and provincial governments have an obvious interest in eliminating any uncertainty over the validity of land title in a claim and will therefore require a full release of the First Nation's legal claims as part of a final settlement. While First Nations inevitably agree to provide this legal release, in many cases they do not wish to approve what appears to be a severing of their continuing relationship to their traditional lands. The First Nation may want the settlement agreement to include a confirmation that certain rights of the First Nation's members will continue, for example, the pursuit of traditional activities in lands under claim.

Where the First Nation has never consented to the taking of lands it is claiming, the federal government will also generally seek a formal surrender of those lands by the First Nation under a referendum procedure set out in the Indian Act. (Chapter 2 discusses in greater detail the surrender of First Nation lands.) Partly perhaps because of the colonialistic implications of the concepts of surrender and extinguishment, First Nations are often reluctant to agree to such a surrender process. As a result, the drafting of the terms by which the First Nation releases any rights to the claimed lands can be a difficult issue in the land claims negotiations.

Government claims policies now stipulate that they will not agree to a settlement that would prejudice the legal rights of non-Aboriginal people in the area. So far as possible, claims settlements are intended to rectify historic wrongs without creating new ones.

f. UNDERLYING CHALLENGES

If reaching agreement on the appropriate form of compensation and achieving finality are the key formal issues in a typical land claims negotiation, it is nonetheless true that there are other important challenges the parties must address if the negotiation is to be successful.

1. Antagonism at the negotiating table

First, Canada does not have a history it can be proud of in its dealings with Aboriginal grievances. In most of the key decisions regarding lands Aboriginal people claimed up to the middle of this century, Aboriginal people were not even represented before the courts. Indeed, from 1927 to 1951 it was a criminal offence under the Indian Act for a lawyer to be retained by an Aboriginal group to press a claim on its behalf. Status Indians did not receive the right to vote in federal elections until 1960 and the federal government did not adopt a formal policy of negotiating land claims until 1973.

Because of Aboriginal peoples' experience in their dealings with Canadian governments, Aboriginal communities are often frustrated by and distrustful of the Department of Indian Affairs and Canadian governments generally. This frustration and suspicion will spill over into land claims negotiations regardless of the approach the particular government negotiator takes at the table. The result, unless all sides are particularly sensitive to this issue, is that negotiations can become adversarial and antagonistic instead of focusing on effective problem-solving approaches.

2. Lack of dispute resolutions processes

Second, successful land claims negotiations, as we have seen, may require agreement on a number of issues on which the parties may legitimately disagree, particularly where the law is uncertain. But there are no dispute resolution processes built into Canada's land claims compensation policies. If the parties reach an impasse once they have agreed a claim has merit and negotiations have begun, there is simply no way for one party to force the others to reconsider their approach. And impasses occur regularly. The government and the First Nation may disagree over how the courts would access the First Nation's rights, or over how the courts would place a modern value on the claim. Alternatively, the federal and provincial negotiators may disagree over their shares of responsibility for a particular claim.

Theoretically, if the parties to a land claims negotiation are unable to work through a disagreement, they could hire a neutral expert to give them advice on the issue. That advice could be binding or non-binding and would serve as a reality check for the negotiators and lawyers involved. Although formal mechanisms could help the parties get beyond impasses in this way if all agree, in practice, once negotiations begin, if an important legal issue is disputed, nothing forces the parties to obtain neutral advice or to take any other action to try to break the impasse. Instead of making progress on the claim, all too often the parties will simply stop meeting for months or years at a time, waiting presumably for a change in the political climate.

3. Imbalance of bargaining power

There is another fundamental challenge underlying all land claims negotiations in Canada, one that helps explain the delays encountered in resolving claims and the frustrations with the process that often spill over into confrontation or legal action. Simply, there is generally a huge imbalance of power between the parties at the table.

Consider a negotiation involving only the federal government. Assume that the federal claims policy is fair and that the government representatives are ready to negotiate "in good faith." Think of the difference between the financial, technical, and legal resources available to the federal government and those accessible to a community of a few hundred, perhaps a few thousand, Aboriginal people. Then consider that it is the government that decides how much research and negotiation funding the party it is negotiating against will receive. The government determines which claims it will negotiate and how much it is prepared to put on the table to settle those that it does negotiate. Recall that the Aboriginal . side cannot force the government to hear even a neutral view on any disputed issue in the compensation negotiations.

Using another common measure of negotiating power, consider each party's options if the negotiations do not succeed. Options are usually very limited for First Nations: court is a lengthy, often impossibly expensive process and physical confrontation or other "self-help" approaches such as roadblocks are a very risky method of trying to obtain public sympathy that would put pressure on the government. Now consider the government's options. If the negotiations fail to reach agreement or if they drag on indefinitely, the government defers paying money to settle the claim. If the issue goes to court, the process will take years and a different department will be involved (and usually different political leaders too, by the time the litigation is over). Even if the courts decide in favor of the First Nation, the government appears to have lost nothing in comparison to the negotiation process and indeed now has the comfort of a court decision to justify its compensation to the First Nation.

Society may have lost, since an injustice was not resolved voluntarily or in a timely way by the government, the investment climate may have been undermined, and Aboriginal frustrations may have been heightened to the breaking point. But these considerations need not necessarily affect the government's approach to the negotiation, particularly if the claim poses no immediate threat to the investment climate and if the First Nation seems unwilling to participate in confrontation.

The lack of a level playing field in negotiations does not, of course, mean it is impossible to reach an acceptable solution for all sides, and to some degree the imbalance will always exist. In fact, from the federal perspective some senior policy advisers candidly argue that the imbalance of power must be maintained in any claims so that the government will always have the final say on whether a proposed settlement meets the public interest. Still, the imbalance in bargaining power is an important point to understand in assessing the backlog of unresolved claims in this country and those remaining to be negotiated. It is also the subject of some of the most prominent proposals for reform of Canada's negotiation policies, as we will see shortly.

g. THE ROLE OF INDEPENDENT COMMISSIONS AND MEDIATORS

Three commissions have been established in Canada to address some of the challenges facing Aboriginal peoples at the negotiating table and assist in land claims negotiations: the Indian Commission of Ontario, the Indian Specific Claims Commission, and the British Columbia Treaty Commission.

1. Indian Commission of Ontario

In Ontario, First Nations may ask the federal and provincial governments to have their claims facilitated by the Indian Commission of Ontario (ICO). Established in 1978, the ICO chairs land claims negotiations as well as other negotiations important to First Nations and the federal or provincial governments. Although the ICO has a wide range of tools within its mandate that may be used if all parties agree, its main role is to act as an independent mediator and keeper of the record of undertakings and agreements reached by the parties. The ICO is also mandated to acquaint the public with the status of the negotiations with which it is involved, making it another place where the public and media can obtain information about claims negotiations in Ontario.

Although the ICO has a small staff and is involved only in claims where all parties request its assistance, it has facilitated the largest claim settlements to date in Ontario and is chairing the majority of active land claims negotiations in the province. The strengths of the ICO are the strengths of mediation generally. ICO staff may discourage all parties from taking adversarial approaches, monitor the parties' completion of undertakings, suggest options for the parties' consideration, coordinate the completion of joint historical and compensation studies, and prepare draft agreements for review. In these ways, the ICO can increase the chances of successful negotiation.

On the other hand, the ICO has no power to compel any party to take a particular action on a claim. It can do little apart from express concern if one party, for example, has failed to attend a negotiation meeting for months or years.

2. Indian Specific Claims Commission (ICC)

The Indian Specific Claims Commission (ICC, also known as ISCC) was created by a federal order-in-council in 1991. Unlike the ICO, this commission has the power to mediate, on the parties' consent, any specific claims negotiation in the country. The ICC also has the authority to hold formal inquiries and make recommendations to the federal government in specific claims where a First Nation disagrees with the federal government's initial assessment of the claim. Reflecting its national mandate, the ICC's budget is about six times as large as the ICO's, and it has five commissioners appointed at the request of the federal government and Aboriginal leaders. The ICC power to hold inquiries is limited to the stage preceding actual compensation negotiations: when a First Nation disagrees with the federal government on which compensation criteria should be applied to the negotiations in accordance with the Specific Claims Policy, or when a First Nation disagrees with the federal government's proposal to reject its claim completely.

After completing an inquiry, in which oral evidence and written documents may be submitted, the ICC forwards a public recommendation to the federal government. The commission's independence and the force of its argument may persuade Canada to reconsider its initial position on a claim.

However, the ICC's mandate has four noteworthy limitations: it has the power to make recommendations only, it can deal only with specific claims, it has no authority over the position or role of provincial governments in claims, and it has no powers of inquiry on any issue once claims compensation negotiations have begun.

Partly because of these limitations, the future of the ICC and its mandate is uncertain. The ICC has advised that as of September 1, 1996, it will not hear any new claims, and as of March 31, 1997, its commissioners will resign unless changes are made to ICC's mandate. That mandate is now being reviewed by the federal government and national Aboriginal leaders.

3. British Columbia Treaty Commission (BCTC)

The British Columbia Treaty Commission (BCTC) was created in 1993 to manage a voluntary, "made in British Columbia" process to facilitate modern treaty negotiations in that province. Like the ICO, the BCTC is a tripartite commission established by the province, Aboriginal leaders, and the federal government. And like the ICO and the ICC, the BCTC has no powers to compel one party to make progress on a particular claim.

But unlike the other commissions, the BCTC is designed specifically to manage a process that will resolve issues of Aboriginal title. To do so, the BCTC is mandated to ensure each party is adequately prepared for negotiations to begin — that each has identified the negotiation issues, appointed negotiators with clear mandates, and adopted a ratification procedure for dealing with proposed settlements. First Nations must have put in place a means for addressing any overlap in claims from other First Nations. The governments of Canada and British Columbia must each have put in place mechanisms for consulting with non-Aboriginal interests affected by the negotiations.

It is not clear to what extent the BCTC will participate in claims negotiations once they begin, although the commission is available to provide advice to the parties on dispute resolution. Tripartite treaty negotiations in British Columbia are new, as is BCTC's process, and to a large extent the role the BCTC will play in facilitating the negotiations remains to be defined.

4. Summary

In summary, the governments' existing policies and the willingness of all parties to make progress in the negotiations limit what each of these commissions can do. Both the ICO and ICC have publicly expressed the view that a new negotiation process is required, recommending a new independent organization be established in Canada with the necessary authority to ensure that undue delays do not occur in land claims negotiations, to adjudicate independent of the federal government as to whether a particular land claim has merit, and to ensure that the parties receive a neutral opinion when negotiations reach an impasse.

The ICO and ICC argue that fairness and the public interest in an efficient claims process require these changes and that the changes should be negotiated by Crown governments and Aboriginal leaders to improve the effectiveness of claims negotiations in the future. As both the national Chiefs' Committee on Claims' 1990 report and the federal Liberals' 1992 Red Book of policy directions call for the creation of a new national body to deal with land claims, it is possible such a reform to the claims negotiation process may be in the offing.

h. THE ROLE OF THE CANADIAN PUBLIC IN CLAIMS NEGOTIATIONS

Where does the public fit into all of this? Why is the public not at the table in claims negotiations today? Well, in fact it *is* at the table if we accept that the role of federal and provincial negotiators is to represent the interest of taxpayers and the public at large. In this sense, the non-Aboriginal public speaks at the table in the same way as the Aboriginal community: through its elected representatives. We have also seen that the federal government and, in practice, every provincial government has a general policy of not agreeing to any land claims settlement that would interfere with the legal rights of other Canadians.

1. During negotiations

In practice, there are two stages in a land claims negotiation at which the public can obtain direct information or participate in discussions about the issues in dispute. During the negotiations themselves, the negotiators will normally agree to appoint one representative of each party to be responsible for updating news media on the issues under negotiation. There are no set government guidelines for the level of detail that should be provided to the public prior to tentative agreements being reached at the table.

On the one hand, there is an understandable desire to avoid appearing to negotiate the issues in the media. In any negotiation, commercial, legal, or otherwise, allowing cameras into the room or negotiating in the public eye guarantees that the parties will be reluctant to speak freely and creatively.

Still, the public at large, the news media, and interested local elected officials are free to insist that all parties keep them regularly informed of the status of the negotiations and progress on the issues. They may also supplement what they learn in this way through applications under federal and provincial access to information legislation to obtain background information about the negotiations. Information on how to make such applications federally is available at the local Indian Affairs office; advice about making an application under provincial legislation is available at the provincial Attorney General's Ministry.

2. During consideration of public land as part of settlement

Next, if public land is being considered as a possible element of a land claims settlement, the federal and provincial governments require full public consultations before making a final commitment to include the land in a settlement. Public consultation policies vary from province to province, and the specific approach taken on a particular claim depends on the size of the claim and how widely members of the public feel they have an interest in the settlement.

Typically, though, the parties will issue a press release and information package describing the options being considered, and meetings and open houses will be arranged to discuss the basis of the claim, the reasons for the proposed settlement, and the possible effects of the settlement. Meetings will also be arranged with local municipal councils and the First Nation community. The consultations and opportunity for public concerns to be expressed normally continue for several months before the federal and provincial governments reach their final decisions on how to proceed.

3. Summary

Canada's recent experiences with land claims consultations show they can be a very trying experience for the local communities involved. The non-Aboriginal community may feel it has not been kept sufficiently informed during the negotiation process to be able to put the settlement proposal in context. And among them there may be many who are distrustful of big government and many who, through no fault of their own, do not understand the constitutional and legal background to the issues.

As for the Aboriginal community, it may feel that since the Crown has admitted it allowed the community's land to be taken away illegally, the Crown should simply replace the land if public land is available — without asking the opinions of outsiders to the legal dispute. And many Aboriginal communities suspect they will face overt criticism of their role in Canadian society and hostile questioning from their neighbors about their legal and constitutional rights.

As controversial as the land claims process may be — both for Canadians at large and Aboriginal communities — consultations with both communities appear likely to continue in the future. Canada's history demonstrates that the issues raised by land claims will not simply go away. For those Canadians who believe in principled dialogue, negotiation will remain the forum of choice to resolve the issues. And for land claims negotiations to be able to lead to enduring settlements that will be respected in both communities, fairness in the negotiation process — to all parties — will be indispensable.

4

INJUNCTIONS AND ROADBLOCKS: LAW AND TACTICS

by Stephen B. Smart

a. BACKGROUND

Modern-day Canada got its first understanding of the power of Native standoffs with the three-month Mohawk occupation at Oka in 1990. The standoff was sparked by a municipal council decision permitting the extension of a golf course onto an ancient Mohawk burial ground, despite Mohawk demands that the burial grounds be left alone. Mohawk warriors responded immediately, occupying lands and erecting a barricade.

The protest proved to be a powerful lesson that educated non-Aboriginal Canadians about the plight facing many First Nations. For the first time, many non-Aboriginal Canadians, raised in an educational and political system that virtually ignored Aboriginal history, understood the historical background of these issues.

Aboriginal communities across the country learned to be more assertive of long outstanding rights, even if they were not specifically provoked into action. They also learned that electronic and media networks could be powerful tools to get their message out, nationally and internationally.

Oka taught the federal and Québec governments that law and order must involve coming to terms with long outstanding and often legitimate Aboriginal concerns for appropriate dispute resolution.

However, the object of Oka was not to attract public attention, although it certainly did do that. Rather, its aim was to use the immediate and decisive remedy of "self-help" to bring to a head disputes that generations of traditional efforts at problem solving had failed to resolve. The Mohawk warriors did not have time to debate issues or consult elders or band councils on whether to start a legal proceeding against the municipality to prevent the proposed development. Community frustration resulted in a call to arms, and the occupation began. During the standoff, a police officer was killed.

Public sentiment was piqued by the manner in which Brian Mulroney's Conservative government dealt with the crisis. For the first time, contemporary Canada seemed to understand that "law and order" (the buzz phrase of the Conservative government) could be looked at from more than one viewpoint. The apparent lawlessness had a resonance in which some Canadians could see the justice and legality of the Aboriginal viewpoint as a distinct counterpoint to the European-inherited legal system that was attempting to quell the "disobedience." While there was never any doubt that once the struggle was over, the federal arm of the law would lay criminal charges against the protesters, the Oka crisis revealed to many Canadians that there was a justifiable background to the Mohawk actions.

Oka gave impetus to other Aboriginal groups throughout the country. Many capitalized on the available national press. In the same summer, the Pic Mobert and Pays Plat First Nations north of Lake Superior blocked both the Canadian National and Canadian Pacific rail lines crossing their reserves, bringing train service between Toronto and Winnipeg to a temporary standstill. The Ontario Attorney General's Department responded with an injunction to halt the railway blockades. Fearing that this bonfire could flare up into another Oka, or, alternatively, act as a spark to other Aboriginal communities, the provincial and federal governments promised immediate negotiations on the outstanding claim.

By November 1990, after subsequent negotiations, Ontario's Minister of Indian Affairs agreed to transfer land back from the province to Canada so that Long Lake No. 58 Indian Reserve could be enlarged from its one square mile, in an effort to increase the economic independence of the residents and to attain acceptable living conditions.

Another Native group making significant strides directly as a result of, and during, Oka was the Six First Nations of the Nishnawabe-Aski of northern Ontario. Justice Harry La-Forme, then head of the Indian Commission of Ontario, brought, through several prime-time television interviews, the plight of these poverty-stricken First Nations to national attention in an attempt to shame the government into providing six separate reserves to the Six Nations. Before Oka, the federal government had failed to provide these First Nations with land or decent living conditions.

Oka also acted as a catalyst to compel the federal government to move land claim settlements off the back burner. The government was forced to rethink its previous policy and finally agreed to consider pre-Confederation land claims, such as the Oka claim.

Events of the summer of 1990 played a role in compelling many Canadians, Aboriginal and non-Aboriginal, to ask soul-searching questions: What is our country really all about? Who are we? How do we want to redefine the important relationship between Aboriginal and non-Aboriginal peoples in a more just society? These questions were asked not only on a national basis but also on a community basis and triggered the federal government to set up the far-reaching Royal Commission on Aboriginal Peoples.

By 1995, it seemed that Aboriginal standoffs had become a distinctive feature of Canada's contemporary political life. High-profile self-help situations occurred like flash fires across the country: the Mi'kmaq in the Miramichi River of New Brunswick, the Chippewas of Kettle Point and Stoney Point First Nation at Ipperwash Provincial Park on the shores of Lake Huron, and Aboriginal protesters on private lands at Gustafsen Lake in south central British Columbia all initiated standoffs. In one case, Aboriginal fishing rights were at stake; in another it was a wrongful holding of Aboriginal burial grounds; in the third, Aboriginal people wanted to regain control over sacred lands held in private ownership. In one case, an Aboriginal person was killed; in another, several persons were injured.

What has become apparent is that within each occupation site there are clear differences of opinion about the appropriate course of action for the Aboriginal community to take. In the Mi'kmaq standoff, some of the elders and chiefs publicly disagreed with the actions of non-resident itinerant warriors who had involved themselves in the fishing rights issue. At Gustafsen Lake there was only nominal public support and considerable community backlash; the high tide of public support existing in 1990 had ebbed considerably. Minister of Indian Affairs Ron Irwin told the *Globe and Mail* newspaper in January 1996, "I keep telling the chiefs: Wake up. Roadblocks hurt your case with whites," and cited the summer 1995 blockades at Adams Lake, Douglas Lake, and Gustafsen Lake in British Columbia.

Both groups, Aboriginal and non-Aboriginal, were becoming more discerning and rather than rashly setting up a roadblock, would analyze each situation on a case-by-case basis. Few would disagree that negotiating claims and grievances is ideally a superior way to solve problems. However, many Aboriginal groups are simply worn out by the length of time it takes to resolve matters because of bureaucratic foot dragging and constantly changing government policies. To some, the process of dispute resolution can only be advanced by increasing public attention to their grievance by using self-help remedies — standoffs.

This was the position of the Chippewa on Lake Huron in the summer of 1995. After years of disheartening and unproductive negotiations, they took assertive action to embarrass the federal government into returning lands taken from them in the 1940s for use as a temporary military base under the War Measures Act. The Chippewa also asserted a claim against the Ontario government for adjoining lands forming part of a provincial park. The park was occupied after its summer closing and the occupation of both park and military base continues as of this date. It was not until after the Ontario government obtained an interim injunction halting the Chippewa's occupation of the park that the government was embarrassed to learn that their claim of burial grounds in the park may indeed be legitimate. Had this occupation not occurred, how many more generations would it have taken for the governments to effectively respond to this claim? In the meantime, one Aboriginal youth had been killed and several others injured by police gunfire.

In 1989, the Algonquins of Barrière Lake protested clearcut logging in the La Vérendrye reserve. Algonquin protesters set up roadblocks to attempt to force the Québec government to improve its conservation practices in the wildlife reserve. Gérard Guay, the Québec lawyer acting for the Algonquins, prepared a press release setting out their position: "The Algonquins have a right to do what they are doing and the logging companies also claim to have a right. Obviously, the Algonquins have a greater right based on their constitutionally recognized ancestral title and environmental law, as well as the fundamental freedom of expression and peaceful assembly. The logging companies only have a permit." Guay pointed out that while it was for the civil courts to balance the different competing rights of the Algonquins and the logging company, it was abusive for the police to lay criminal charges at that stage against the Algonquins, when the civil matter before the courts had not yet been resolved by a judge.

This chapter neither condones nor promotes self-help tactics to resolve disputes. Such actions, apart from being in some cases illegal, clearly put peoples' safety and lives at risk. As well, self-help actions can cause considerable negative public reaction, which can backfire on the Aboriginal peoples' attempt to resolve the issue. However, the reality of any given situation might justify use of the self-help remedy. Why, for instance, in a case of competing legal interests, should it be the Aboriginal community that must take a back seat to the legal right being advanced by a non-Aboriginal party?

b. GROWING RECOGNITION OF ABORIGINAL RIGHTS

Aboriginal communities have received much-needed support for the recognition of their rights and status in three important areas.

The first is simply society's recently acquired understanding of the difficult plight facing Aboriginal communities in Canada. This understanding has come through radio, television, and the many articles in newspapers and magazines discussing Aboriginal issues. Courses on Aboriginal history are now available at many colleges, universities, and law schools across the country. As well, a number of excellent books have been published on Native issues. While much research and education remains to be done, Canadians are more literate on Aboriginal issues than they were 20 years ago, and more able to understand and discuss these issues.

Courts in Canada, in particular the Supreme Court, have slowly but significantly played an important role rendering judgments that recognize Aboriginal rights. For instance, Conrad Sioui, a Huron, persuaded the Supreme Court of Canada that he was properly acquitted from charges laid against him for breaching Québec provincial park regulations when he cut timber in the park as part of his Aboriginal spiritual practices. Similarly, certain Musqueam fishers in Vancouver persuaded the Supreme Court of Canada that they had the right to fish salmon to feed their peoples without being charged under provincial fishing quotas.

Most important, the enshrinement of Aboriginal and treaty rights in Canada's constitution has significantly altered Canada's constitutional environment. While these rights are not enumerated or defined, the general recognition of Aboriginal and treaty rights provides the important base from which many Aboriginal communities and individuals may now assert rights that in the past were less clear.

c. EXAMPLES OF SELF-HELP SITUATIONS LEADING TO LEGAL ACTION

Any Aboriginal community facing a particular local problem might feel alone in its attempt to assert an Aboriginal right. It need have no such fear: Aboriginal communities have for some time been actively pursuing and protecting their legal rights across the country. Self-help situations using roadblocks sometimes end up in Canadian courts. Apart from the civil law suits, Aboriginal persons have often been prepared to face criminal charges to prove their point, as part of their plan of action. The issues raised in these cases are complex and require strong determination to bring about solutions.

1. New taxes in New Brunswick

In 1993, Maliseet Indians, upset with the New Brunswick government's proposal to take away provincial sales tax exemptions for certain Aboriginal transactions, put up blockades on roads through their reserves — located within the city limits of Fredericton and also on the Trans-Canada Highway. The result: police ended the blockade peacefully, but criminal charges of mischief were laid against some protesters, leading to a number of convictions.

2. Ski resorts on traditional Aboriginal lands

For several years, members of the Penticton Indian Band in British Columbia have used roadblocks during the winter months to attempt to bring into focus their frustration with unresolved land issues. Green Mountain Road, the shortest route to the Apex Mountain Resort, runs through the Penticton lands. The Penticton, upset because of the lack of an effective solution to their problems, were all the more infuriated because the British Columbia government was financially supporting the Apex ski resort's expansion program by guaranteeing outstanding corporate loans. The Pentictons were also concerned that the development would cause serious environmental damage. Thus, the roadblocks.

In 1994, the Apex company requested a temporary halt to the trading of its stocks on the Vancouver Stock Exchange because it felt the media reports and controversy about closed roads to the resort were harming stock prices. In July 1996, the media reported that the Apex ski resort was in deep financial trouble and on the brink of receivership. The British Columbia government was demanding repayment of its $8.4 million loan guarantee. This example shows how important it is for outstanding land claims to be resolved, not only for the benefit of First Nations but also for the benefit of companies such as the Apex Mountain Resort and skiers using the resort.

3. Cottage access across a First Nation's lands

The Shawanaga First Nation on the eastern shores of Georgian Bay has had a long simmering dispute with the Skerryvore Ratepayers Association, a group of cottagers who cannot access their cottages on Georgian Bay except by a road running through the Shawanaga Reserve. The First Nation has for years claimed that the roadway through the reserve is not a public highway and cottagers should not be able to use it without first obtaining a licence from the First Nation. At trial, the cottagers won a declaration that the roadway was a public highway, along with a permanent injunction preventing the First Nation from interfering with the cottagers' use of the roadway.

The Ontario Court of Appeal overturned the trial judgment, deciding the reserve land had never been surrendered and the road could not be a public highway. After years of litigation, this decision confirmed the Shawanaga First Nation's ability to block the cottagers' use of the roadway unless the cottagers entered into satisfactory arrangements with the First Nation. A subsequent legal action by the Skerryvore Cottagers Association, whose members had difficulty accepting that they did not have the right to open passage to their cottages, was promptly dismissed by the court. The matter is now at the negotiating stage. At one point during this deadlock, the Ontario government suggested that it might fly the cottagers in at public expense!

4. NATO low flying in Labrador

In 1989, four Innu occupied the airport runway of the Goose Bay Canadian Forces Base in Labrador to protest low-level flying by NATO aircraft over Innu communities and their traditional hunting grounds. The Innu were charged with wilful interference with the lawful operation of property. In one of the few significant cases decided by an Aboriginal judge, provincial court Judge Igloliorte acquitted the Innu because of the reasonable belief they held that Aboriginal title to lands they occupied had never been given up or surrendered.

d. HOW TO APPROACH PROBLEMS

The above examples make clear that Aboriginal communities across the country have had to wrestle with some very difficult issues. Band councils, chiefs, elders, and warriors often debate at length the appropriate strategy to resolve the particular issue at hand. Here are the kinds of questions that might be discussed and analyzed when developing an appropriate strategy to resolve outstanding issues.

(a) How carefully have we assessed the validity of the legal right we are about to assert? How strong a legal case do we have? What are the weaknesses to our case? Have we done adequate legal and historical research to provide a sound footing for our proposed actions?

(b) Have we, as a community, exhausted our efforts to negotiate the issues with the appropriate government officials? Should our priority be to continue negotiating or are we simply wasting our time?

(c) Have we exhausted all efforts of getting our story out to the public? Are the local radio and television stations aware of our problem? Have we educated the community — both Aboriginal and non-Aboriginal — about these issues? Have we hired a press agent or a public relations expert to make sure our message is projected in a positive and supportive way?

(d) Can we involve a mediator or arbitrator to assist in problem solving? Could a private individual be appointed as mediator or arbitrator, or could we use government-funded mediation facilities? Mediators can develop agendas for negotiation and then set and monitor timetables for action.

(e) Have we enlisted the support of special interest groups, such as environmentalists, that may help advance the cause? Do we want or need such support?

(f) If we adopt a self-help remedy, are we prepared for the reaction it will cause both within our own community and in the non-Aboriginal community? How united is our own Aboriginal community behind the issue? Have we mobilized and organized ourselves so that when we proceed with our plan, our community will be seen to be clearly behind our action?

(g) If we take self-help action, are we aware that our actions may cause a reaction by other non-Aboriginal groups — that our actions may interfere with their legal rights?

(h) Do we realize that our actions, even though they are legal from an Aboriginal viewpoint, might result in criminal charges being laid against us?

e. COURT ACTION — USING INTERLOCUTORY INJUNCTIONS

Temporary injunctions, known as interlocutory injunctions, are court orders prohibiting a party from continuing to act in a certain manner until the trial. Temporary injunctions are a useful tool to prevent damages or "unlawful" conduct until the trial is held and can be applied for and obtained within a reasonably short time. In urgent cases, it is possible to be in court and before a judge in a matter of days. Such injunctions are very important because they often set the stage for parties to finally resolve matters. Obtaining such an injunction may help an Aboriginal community prevent, for instance, a resource development company from continuing to log, mine, or build a pipeline across reserve lands until the full legal rights of the parties are resolved at a trial.

Legal principles developed by the Canadian courts for the granting of interlocutory injunctions apply equally to Aboriginal law as to other areas of law. Canadian courts have developed clear legal rules as a result of dealing with a great variety of situations coming before the courts over many years. These legal rules can be of great use to Aboriginal communities wishing to stop unwanted conduct.

This same body of law is equally available to resource development companies or other persons or groups. While temporary injunctions might be used by Aboriginal communities to prevent others from affecting their rights, resource development communities also may wish to pursue their legal right to log, mine, or fish commercially. The law of injunctions often occurs where competing legal rights of the two parties intersect. A classic example of this interplay of legal rights is where the logging or mining company harvests resources according to a government permit while the Aboriginal community claims ownership of the lands on which the forests or minerals are located.

f. THE GRANTING OF AN INTERLOCUTORY INJUNCTION

Canadian courts have developed a number of rules to help them decide whether a party should be prevented from continuing a course of conduct, pending a trial. The rules put forward in this chapter are not exhaustive, and any group or individual should seek legal advice for a more detailed consideration of legal principles applying to a particular situation. Four important factors a court will consider when deciding whether to grant an interlocutory injunction are as follows.

1. Does the person seeking the injunction have a serious claim to be decided at trial?

The applicant must establish that there is a serious issue for the trial judge to deal with, which in the meantime should be protected. If the claim being put forward appears frivolous or far-fetched, the court will not consider granting an interlocutory injunction. The following examples illustrate how courts have dealt with this principle.

(a) *Attorney General of Ontario v. Teme-Augama First Nation*

In 1989, Aboriginal groups and environmentalists unsuccessfully opposed a government permit issued for the extension of the Red Squirrel Road in the Temagami forests of northern Ontario. The group publicly announced an intention to blockade the road construction and advertised for volunteers to participate in the blockade. Volunteers would first need to take what the group called "peaceful resistance training." Ontario's Attorney General sought an injunction to prevent the protesters from conducting the blockade, alleging that the safety of the construction workers was at stake and that the road would not be completed in the time required by law.

The motions court judge decided that the government's legal proceeding was premature: no actual blockade had yet begun; the protesters were entitled to express their opinions freely; it was quite possible that the demonstration that might ultimately occur would be without violence, would be lawful, and would not violate any of the Crown's rights.

(b) *Mohawk Bands of Kahmawake et al. v. Glenbow-Alberta Institute*

In 1988, the Mohawks tried to prevent Calgary's Glenbow Museum from exhibiting certain spiritual objects, in particular an Iroquois False Face mask, in an exhibition timed to coincide with the 1988 Olympics. When the Alberta court dealing with the claim discovered that these sacred masks had been on public view for a number of years in different museum locations across Canada without protest, the judge concluded that there could be no irreparable harm to the Mohawks pending the trial of the action, since masks had been publicly exhibited previously.

2. Will the court's intervention prevent irreparable harm?

If money can compensate for the wrong that is done, the court will not usually grant an injunction. On the other hand, the Canadian legal system also recognizes that some conduct causes irreparable damage and should be stopped pending trial. "Irreparable damage" means that money simply cannot replace what will be destroyed by the actions of the other party or that calculating those damages would be far too complex. Clear-cut logging, flooding of lands, mining, and digging up sacred burial sites are all activities that irreparably damage Aboriginal communities, destroying the environment or otherwise adversely affecting Aboriginal settlements. All of these activities have been litigated in Aboriginal cases in Canadian courts over the years.

One famous early case involves the Inuit community of Baker Lake. In 1978 and 1979, Inuit applicants sought to prevent prospecting permits and mining licences being issued for mining exploration and activities within the Baker Lake Study Area on the grounds that the mining activity would have permanent, lasting effects on the caribou population, an essential part of the Inuit life and livelihood. Finding that the Inuit had a serious question for trial, the Federal Court of Canada granted an interlocutory injunction because if it did not do so, the Inuit community would be irreparably harmed. As well, the defendants would not suffer by having an interlocutory injunction against them pending trial. The judge noted: "The minerals, if there, will remain; the caribou, presently there, may not."

In 1986, the Kwakiutl Indian Band on Vancouver Island locked horns with Halcan Log Services, which had purchased lands from MacMillan Bloedel and obtained government permits to log these lands. The Kwakiutl claimed that logging should be stopped and asserted Aboriginal and treaty rights to hunt, fish, and trap. The court granted the injunction against the company, concluding that the logging company's interference with Aboriginal rights would cause irreparable damage to the Kwakiutl Nation and the trial judge would have great difficulty assessing those damages, whereas the calculation of the lost profits to the logging company would be much easier to calculate.

This view contrasts with the much-criticized 1975 Québec Court of Appeal overturning of an interlocutory injunction on appeal when the court decided that widespread flooding of large areas of traditional Aboriginal territories by Hydro Québec would not constitute irreparable harm.

3. Will the applicant be responsible for the defendants' damages incurred should it lose at trial?

A court will normally not grant an injunction unless the applicant gives a binding promise to the court that it will be responsible for any damages the defendant incurs from being restrained, should the applicant not be successful in its claim at trial.

Unfortunately, many Aboriginal groups do not have the financial resources to meet what might be considerable monetary damages if they lose at trial. On the other hand, these groups are compelled to take action to prevent actions of others. Accordingly, this rule has been altered on a number of occasions to recognize the poor financial situation many Aboriginal groups find themselves in. In *Baker Lake*, an interlocutory injunction was granted even though the Aboriginal community may not have been able to satisfy a damage claim the mining companies might ultimately have against them.

4. The balance-of-convenience test

The balance of convenience of the parties pending the trial is another factor the motions court judge will consider when deciding whether to grant an interlocutory injunction. If the applicant has a clear legal right that is being violated by the other party and that party's conduct is not legally justified, a temporary injunction will be granted. If both parties appear to be acting legally, the court will assess whether one legal right is clearly stronger and will protect that stronger right. If both parties seem to have legal rights of similar weight, the court will consider the practical balance of conveniences to each party — which will be disrupted the most by granting or not granting an interlocutory injunction? If one party will be affected significantly more than the other, the court is more likely to give that party the legal protection it needs. In other words, the court will try to minimize the damage to the party that might otherwise suffer the most pending the trial.

If it is not clear which party will be affected the most — if both parties will be affected similarly — the courts may simply choose to maintain the status quo pending the trial rather than tipping the balance in favor of either party. Curiously, maintaining the status quo in some cases might mean the court will make no order, while in other cases maintaining the status quo means granting injunctions against one party or in some cases, against both parties.

Between 1986 and 1989, the McLeod Lake Indian Band from British Columbia appeared in court on a number of occasions to assert and clarify its Aboriginal and treaty rights to a significant portion of land in northeastern British Columbia. Various lumber companies were attempting to log this land under provincial licences. The history of this litigation sheds light on how different judges have applied the principles of law for the balance of convenience.

In June 1987, the McLeod Lake Indian Band erected a road blockade to restrain Balcaen Consolidated Contracting, which had a six-week licence to harvest forests worth a quarter of a million dollars. Having found that each party had serious legal rights to advance at trial, Justice Davies decided that he would maintain the status quo which, in his opinion, favored the established government system of harvesting the forest by permit. Accordingly, he ordered the McLeod Indian Band to dismantle its roadblock.

In November 1988, the McLeod Lake Indian Band claimed Aboriginal title to some 166 000 acres of land. Under Treaty 8, the band agreed it was entitled to only 40 000 acres of the original claim. The exact 40 000 acres had not been resolved. The band sought to prevent logging by a number of different forestry companies anywhere in the 166 000 acres until its claim was settled.

Justice McLachlin, then Chief Justice of the Trial Division of the British Columbia Supreme Court (and now a member of the Supreme Court of Canada), found that the McLeod Lake Indian Band passed the threshold test of having a serious question to be tried, but she concluded that the balance of convenience was against the granting of an injunction. Justice McLachlin found that the logging companies would suffer irreparable harm if they were restrained — some might even go out of business. However, she dismissed the claim for a temporary injunction because the band could not prove that the proposed logging would in fact affect the specific 40 000 acres of land which the McLeod Lake Indian Band had not yet identified as part of its treaty settlement.

One month later, in December 1988, the parties appeared once more before Justice McLachlin when the band narrowed its previous claim to title for 166 000 acres down to its entitled acreage under the treaty, of which 1 000 acres were slated for immediate logging. Justice McLachlin felt that because the parties each had valid claims, the status quo should be maintained until trial. Accordingly, she permitted the logging of the 1 000 acres to proceed in the meantime. However, she imposed a moratorium on further logging in the balance of the logging area for a two-year period, within which time the matter would reach trial.

Justice McLachlin's order imposing a moratorium did not anticipate nature. In November 1989, spruce bark beetles infested a good portion of the area subject to the court order, preventing further logging. Because the spread of the beetle disease was serious, all parties agreed that timbers be harvested to curb its spread. But who should have the right to harvest — the McLeod Lake Indian Band or the private commercial forestry companies licensed by the government? Justice Donald had no difficulty altering Justice McLachlin's order based on the new facts. He did so creatively:

The public has an interest in the maintenance of the overall forestry scheme under the statute but I believe that the public also has an interest in the fair and orderly settlement of aboriginal claims....It is to everyone's advantage that the native peoples have confidence in the rule of law. They will not see the need to resort to civil disobedience and other self-help remedies if they know that while their legal claims are pending the land will not be stripped....

Here, logging must proceed, and the question is by whom and under what auspices....The Band has hired well qualified experts whose opinions are worthy of careful consideration [and] the ministry will create a steering committee "in order to ensure that all interested parties are involved in the planning process...."

In my view the best way to proceed is to give the consultative approach a try and to lift the logging moratorium only for the first phase. This will require the parties to return to court at the conclusion of the winter logging operations, at spring break-up, for a continuation of the variance and at that time the initial cutting and the trap tree plan can be assessed.

These examples illustrate the flexibility and variety of approaches used by the courts to resolve matters before trial. They also illustrate how the very specific facts of each case are important in affecting the result. Because judges use their discretion in granting interlocutory injunctions, even though they are to apply well-developed legal principles, the result of the application is not entirely predictable.

5

DECISION MAKING ON RESERVES — THE CURRENT SITUATION

by J. Stephen O'Neill

This article is dedicated to the Aboriginal peoples of Manitoulin Island and of the Robinson-Huron Territory in northern Ontario.

The Aboriginal communities of Canada are at a crossroads with self-government. On the one hand, they are faced with the ever-present reality of the Indian Act, an act reflecting a 19th-century vision of the role and place of Aboriginal peoples in Canada. On the other hand, since the entrenchment of Aboriginal and treaty rights in the Constitution Act, 1982, and the handing down of some important decisions by the Supreme Court of Canada since 1984, there has emerged a growing recognition by Canadians of the inherent right of Aboriginal peoples to self-government. Such recognition would establish Aboriginal peoples as a third order of government in this country.

Although self-government negotiations are being carried out between the federal government and a number of Aboriginal communities and organizations across the country, the approach remains disjointed. A central agreement has not yet been reached on how to enshrine and articulate, within the framework of the Canadian constitution, the reality of self-government in its everyday workings. However, until it has been substantially modified or even repealed, the Indian

Act will continue to factor largely in decision making and government issues on reserves.

Many, if not most, Aboriginal communities do not accept the legitimacy of the Indian Act, and in virtually all Aboriginal communities, traditional ways and institutions still greatly influence the way these communities are governed. Hereditary councils, the advice of elders, and traditional, consensual approaches to decision making continue to play a vibrant and unique role in Aboriginal communities from coast to coast. The strength and adaptability of these traditions have in large part formed the basis of the cultural survival of Aboriginal peoples in Canada and of their hope for the future.

Nevertheless, almost every Indian reserve must deal with the effects of the Indian Act. While this chapter is intended as an introduction to this act, it is impossible to describe all of its workings and sections. Rather, I attempt to describe and point out those particular provisions of the act dealing specifically with the decision-making powers of band councils.

a. THE INDIAN ACT AND DECISION-MAKING POWERS

The Indian Act is one of the most outmoded and archaic pieces of legislation in this country. This act, first put on the statute books in 1876, clearly reflects a century-and-a-half-old view of the rights and responsibilities of Canada's Aboriginal peoples. The Indian Act is a sweeping code by which the federal government sets out rules and procedures affecting almost all aspects of life on an Indian reserve. Throughout the sections of the act, the Minister of Indian Affairs is given the authority to make ultimate decisions on behalf of a band, either by approving decisions or by overruling them.

The act deals with fundamental issues such as the transfer of reserve lands between band members, the inability to pledge or mortgage reserve lands to outside parties, membership in a band, and the spending of a band's money.

To appreciate the decision-making powers of bands and band councils and how decision making is carried out on a reserve under the act, you must consider the following questions:

(a) What is the legal status of a band or First Nation?

(b) What are the powers of a band council?

(c) Are there rules for meetings and decision making by band councils?

(d) How and by whom are band councils elected?

(e) What are the decisions requiring approval of the membership?

b. WHAT IS THE LEGAL STATUS OF A BAND OR FIRST NATION?

The terms *band* and *First Nation* are quite often used interchangeably. There is no definition of *First Nation* in the Indian Act, but the term has become relatively popular among a good number of Canada's 608 Indian bands. (It is important to note, however, that while Indian bands are often referred to as First Nations, all First Nations may not necessarily be Indian bands: Inuit communities, for example, are also First Nations.)

A First Nation, or a body of Indians, is a *band* under the Indian Act, if —

(a) it has a reserve,

(b) Canada holds trust money on its behalf, or

(c) the federal government declares it a band.

A band clearly has the legal status and capacity to sue or be sued in its own name and to assume obligations and responsibilities separate from its individual members. An

Indian band may enter into commercial contracts in the open marketplace. For example, an Indian band may contract with architects, builders, or construction companies for services, buildings, and infrastructure projects on a reserve. A band may also borrow money or enter into joint venture projects with commercial interests, contractors, or third parties outside a reserve. In any of these cases, a band can be held responsible for fulfilling its contractual obligations and it can bring a legal action to enforce agreements and contracts it has entered into.

c. WHAT ARE THE POWERS OF A BAND COUNCIL?

1. Broad versus narrow powers

A band council, elected under the Indian Act or chosen according to a band's special custom (see section **e.** below), has specific powers that are dealt with under the act; it may well have additional and wider powers, given the entrenchment of treaty and Aboriginal rights in the Canadian constitution and the growing recognition and acceptance of the Aboriginal right to self-government. The wide range of governmental powers that may be handed over to the band council by its electors, when fully understood and recognized, could well elevate a band, acting through its band council, to a government status above that of a Canadian municipality or, as stated earlier, to a third order of government in Canada.

It is perhaps because of the tension between band council powers under the Indian Act and a recognition in the Canadian constitution of a right to self-government that two lines of thought about the Indian Act powers of a band council have developed. The narrow interpretation of such powers is that because band councils are created under the Indian Act and derive their authority to operate from that act, they have no source of power other than the powers of administration and decision making described in the act.

A more flexible and understanding view of a modern-day band council is that, as well as the strict powers set out in the Indian Act, a council must have additional or implied powers necessary to carry out its decision making on a day-to-day basis.

A strong argument is now made that since 1982, following the affirmation of Aboriginal and treaty rights in the Canadian constitution, an Aboriginal community or an Indian band has an inherent right to govern itself, so that its powers cannot in any way be solely restricted to or interpreted from the Indian Act.

2. Bylaw-making powers

A band council has a large range of bylaw-making powers under the Indian Act. For example, a band council's bylaw-making authority includes:

- Regulation of traffic on the reserve

- Zoning for land use on a reserve

- Regulation of construction and repair of buildings

- Management of game and fish on a reserve

- Taxation, licensing, and certain miscellaneous spending bylaws

The difficulty with making bylaws is that the procedure under the Indian Act is relatively complex.

More important, a council's bylaw is not effective unless it is restricted to matters outlined in the Indian Act and unless it is ultimately approved by the Minister of Indian and Northern Affairs. In short, band council bylaw-making authority is squarely under the control of the minister, a situation that does not rest well with many communities that feel strongly about their Aboriginal right to self-government. For these reasons, many First Nations have chosen not to become involved in the drafting and passing of overly complicated bylaws.

However, a certain class of bylaws described in section 83 of the Indian Act may have tremendous potential for First Nation communities as they move toward self-government and as they look for functional ways to raise money. These bylaws provide for "taxation for local purposes of land, or interests in land, in the reserve, including rights to occupy, possess or use land in the reserve."

Many Indian bands and First Nations in Canada occupy and control land in strategic geographic locations through which pass rail lines, highways, telephone lines, power transmission lines, and gas pipelines. The companies controlling and managing these various utilities and transportation services should be aware that band councils may tax or assess monetary amounts in return for granting these companies the right to occupy, possess, or use land in or across a reserve.

The Supreme Court of Canada recognized this important taxation power when, in a 1995 decision (*Matsqui Indian Band v. Canadian Pacific Ltd.*), it stated that the provincial and federal authorities had relinquished their historical field of taxation over reserve lands and had recognized the legitimacy of Indian band councils running their own system of taxation.

3. Spending of capital and revenue moneys

Indian and Northern Affairs Canada maintains two separate bank or trust accounts for many Indian bands. Money from the sale or surrender of Indian land or assets on land (most often timber or oil and gas) are deposited into one of the accounts. This money is known as *capital moneys* under the Indian Act. All other band money — from whatever source — is managed and maintained in a separate account; this is known as *revenue moneys*.

A band council has important powers vested in it for the spending of a band's capital or revenue moneys. Even though the spending power is subject to the approval of the minister, a band council may request and direct the spending of capital moneys to:

- Distribute per capita to the members of the band an amount not exceeding 50% of the capital moneys of the band derived from the sale of surrendered lands

- Construct and maintain roads, bridges, ditches, and watercourses on reserves or on surrendered lands

- Construct houses for members of the band

- Meet expenses necessary for the management of reserve lands

A band council may request that the minister authorize and direct the spending of the band's revenue moneys for any purpose that, in the opinion of the minister, will promote the general progress and welfare of the band or any member of the band.

Although the minister once again has overreaching authority, in practical and real terms it is very unusual for the minister not to consent to a decision taken by a duly constituted band council to spend capital and revenue moneys for specific purposes.

4. Borrowing of money

The council of a band may, according to the Indian Band Council Borrowing Regulations (made according to the Indian Act), borrow money for band projects or housing purposes and may make loans out of this money to members of the band for housing purposes, on terms and conditions determined by the council.

Lenders and persons contracting with a band should not assume that Indian and Northern Affairs Canada will directly or indirectly guarantee repayment of a loan or performance of a contract. As a general rule, if the contract or agreement is not entered into or signed by Her Majesty the Queen in Right of Canada (represented by Indian and Northern Affairs Canada), the performance and obligation of the contract rests solely with the band, and the benefits of the contract will flow directly to the band.

5. Superseding provincial and federal jurisdiction

A validly enacted band council bylaw takes precedence over all laws of general application in force in any province, according to section 88 of the Indian Act. In situations where validly enacted bylaws conflict with regulations of general application under other federal statutes, the bylaws have prevailed.

For example, if a conflict has developed between band fishing bylaws passed under the Indian Act and regulations made under the federal Fisheries Act, the band bylaws have been held by the courts to prevail. *R. v. Baker* dealt with a bylaw the Squamish Indian Band passed under section (81)(1)(o) of the Indian Act. The bylaw permitted band members to fish on band waters "at any time and by any means." The court held that, through the operation of the Indian Act and other federal statutes, the bylaw had become a statutory instrument and was effective on the reserve. The court also held that the Fisheries Act and regulations would not apply on the reserve if they conflicted with a band bylaw.

While validly enacted band bylaws have the potential to establish, in some respects, a band council as a third order of government in Canada, in most instances a mixture of federal laws, provincial laws, and band bylaws exists on reserves. The co-existence of laws from these three levels of government, along with the entrenchment and recognition of a band's treaty and Aboriginal rights, is often a recipe for confusion, conflict, and misunderstanding. The potential for such conflicts and misunderstandings will continue to be reduced as more progress is made in the area of self-government and as much-needed clarification of treaty and Aboriginal rights takes place.

d. ARE THERE RULES FOR MEETINGS AND DECISION MAKING BY BAND COUNCILS?

1. Band council meeting formalities

Meetings of band councils elected under section 74 of the Indian Act are regulated by the Indian Band Council Procedure Regulations, which deal with procedural requirements such as meeting times, quorum for council meetings, the order of business at each regular council meeting, and the establishment of standing committees of the council. Usually, the presiding officer or chairperson for the meetings will be the chief of the band. Questions before the council are decided by a majority vote of the councillors present, provided there is a quorum for the meeting. The presiding officer is not entitled to vote except when the votes are equal; he or she will then cast the deciding vote.

Despite these regulations, many Aboriginal communities have, by tradition and custom, adopted their own procedures for band council business and meetings. However, some practices are common to all these traditions: regular meetings of band councils are open to all members of the community, decisions on major issues are taken only after community consultation, and an ultimate decision is made only after a majority vote of the band councillors.

2. The role of the elders

Elders in Aboriginal communities have great influence on the decision-making process. The views and advice of a respected elder carry great weight on any given issue for which community input and support are required, and an elder's influence on how a band councillor will vote on an issue cannot be underestimated. Seeking input and support from an elder is usually done informally.

Including the elders in discussions and seeking their advice will greatly assist the process of reaching a consensus, whether that process is informal — through community discussions — or formal — at a public council meeting. Input from the elders is also extremely important on sensitive community issues or unique issues arising in the community.

3. Band council resolutions

Most councils use a document called a "band council resolution" (BCR) to record all band council decisions that require action or approval of Indian and Northern Affairs Canada or that approve contractual arrangements and decisions the band council has made on behalf of the band. While it is not necessary to use these BCR forms, the great majority of band councils do, since they can be extremely useful in documenting that a decision taken by a band council was made according to the proper formalities.

In a recent court decision (*Heron Seismic Service Ltd. v. Muscowpetung Indian Band*), a company sued a band for the balance owing on an account for the drilling and development of wells on the community's reserve. The trial judge concluded that the company assumed the risk of nonpayment by carrying out work on the reserve without first ensuring that the band council, supported by the required band council resolution, had approved the work. The court stated:

> Even if there was some form of contract, that contract would have to be discussed at a properly called band council meeting with a quorum present, followed by a resolution being passed and signed by a majority of the council members present as provided by section 2(3)(b) of the Indian Act. No resolutions were passed authorizing the plaintiffs to do any well drilling and no resolution was passed authorizing any elected officials or staff to conclude a contract for the drilling

106

and development of wells. There was no contract between the plaintiff and the defendant. There was no authority for the expenditure on wells in the budgets.

Even if a band council resolution is merely a formal document evidencing a resolution passed at a band council meeting, the importance of ensuring that a band council properly follows the decision-making formalities when dealing with commercial or business contracts should not be overlooked.

4. Business communication

Band councils are transacting more and more business both inside and outside reserves and entering the commercial marketplace much more often today than ten years ago. The influence and power of band councils is growing as a result of reserve lands expanding across the country and the increasing recognition of a First Nation community's inherent right to self-government. Those wishing to conduct business relationships with band councils should attend reserves to meet and interact with the chief, councillors, and elders to develop trust and respect.

Gone are the days when third parties trying to secure a decision or contract with a First Nation community could communicate only through a local official of Indian and Northern Affairs Canada. A direct relationship between those residing outside of reserves and decision makers residing within Aboriginal communities is now a practical requirement.

e. HOW AND BY WHOM ARE BAND COUNCILS ELECTED?

An understanding of how band councils govern activities on reserves, make decisions, and interact with persons residing both on and off reserve lands would not be complete without understanding how and by whom chiefs and band councillors are elected. Councils established according to the Indian Act (elected councils) are distinct from those councils chosen according to the custom of the band (custom councils).

1. Elected band councils

Roughly 50% of the band councils of the 608 Indian bands or communities in this country are elected according to elections held under the Indian Act. Rules and provisions governing the election of Indian band councils according to the Indian Act are set out in section 74:

(a) A council of a band must consist of 1 chief and 1 councillor for every 100 members of the band, with a minimum of 2 councillors and maximum of 12 councillors.

(b) The councillors of a band must be elected by a majority of the votes of the electors of the band.

(c) The chief of the band must be elected by a majority of the votes of the electors of the band or a majority of the votes of the elected councillors of the band.

(a) Band electors

An *elector* is defined under the act as a person who is —

(a) registered on a band list,

(b) of the full age of 18 years, and

(c) not disqualified from voting at band elections.

According to the Indian Act, a qualified elector must be a band member who "is ordinarily resident on the reserve." According to the Indian Band Election Regulations, a band member is ordinarily resident on the reserve if his or her place of ordinary residence is on the reserve and if this place has always been, or has been adopted as, his or her home. Residency status for voting purposes will not be lost or changed because of temporary absences from a place of ordinary residence.

(b) Non-resident voters

When the issue of the residency status of band electors was recently dealt with by the Federal Court (*Corbiere v. Canada*), the court struck down provisions of the Indian Act that denied non-resident band members a right to vote directly at a meeting or in a referendum — or indirectly through voting for the band council — on the potential surrender of all or part of a reserve or on any use of capital or revenue moneys. The court went on to state that, except for these two qualifications, only on-reserve voters could elect a band council.

This case was largely upheld on appeal. The appeal court granted a constitutional exemption, exempting members of the Batchewana Indian Band from the residency requirements of Section 77 (1) of the act, relating to band council elections. It remains to be seen whether or not this decision, applicable only to one band, will lead to an amendment to Section 77 (1) of the Indian Act, which would be effective across Canada.

2. Custom councils

Traditional forms of government continue to play a major role in many First Nations communities in Canada, despite the Indian Act. For example, within Iroquois communities in Ontario and many communities in British Columbia, traditionally chosen councils continue to receive wide support. Some of these traditional councils continue to operate without reference to the act. Many, however, have chosen to formalize their traditional government practices by reverting to custom councils and elections.

Often, the election of a custom council has its roots in the custom the band used before elections were held under section 74 of the act. The First Nation membership, through a vote or plebiscite, determines how a custom council will be chosen, who may vote for the council, and the length of the council's term in office.

The Minister of Indian and Northern Affairs Canada must approve a change toward band custom elections. Band custom elections and councils will be recognized by Indian and Northern Affairs Canada provided that —

(a) the custom elections follow the basic principles of natural justice and are consistent with the Charter of Rights and Freedoms,

(b) custom election regulations include a provision for the settlement of election appeals,

(c) custom election regulations include a provision for amending the rules for elections, which involve concurrence by a band's membership, and

(d) custom election regulations follow rules and procedures supported by the band membership and that protect the rights of individual band members.

Many bands favor a return to custom elections, as their custom does not distinguish voting eligibility between band members who reside on reserve and those who reside off reserve. In 1995, the election of the chief and council of the Garden River First Nation in Ontario was set aside, partly because the minister determined that band members residing off reserve had been permitted to vote in the band council elections. The Garden River First Nation community is now in the process of reverting to band custom for the purposes of choosing its council.

f. WHAT ARE THE DECISIONS REQUIRING APPROVAL OF THE FIRST NATION MEMBERSHIP?

While most band decisions are made by a band council, there are some powers and decisions outlined in the Indian Act that may be exercised only by the band acting as a whole. In these instances, it is the band members themselves, rather than the band councillors, who make decisions that will ultimately affect the community. Included among those decisions are the following:

- The amalgamation of bands by a vote of a majority of their electors

- The approval of a land claims settlement

- The surrender or sale of band land or the designation of land for leasing purposes

Referendums are held to make decisions on these and other specific issues.

The Indian Referendum Regulations set out a code of procedure for holding referendums on reserves. If a referendum is organized to approve a land claims settlement or to adopt regulations for band custom elections and councils, the result of the referendum vote will be recognized if it is supported by a simple majority of those band electors who are qualified to vote. If an insufficient number of electors vote at the referendum, a second referendum may be held. A simple majority of those electors voting will be sufficient to support the referendum results.

As we have seen, until changes come about, most of the governing on Indian reserves and within First Nation communities will undoubtedly be carried out under the Indian Act. In the meantime, it is hoped that the provisions under the act will at least be interpreted and used in a more flexible manner to mirror the particular culture, customs, and traditions of a First Nation community.

6

THE LEGAL BASIS FOR ABORIGINAL SELF-GOVERNMENT

by Derek T. Ground

a. OVERVIEW

Self-government is conceptually simple yet logistically complex, and a brief chapter in a book of this nature can hardly do justice to the historic and legal background to the assertion of this right by the Aboriginal groups of this country.

As a result of recent attempted changes — constitutional and otherwise — to the Canadian federation, more Canadians than ever before are aware of Aboriginal aspirations of self-government. Aboriginal people assert that their right of self-government is inherent. There is increasing legal and political support for this position, although it has not yet been acted on to any meaningful degree. An inherent right is a right founded to some degree in historical fact, and so it is to history that we must first briefly turn in order to understand this issue.

1. Aboriginal history

Much of what we know about the history of Aboriginal societies before European settlement is taken from oral histories handed down through generations, from archeological records, from anthropological extrapolation, and from other more traditional (in a western sense) historical sources.

One of the great failures of all western historians is not listening and according respect to the histories of Aboriginal peoples. This failure leads, unfortunately, to a more fundamental one: the failure of non-Aboriginal Canadians to understand their own history which, certainly in Canada, is integrally connected to the history of the Aboriginal people.

2. The arrival of the Europeans

When Europeans arrived on the shores of what is now called North America, they encountered a variety of self-governing societies which were treated as — and for all intents and purposes were — self-governing nations. Among the most famous of these was the Iroquois Confederacy, whose system of governmental checks and balances influenced the United States Constitution, as acknowledged in a 1987 Congressional resolution:

> ...the confederation of the original Thirteen Colonies into one republic was explicitly modeled on the Iroquois Confederacy as were many of the democratic principles which were incorporated into the Constitution itself.
>
> *100th Congress, 1st Session S. CON. RES. 76,*
> *September 16, 1987*

There are countless references to the Indian "Nations" in early historical and legal documents. Treaties of peace and friendship, and military and trading alliances characterized the early relations between First Nations and European settlers. This approach, from the European point of view, was largely one of self-interest: the Aboriginal people had been living in North America since time immemorial and had important knowledge of the land and how to survive there, not to mention their knowledge of trading routes and resources. In fact, many of the most successful early colonial economies were built using knowledge and practices taught to the Europeans by Aboriginal peoples, particularly the fur trade in what is now Canada and of the tanned deer-hide trade that formed the first economy of the Carolinas.

Generally speaking, the Europeans were welcomed in the spirit of cooperation and friendship by First Nations — first by the Mi'kmaq and Algonquians in the Gulf of St. Lawrence and then further inland by the Iroquois Nations. This spirit is best exemplified, and can perhaps be best understood, through the profound symbolism of the two-row wampum belt, representing the Mohawks and Europeans proceeding on separate but parallel tracks. These tracks, although they were never to intersect, would nonetheless run together. For many Aboriginal peoples, the principle of the two-row wampum remains potent today. It is essential to understand that Aboriginal peoples have never forfeited the right to govern themselves. In Canada, no Aboriginal nation was ever defeated at war. Despite the rhetoric now emanating from some sources within the Canadian political spectrum, Aboriginal people are not a "conquered people."

3. Aboriginal title and the courts

In non-treaty areas, Aboriginal title was never validly extinguished, and the validity of extinguishment in some treaty areas is, at best, questionable. Many Aboriginal rights that have not been exercised for decades have never disappeared completely. Many Aboriginal peoples who signed treaties regarded them as nation-to-nation agreements. Canadian courts, however, generally have not recognized treaties between the Crown and First Nations as such, but, rather, have concluded that these agreements are *sui generis* or unique, entailing special Crown obligations.

Whether the self-governing Aboriginal societies were — or are — nations, in the sense of having rights under international law, remains very much an open question. International law doctrines have assisted the courts' interpretation of Aboriginal rights but although "peoples" under certain international law doctrines have the right to self-determination, Aboriginal government rights akin to those of nation states remain unrecognized under international law.

Although international law is constantly evolving, international law doctrines are something of a self-fulfilling prophecy; they were developed by nation states for the benefit of nation states. The idea of the right to self-determination of colonized peoples attained international currency only after World War II.

The perception of Aboriginal peoples is essential for an understanding of the treaties. In attempting to understand and analyze Indian treaties, the courts have frequently used analogies to more common western legal concepts such as international treaties (notably in *R. v. Sioui*) and standard contracts, thus slotting Aboriginal peoples into the courts' own precepts of understanding while too often ignoring the very real and valid perspective of the people whose ancestors signed them.

In the minds of Aboriginal peoples, the right to govern themselves never disappeared — in fact, in law, or as an issue for discussion. Federal and provincial governments, after years of hoping that the issue would simply vanish, have finally begun to recognize this reality, although for the most part their understanding of its implications lags severely.

Aboriginal peoples are seeking nothing less than many of the rights of government that the Europeans assumed when first arriving on these shores. While there are few Aboriginal peoples who would argue that the exercise of this inherent right will result in societies that function largely as they did before contact or that these societies will be completely independent from Canada — in constitutional and other terms, the exercise of the inherent right of self-government will nevertheless put many Aboriginal rights and many traditional forms of Aboriginal government into a modern context.

b. WHAT IS THE LEGAL BASIS FOR ABORIGINAL SELF-GOVERNMENT?

There are many politicians who make much of what they call "special interest groups" seeking special rights or treatment. This sort of rhetoric has been used to attack gay rights, women's rights, employment equity, and Native rights. Because of the disdain in which the word "special" is now held in some quarters, there are some Aboriginal people who prefer to characterize their rights as "different" rather than special. As Pat Brascoupé, a former adviser to the Native Council of Canada on constitutional issues, says, "Aboriginal people have different rights, for different reasons."

The reasons are rooted in the historical fact that Aboriginal peoples had the same rights that any other self-governing societies had at the time of contact. Because of the nature of the relationships that developed between the First Nations and European settlers, the scope of these rights was often unilaterally altered, and some of these rights, especially land rights, were — in the parlance of the times — extinguished through the treaty-making process. Most treaties, however, enshrined and ensured that other rights (for example, harvesting rights) would continue in perpetuity.

Treaties are but one source of these different rights, and the historical necessity for the federal government to enter into treaties is but one of the different reasons that these rights exist and endure. In fact, a threshold question can be extrapolated from the very fact of the treaty process itself: if a society has the capacity to enter into a treaty, how can that society be any other than self-governing? Many, if not all, of the rights of Aboriginal peoples are guaranteed in the Canadian constitution and thus form the supreme law of the land. Those who complain about, or do not understand, these different rights for Aboriginal people are operating in ignorance of the laws of Canada.

116

1. The Royal Proclamation of 1763

The Royal Proclamation of 1763, which spoke of the "great frauds and abuses" visited on Aboriginal people, set out a method by which Aboriginal lands were to be purchased (this could be done only by the Crown). This method formed the basis for the treaty-making process. The Proclamation reads in part:

> ...where it is just and reasonable, and essential to our Interest, and the Security of our Colonies, that the several Nations or Tribes of Indians with Whom We are connected, and who live under our Protection, should not be molested or disturbed in the Possession of such Parts of our dominions and Territories as, not having been ceded to or purchased by Us, are reserved to them, or any of them, as their Hunting Grounds...
>
> *(Royal Proclamation, 1763, R.S.C. 1989,*
> *Appendix II, No.1.)*

This has been taken to mean that the imperial government of the time clearly believed that the Indian nations had some form of self-governing powers and their protection was essential because the Crown depended on its Aboriginal allies to help defend it.

The Royal Proclamation is by no means ancient history as far as Canadian law is concerned. The method of obtaining Aboriginal lands outlined in the proclamation remains, by and large, the way in which land is obtained today. As well, there are land claims still pending in Ottawa based on the alleged failure of the federal government to live up to the promises in the Royal Proclamation. The Royal Proclamation has been called the "Indian Magna Carta" and has been likened to a statute that has never been repealed.

2. The Indian Act, the White Paper, and the policies of assimilation

Section 91(24) of the Constitution Act, 1867, grants the federal government legislative authority over Indians and lands reserved for Indians. This authority enabled the federal government to enact, in 1876, the Indian Act — the legislative mechanism by which this power was exercised. The Indian Act imposed a system of government on First Nations and is probably the most infamous and readily available example of the federal undermining of First Nations' governmental authority. As it developed, the Indian Act granted the Minister of Indian Affairs final authority over virtually everything that an Indian band government did.

Through the 19th century it became increasingly clear that the Canadian government policy toward Indians was one of assimilation. As Sir John A. Macdonald stated in 1887, "The great aim of our legislation has been to do away with the tribal system and assimilate the Indian people in all respects with the other inhabitants of the Dominion, as speedily as they are fit to change."[1]

European forms of government were imposed on Indian peoples, who were forced to function in a society where they often did not understand the rules and where, when they did, those rules were simply incompatible with the ways in which their cultures and governments functioned.

The Indian Act fostered a culture of dependence; its remnants are still very much apparent in many Aboriginal communities. Those communities that did not play by the imposed rules found themselves paying dearly for their assertions of independence: laws were passed outlawing Indian cultural practices such as the potlatch; guns were drawn on the Métis who asserted their independence, land interests, and cultural distinction on the prairies.

Until 1924, a traditional government system remained on the Six Nations Reserve near Brantford, Ontario. Despite the success of the Six Nations people in getting international support for their rights to govern themselves according to their traditions and not to succumb to the provisions of the Indian Act, the RCMP raided the reserve and longhouses and imposed an Indian Act regime on the reserve. The scars remain to this day.

Indians who sought an education or voluntarily fought for their country found that they were no longer considered Indians for the purpose of the Indian Act: their status was taken away by Ottawa. Those who remained Indians despite being encouraged to give up status, found themselves collected on reserves, often in the most barren, inaccessible, and inhospitable parts of their traditional territories, and (still) comprising only approximately 1% of the land mass of the country. Indians were then blamed for their own poverty, for their dependence on welfare, and for the degree of alcoholism and abuse in their own communities.

Despite these overwhelming odds, the Indian people survived, as did their cultures and values. Their leadership grew stronger and, throughout the 1960s, they began to assert their rights. The Indians, who were not supposed to be around a hundred years after Confederation, had become a force to be reckoned with.

One attempt to reckon with Aboriginal peoples was the White Paper of 1969. Among the policies proposed by the framers of the document was the abolition of the Department of Indian Affairs (as it was then called), of the Indian Act, and of Indian reserves. This was proposed in the apparent interests of equality. Had the policies of the White Paper been implemented, the result would have been the abolition of the so-called special status of Indians, meaning, essentially, that Aboriginal rights and Aboriginal title would no longer exist or be relevant in Canada.

The Aboriginal response to the White Paper was one of predictable outrage. In fact, the White Paper was in great part responsible for a new era in Aboriginal politics: the National Indian Brotherhood, the predecessor to the Assembly of First Nations, took on a truly national scope, and the Native Council of Canada (now called the Congress of Aboriginal Peoples) was formed in 1971. Both these organizations would, over the next 20 years, place increasing reliance on the constitution as a vehicle for safeguarding Aboriginal rights.

3. The constitutional front

Until the patriation of the constitution in 1982, the only section of the constitution dealing directly with Aboriginal peoples was section 91(24). The inclusion of sections 25 and 35 on Aboriginal rights in the Constitution Act, 1982, was accomplished amidst considerable acrimony, both between Aboriginal groups and the federal government and among the Aboriginal groups themselves, over the precise wording of the sections. After many protests and much political wrangling, however, section 35, recognizing the "existing" rights of Aboriginal people, was included and was present in the constitution when it was proclaimed in April 1982. Section 25 reads:

> The guarantee in this Charter of certain rights and freedoms shall not be construed so as to abrogate or derogate from any aboriginal, treaty or other rights or freedoms that pertain to the aboriginal peoples of Canada including
>
> (a) any rights or freedoms that have been recognized by the Royal Proclamation of October 7, 1763; and
>
> (b) any rights or freedoms that now exist by way of land claims agreements or may be so acquired.

Section 35 reads:

> (1) The existing aboriginal and treaty rights of the aboriginal peoples of Canada are hereby recognized and affirmed.
>
> (2) In this Act, "aboriginal peoples of Canada" includes the Indian, Inuit and Métis peoples of Canada.
>
> (3) For greater certainty, in subsection (1) "treaty rights" includes rights that now exist by way of land claims agreements or may be so acquired.

(4) Notwithstanding any other provision of this Act, the aboriginal and treaty rights referred to in subsection (1) are guaranteed equally to male and female persons.

In addition, section 37 committed the federal and provincial governments to a first ministers conference on "constitutional matters that directly affect the aboriginal peoples of Canada." Ultimately, the three conferences that were held resulted in virtually no gains for Aboriginal peoples beyond the vagaries of section 35 of the Constitution Act, 1982.

The wording of section 35 was deliberately general and therefore open to debate. Some see that as a service of confusion, while others see it as an opportunity to advance and clarify the place of Aboriginal rights within Canadian society. The acknowledgment of existing Aboriginal and treaty rights was, for many Aboriginal people, tantamount to recognizing an inherent right of self-government.

But is the inherent right of self-government an existing aboriginal and treaty right recognized and affirmed in section 35(1) of the Constitution Act, 1982? Historically, there is no denying that Aboriginal peoples were self-governing. Such a right can be terminated only by surrender or, according to some international law scholars, willful integration within another sovereign state. Aboriginal peoples can hardly be said to have willfully integrated into Canada, and the existence of treaties goes a long way toward confirming that. As such, any recognition of the inherent right to self-government must be a recognition of a right that already exists.

For the historical and legal reasons given above, many are of the view that the "existing" rights of section 35 include the inherent right of self-government. It is significant that this view has now come to be accepted by the current federal government and by the Royal Commission on Aboriginal Peoples (see the Interim Report of the Royal Commission on Aboriginal Peoples).

4. Policy and legal developments in 1990

Sparrow was handed down in May 1990. In June of that year, the Meech Lake Accord was defeated, in part because of the trenchant "No" of Elijah Harper, an Ojibway-Cree from northern Manitoba. Harper, now a federal Liberal member of parliament for Churchill, came to be seen as a spokesperson for the Aboriginal peoples of Canada, a group which had once again been the victim of constitutional politics of exclusion based on the myth of the "two founding peoples." In July of that year, tensions at Oka over Mohawk land rights grew into an armed confrontation between the Canadian army and Mohawk warriors. Press coverage of Oka was seen around the world and brought the Canadian government much unwanted international attention. These events brought Aboriginal issues to the forefront of Canadian political discourse.

On September 25, 1990, the final day of the Oka crisis, Prime Minister Mulroney announced his Native Agenda in the House of Commons. The stage had been set for what many Aboriginal people hoped would be a new beginning.

5. The Charlottetown Accord

The importance of Aboriginal issues to the Canadian public was one of the central themes of the report of the Citizens' Forum on Canada's Future (the Spicer Report), released in July 1991. That same summer, leaders of the four national Aboriginal groups — Assembly of First Nations, Inuit Tapirisat of Canada, Métis National Council, and Native Council of Canada — were "invited" to a premiers' conference on constitutional issues held in British Columbia. (Although the press ran the story as an invitation and several premiers, including host Premier Rita Johnson, took credit for it, Aboriginal participation at the conference was actually the result of aggressive lobbying.)

The national Aboriginal leadership's presence at this forum was, in part, responsible for their inclusion at the constitutional table during the Charlottetown Accord negotiations and ultimately resulted in the official recognition of the inherent right of self-government in the 1992 Charlottetown Accord, which contemplated the notion of a third order of government.

It may seem odd to the casual reader that the Aboriginal leadership of Canada still puts so much emphasis on the Charlottetown Accord, especially because it was overwhelmingly defeated by a majority of Canadians, including Indians on reserves. In the wake of the defeat of the accord, however, the national Aboriginal leadership by and large agreed that the accord represented a victory insofar as the inherent right of self-government for Aboriginal peoples had been recognized by all provinces and, in fact, seemed to have some wide support among the Canadian population. A survey of six urban centres throughout the country, conducted by the Native Council of Canada for the Royal Commission on Aboriginal Peoples in 1993, found that 84% to 95% of people living in those cities supported the idea of Aboriginal self-government.[2]

c. THE 1995 FEDERAL INHERENT RIGHT OF SELF-GOVERNMENT POLICY

In early August 1995, the federal government released its long-awaited policy on Aboriginal self-government, a statement both of political will to negotiate self-government agreements and of limitations the government would impose on self-government. The policy had been in the works for some time and was a direct result of the promise in the Liberal's election platform that a Liberal government would act on the premise that an inherent right of self-government was an existing Aboriginal and treaty right.

The Speech from the Throne on January 18, 1994, that opened the first session of the 35th Parliament of Canada promised that "the Government will forge a new partnership with Aboriginal peoples, particularly in respect of the implementation of the inherent right of self-government." The policy, in effect, proposes that Aboriginal governments will have powers that are somewhere on the continuum between municipal and provincial powers.

The general reaction to the policy was mixed. While many Aboriginal groups have found some aspects of the policy worthwhile, there is controversy over whether the policy is largely being imposed on Aboriginal people and whether it reflects true inherency or is in fact closer to a devolving of administrative authority. The federal government is emphasizing the policy's pragmatic approach, while many Aboriginal groups regard the range of subjects for negotiation as falling well short of a third order of government as contemplated in the Charlottetown Accord. As one commentator noted, "What is missing from the inherent right policy is any notion of inherency."[3] Both the Assembly of First Nations and the Chiefs of Ontario, among others, have taken the position that they were not adequately consulted in the development of the policy.

The policy sets the parameters for self-government negotiations by outlining a range of subjects in which the federal government is willing to negotiate some degree of Aboriginal jurisdiction and in which "there is no compelling reasons for Aboriginal governments or institutions to exercise law-making authority." The latter subjects are, generally, related to Canadian sovereignty, defence, and external relations.

The policy will apply to Aboriginal groups and First Nations with a land base and to Aboriginal groups living off reserve. Different considerations will govern negotiations with on- and off-reserve groups. The policy also stresses the need for provincial involvement and contemplates an expanded role both for provinces and for third-party interests. In fact, an annex to the policy states that provincial governments bear the primary responsibility for Métis and off-reserve Aboriginal people, a position which is at odds with the understanding of most Aboriginal people.

As well, the federal policy proposes that the Canadian Charter of Rights and Freedoms applies to Aboriginal governments. This is a divisive issue within the Aboriginal community and generated a good deal of comment on the policy's release. Many Aboriginal people see it as a potential intrusion on the right of Aboriginal peoples to decide their own principles of government, part of a divide-and-conquer strategy (of which governments are often accused, often for good reason). Others see the application of the charter as a necessary imposition of broad general principles to Aboriginal government and openly wonder why anyone would have trouble with it.

d. THE CURRENT PICTURE

Out of that entire journey, from the treaty process through the Indian Act, from the White Paper to the Charlottetown Accord, several things eventually became clear: Aboriginal people were not going to be assimilated, they were not going to give up their unique rights, and they were dissatisfied with the governing structures available to them.

There is, however, no one model of self-government that will work for all Aboriginal communities. The needs and resources of a small reserve in northern Saskatchewan will be different from the needs of larger reserves near or in major cities. As well, each community is at a different stage of readiness for self-government, and each is prepared to accept different governing powers. Finally, self-government is not necessarily only of reserves (although this appears to be where most self-government arrangements will be successfully negotiated) but also of Métis communities, off-reserve communities, northern Inuit communities, and urban communities. The needs of each will be different as well.

So far there are very few existing examples, apart, perhaps, from the Nunavut Final Agreement (see chapter 14) and other comprehensive land claims agreements where powers and structures of Aboriginal self-government have been implemented.

More commonly, Aboriginal groups such as a First Nation or a group of several First Nations have entered into sectoral agreements that give them control over certain areas of government such as land management, policing, child welfare, or education. (The word "control" here usually means administrative control, as opposed to jurisdictional authority.)

The practical challenges facing Aboriginal communities in implementing self-government are described by Commissioner Philip Goulais in chapter 7. Suffice it to say that the practicalities of implementing self-government remain largely to be determined through consultations and negotiation. The basic reasons for recognizing and implementing Aboriginal self-government are simple. First, there is the historic reality that Aboriginal peoples have never given up the right to govern themselves. Second, existing government institutions have failed to speak to, and meet the needs of, the Aboriginal peoples of this country. Aboriginal self-government may be the one successful way to deal with Aboriginal aspirations.

ENDNOTES

[1] Olive Patricia Dickason, *Canada's First Nations: A History of Founding Peoples from Earliest Times* (Toronto: McClelland and Stewart, 1992), 257.

[2] "Friendship Centres: Service Based Government" (National Association of Friendship Centres, 1994).

[3] Comments made by Alan Pratt, panelist at the program "The Federal Inherent Right Policy: Is That All There Is?" held at the Canadian Bar Association (Ontario) Aboriginal Law Section Program in Toronto, Ontario, December 6, 1995.

7

SELF-GOVERNMENT:
AN ABORIGINAL VIEWPOINT

A conversation between Philip Goulais and
Michael Coyle.

Self-government is a concept most Aboriginal people in Canada consider a key foundation to building a better future. Still, despite the obvious importance of self-government to Aboriginal people and the sincere willingness of most Canadians to learn more about this issue, there are few concrete models of what self-government means in practice.

In this chapter, Philip Goulais provides an Aboriginal perspective on what the term "self-government" means to people at the grass-roots level.

MC: *Canadians have been hearing about Aboriginal self-government for some time now. When did people first start talking about self-government in a modern context?*

PG: The current debate about self-government really began around 1969 in response to the federal Liberal government's White Paper, which proposed to assimilate Aboriginal peoples into the rest of society. Canadians began to hear from Aboriginal leaders in an assertive and persuasive way. National and community leaders were concerned that the Crown would be breaking treaty and other binding agreements.

Aboriginal people were asking, Where does the government of Canada get the right to make decisions for

First Nations? What evidence does Canada have to question Aboriginal peoples' right to govern themselves?

Discussion continued between 1969 and 1981. However, the momentum for self-government increased in 1979. That year, chiefs from all across Canada travelled to England in a failed attempt to secure an audience with the Queen. We were trying to meet with the Queen and request that she not participate in the proposed Canadian constitution until all the First Nations' concerns were dealt with.

It is important to note that from 1969 to 1979 — and to date — the First Nations leaders were extremely busy with concerns at the community level — concerns such as the lack of adequate housing, needs for proper drinking water and healthy, sanitary conditions, infrastructure in general, education, and economic development requirements. While First Nations leaders were trying to improve their living conditions, they were faced with the challenge of leaving their communities and working collectively with First Nations organizations toward securing protection of fundamental Aboriginal rights that were being ignored by the proponents of Canada's proposed Constitution Act.

In 1981, when the patriation of the constitution was proposed, discussions about self-government once again became more prevalent. Native people argued that the Queen couldn't sever her ties with nations with whom she had made treaties.

MC: *What are the roots of self-government — where did the idea come from?*

PG: Younger people today are asking if this is a new idea. But self-government has always existed among Aboriginal people. Historical documents — the Royal Proclamation of 1763 for example — recognized that when Europeans arrived there were already self-governing nations of people living in Canada. There was and is no doubt about that. If you look at treaties — the Robinson-Huron Treaty of 1850, for example — you will see that they are agreements between nations.

Aboriginal peoples at that time had all the basic elements of government — they were distinct peoples, with their own land base and their own languages. They governed themselves and made their own decisions. These elements are present today: Aboriginal people still have land, language, and society.

MC: *So the concept of self-government doesn't have its basis in treaties or the Royal Proclamation of 1763?*

PG: Some people spend a lot of time in libraries looking for a legal document that might be the basis of our right to self-government. But historical and legal documents such as the Royal Proclamation are not the source of self-government. Before the proclamation, no documents were required for First Nations to be sovereign. They governed themselves because they had to have their own ways of dealing with concerns in the community.

Aboriginal peoples in Canada were not conquered in any war. And self-government was never on the bargaining table at the time of the treaties. If you go to a library today and search from now until you have exhausted its resources, you won't find a document that will show where First Nations bargained away their inherent right to self-government. So how could we have lost that right?

As European settlement expanded, it seems that these new Canadians simply assumed that we had given up our right to govern ourselves. Perhaps it was simply their superiority in numbers that made them feel that they had the right to control us. That thinking led to the Indian Act. Whatever led the Canadian people to believe that they could govern us better than we could govern ourselves, we will never know. We do know, however, that the Indian Act system has failed us miserably.

MC: *What did self-government mean in practice in earlier times?*

PG: Self-government meant that Indian societies made collective decisions for themselves that were in their own best interests. Whether it was a matter of someone misbehaving or not sharing game with the community according to traditional values, if people broke rules, there needed to be a way for the community to deal with it.

If you speak with the elders, they will tell you that even as recently as 50 years ago in some areas, First Nations were handling their own justice issues in traditional ways. There were no jails and there might have been only one RCMP officer policing ten remote communities.

Tribes also needed to develop their own rules, laws, and procedures for dealing with other tribes. Decisions needed to be made about war and peace, trading rights, and territorial boundaries.

MC: *Since the first consolidated Indian Act in 1876, the Department of Indian Affairs has exerted a lot of control over life on the reserves. Would you give us some examples of this federal control and some of its effects on First Nations communities?*

PG: Most Canadians I have spoken with who have taken the time to understand the Indian Act agree that they, as citizens of Canada, would simply not put up with this degree of government control over their daily lives.

One well-known example of the high degree of government control, and an issue creating a lot of concern, is the authority the Indian Act has to determine who is Indian. The ultimate decision on who is and is not an Indian in Canada — and therefore who may be a full member of an Indian community — is still made by the federal government!

For many years — until 1951 — lawyers in Canada could not represent Aboriginal clients on a land claim in a court of law. If a lawyer represented Aboriginal people who felt they had been treated illegally by the government in their land dealings, for example, or who felt the Department of Indian Affairs didn't deal fairly with timber or other resources being removed from their communities, he or she could face criminal charges.

The education of Indian children was also controlled by the Department of Indian Affairs. Many people, including people who are among our leaders today, were taken away from their communities to residential schools — for years — and not allowed to use their own language or learn their history or traditional ways. This continued right up until 1970. These things have a dramatic effect on people. Again, civil servants in Ottawa were making decisions that tore traditional Aboriginal family life apart. It is hard today to imagine the devastation caused by those decisions.

In Canada today, when Indians make their will, they go to the grave knowing even their will is subject to approval by the Department of Indian Affairs. I don't believe that any other Canadian people must have a government official in a far-away city review their will!

The Indian Act also contains many barriers to economic development. Leases and other land arrangements require the department's approval in Ottawa. If an Aboriginal community wants to compete in the industrial world and bring in a developer to develop Indian land and create employment, the developer must contend with a lot of red tape. As chief at Nipissing, I've experienced this. Approvals from Ottawa for a shopping-centre lease or other major transaction take six months or longer once the First Nation and developer have reached their agreement.

This puts us at a serious competitive disadvantage compared to our neighbors. Over the past 15 years, our community has recorded at least 25 opportunities for economic development that we have lost because of the delays and bureaucratic red tape involved in getting Ottawa's approval for development projects.

MC: *You've said that the idea of self-government has been widely discussed now for 20 to 25 years. Why don't most Canadians have a clear sense of what fully implementing self-government will mean?*

PG: First Nations have a pretty good concept of what self-government will look like as we approach the next millennium. We are clear that it will not be like it was back in 1850. We must deal with the realities of society today.

I think that Canadians are looking for a blueprint for self-government. Well, there is simply no one blueprint. Nor should there be. It wouldn't work — the needs of Alberta's communities, for example, are not the same as those of British Columbia's. Similarly, the needs of Aboriginal people in the Toronto area would be quite different from those of communities in the far reaches of northern Ontario.

There will be many self-government models. The challenge today is for the leadership of each Aboriginal community to work with people at the grass-roots level to establish their own model of self-government. The first step is for communities to decide whether, in fact, they are going to pursue self-government. This decision must be community driven. The common denominator in successful Aboriginal projects is that the communities decided to develop the project themselves.

For each community, there will be a different starting point. One community may want to initiate self-government around economic development, another around health services. Communities are thinking about how to create employment and how to compete in the business world. The focus of some communities will be negotiations about unfulfilled treaty commitments. Others will want to focus on negotiating arrangements for equitably sharing resources on traditional Aboriginal lands.

Eventually, First Nations will want to have a say in all the government programs affecting the quality of life in their communities, whether it be in the management of their lands, health, education, economic development, or developing a resource base. The quality of life on reserves will improve when First Nations, not civil servants in Ottawa, are making their own decisions about laws and about how their people will live. First Nations will regain pride and responsibility for their own decisions when they manage their own affairs.

The challenge is now for First Nations leaders and communities to present this vision to Canadians. It's up to us to develop concrete models of self-government to make clear to the average Canadian just what self-government will mean.

MC: *Do you see any downside in all of this for surrounding non-Aboriginal communities?*

PG: Self-government has positive economic spin-offs for our neighbors. Once we begin to develop economically, we are creating a market for materials and labor, for infrastructure — water distribution, sewers, community buildings, and residential suburbs.

I also see no downside for other Canadians as we move to self-government. There will be some downsizing of Indian and Northern Affairs Canada — a move that Canadians may welcome, as the department is top-heavy with personnel. The return on the value of the programs aimed at First Nations territories is minimized under the current system and Aboriginal communities receive less benefit. The more Aboriginal peoples move toward self-government, the less work there will be for someone off reserve to do for a First Nation community.

MC: *What are some of the successes in the movement to re-establish Aboriginal self-government?*

PG: Well, many communities are now managing their own education programs. Other communities are active in economic development, creating employment on reserve. The management of health delivery services is now being transferred from Health Canada to Aboriginal communities. This is occurring as we speak, and we are starting to witness the quality of life improving.

As I said earlier, there are many models. Some are being developed at the grass-roots community level and some by First Nations organizations. A recent example is the First Nations Lands Management Agreement, signed on February 12, 1996, at Georgina Island in Ontario. The First Nations from across the country who are signatories to this framework agreement will now be able to manage their lands. Whether it be for residential, agricultural, community, sacred, or ceremonial purposes, or overseeing removal of resources, all decisions affecting land will be made at the community level. The agreement also restricts the ability of outside governments to expropriate First Nations' land and recognizes First Nations' ability to mortgage improvements on land.

As an example of the community-centred model of self-government, the Sechelt Band in British Columbia has a self-government arrangement with Canada which is recognized by special federal legislation. The Sechelt Band has been in the process of managing its own government for years now.

The Manitoba Chiefs are in the process of developing a different self-government model, taking control of all of the programs that Indian and Northern Affairs Canada formerly handled on their behalf. Undoubtedly, other Aboriginal communities across the country will look at what is resolved in Manitoba.

MC: *Some people say that because Aboriginal people often live in difficult social conditions, with high unemployment on many reserves, a simple solution is to abolish Indian reserves and simply treat Aboriginal people like other Canadians. What do you say to that idea?*

PG: I don't know of any First Nation I've worked with in the last 20 years that would ever suggest that the reserve system be abolished. I've experienced substandard housing, I've witnessed sanitary problems and social problems. You know about the higher-than-average suicide rate, the higher-than-average mortality rate among infants in Aboriginal communities — all these terrible and sad things happening in Native communities in larger numbers than in non-Native communities.

These are not issues of "Indianness" — they are problems of resources and control of those resources.

It would be more helpful if the government stopped spending millions of dollars doing more and more studies and simply transfer those funds to the communities for better housing, better drinking water, better sanitary conditions, and for training people to participate in economic development so they are self-sufficient and competitive in society.

MC: *What do you say to people who say that self-government means establishing a racist system of segregation and is therefore morally wrong?*

PG: Some people may respond that way, but if they were to look a little further, they would understand that there is a legal and constitutional obligation on the part of the government and the people of Canada to recognize Aboriginal self-government. If you look back again at the agreements of the last couple of hundred years, there were no provisions in any of those agreements where First Nations surrendered their inherent right to self-government. It was never on the bargaining table. So there is still an obligation on government to deal with First Nations on a government-to-government basis.

You know, maybe the people who feel this way should look at the situation from our viewpoint. How would they like to subject themselves to the laws, institutions, and rules of outsiders? In many ways, the question condones arrogance as an acceptable value in the name of sameness. You know, Canada is both special and unique because of its Aboriginal peoples. I think we can agree that finding just solutions in our society benefits all.

MC: *What does the future hold for Aboriginal self-government?*

PG: Communities must decide for themselves when they're ready to proceed. We see different Aboriginal communities at different levels of progress — some are well underway, economically, some are mid-way, and others are just starting out or contemplating starting out. The responsibility for development rests with the Aboriginal community at the grass-roots level.

Today, I believe the timing is right to move ahead. We still have a lot of our elders with their experience and wisdom, and we have a lot of talented young graduates who are bringing their academic backgrounds and learning back to the community, and we also have people at the grass-roots level who live in the community on a day-to-day basis and who have important insights.

No other government will be able to develop or deliver self-government to the First Nations communities — it's impossible — no other government knows of the concerns at the grass-roots level, and no other government can be sensitive to the vision that First Nations have about where they are going with their future.

Education will continue to be essential. Speaking from experience, education must be given a lot of credit for the improvements in the quality of life in Native communities.

This is an exciting time. Settling all the issues will require a great deal of hard work and creativity on everyone's part. Working toward self-government provides opportunities to create a more just Canadian society.

8

FIRST NATIONS AND MUNICIPALITIES

by Roger Townshend

First Nations and municipalities often live close to each other and affect each other by their actions. Although it has been the tendency for both First Nations and municipalities to ignore each other, it is in the interests of both to be more aware of each other. This must include an awareness that, despite a historic tendency by settler governments to do so, First Nations should not be equated with municipalities, since First Nations' history, social makeup, jurisdiction, and structure are fundamentally different.

a. POWERS OF MUNICIPALITIES

Municipalities are statutory creatures. That is, they have no inherent power — all their powers flow from provincial legislation. Provincial municipal acts typically are complex and detailed, being very explicit about the limits of the powers conferred and the conditions that must be met in order for the municipality to act.

The historic tendency of courts to read the grants of powers to municipalities quite narrowly reinforces these limitations. Courts have not been willing to extend the powers of municipalities beyond those granted explicitly or by necessary implication. Courts have also seen themselves in a supervisory role over municipalities, testing whether bylaws were passed in good faith or in the public interest, or if they were reasonable. Statute modifies the extent of the courts' supervision in some provinces — sometimes to insulate the municipality from this supervision, sometimes to add avenues of recourse to the courts.

b. POWERS OF FIRST NATIONS

In contrast to the single source of limited and delegated authority for municipalities, First Nations have various sources of authority, including inherent powers. First Nations can have powers with sources in international law, quasi-international inherent rights, treaties, Canadian constitutional law, and Canadian statute law.

1. International and quasi-international powers

Some First Nations assert a full right of statehood in international law. Anyone dealing with such a First Nation should be aware of this, since it profoundly affects the type of interactions possible with that First Nation.

Almost all — if not all — First Nations assert some kind of inherent powers, flowing from their very existence. Because these powers exist independently and are not delegated from anywhere, they are best thought of as quasi-international, flowing from the same source as any state's powers. They are *quasi*-international since First Nations often assert an inherent right of self-government that stops short of a claim to full statehood. These asserted rights can have varying scope, depending on the particular First Nation. While different things may be meant by such inherent rights, it is important to know that Canada and a number of provinces recognize that First Nations *do* have inherent powers.

2. Treaty powers

First Nations may also have powers that flow from, or are recognized by, treaties. These may be historic treaties or modern treaties such as land claims settlement agreements or self-government agreements. The particulars of treaty powers depend entirely on the terms of the treaty in question. The historic treaties seldom deal explicitly with First Nations' powers. However, the very fact that the treaties were entered into by settler governments shows their recognition that First Nations were political and legal entities. This presupposes some kind of Aboriginal inherent power. In the minds of most First Nations people, the treaties affirmed a nation-to-nation relationship between the Crown and the First Nation in question.

Modern, comprehensive land claims agreements frequently contain rights for Aboriginal peoples that are governmental in some sense, such as rights to be represented on various decision-making boards. Self-government agreements contain provisions that are much more directly jurisdictional and, in some circumstances, these agreements may now be recognized as treaties.

3. Constitutional powers

The Canadian constitution recognizes and affirms existing Aboriginal and treaty rights of the Aboriginal peoples of Canada. As such, it is not a *granting* of these rights: the right of self-government is considered by First Nations to flow from the Creator, not from the Canadian constitution.

While it is not settled in law that the constitution, by affirming Aboriginal and treaty rights, also affirms the inherent right to self-government, courts have made comments tending in this direction. As well, the federal government and a number of provinces are now conducting themselves on the basis that First Nations have inherent rights of self-government, taking the relationship between First Nations and settler governments outside the scope of purely internal Canadian law and into the realm of a nation-to-nation relationship. This is a key and cutting-edge development which greatly affects the contours of the interaction of First Nations and municipalities — when they do, in fact, interact.

4. Powers granted by Canadian governments

First Nations are also delegated powers by the federal government and, sometimes, by provincial governments (the most notable federal statute delegating powers is the Indian Act). Statutory interpretation, in the context of Canadian administrative law, defines the extent of these powers. These First Nations powers, insofar as they are delegated powers from other governments, are similar to the powers of municipalities. Whether or not, as delegated powers, they are as narrow as municipalities' powers is a complex question that will not be addressed here.

c. DO MUNICIPAL BYLAWS APPLY TO INDIAN RESERVES?

The question of whether, according to Canadian law, a municipal bylaw applies to land on Indian reserves is very complex. The simple answer, however, is that municipal bylaws seldom do apply to Indian reserve land.

The first step in arriving at this answer is to determine whether the boundaries of the municipality encompass a particular reserve. Even if surrounded by a municipality, the reserve lands may be carved out of the municipality, in which case the municipality has no jurisdiction.

If the boundaries of the municipality *do* include a reserve, a three-stage analysis of the municipal bylaw is necessary. (This analysis is also used to determine whether any particular provincial legislation applies to Indian reserve land.) The three issues determined are the following:

(a) Federal and provincial division of powers

(b) Statutory interpretation of the Indian Act

(c) Constitutional guarantee of treaty and Aboriginal rights

1. Federal and provincial division of powers

Since all municipal powers are delegated from the province, the municipality cannot exercise any powers greater than those of the province. It must be determined, then, whether a municipal bylaw stays within the scope of provincial powers as a matter of constitutional law.

Legislative power over Indians and land reserved for the Indians is assigned to the federal government in section 91(24) of the Constitution Act, 1867. On the other hand, the provinces have jurisdiction over property and civil rights (s. 92(13)), municipal institutions (s. 92(8)), and matters of a local and private nature (s. 92(16)). The provinces also have ownership of Crown lands and resources (s. 109). The interaction of these provisions is complicated and has frequently been controversial. The question of whether provincial law applies to First Nations members or lands contains numerous subtleties. For our purposes here, however, provincial legislation of general application does not apply to First Nations members and lands on division-of-powers grounds if the legislation —

(a) affects *Indianness* (the particular status and capacities of First Nations or their members),

(b) singles out Indians for special treatment, or

(c) affects the interests of First Nations or their members in their lands.

Despite the sweeping effect of these exceptions, there is still significant room for the underlying rule to operate. Traffic legislation is one example of this.

It seems uncontroversial that municipal legislation, primarily directed to land use, does not apply to a First Nation reserve if the land is used by the First Nation members, since this would plainly infringe on exclusive federal jurisdiction. The unresolved question is about jurisdiction over *designated lands* leased to non-Indians. Designated lands encompass lands a First Nation wishes to lease to non-Indians. Because of the nature of reserve land tenure, such lands are leased by the non-Indian from Canada. (Before 1988, such lands were called *conditionally surrendered*. The change in terminology has not resolved the constitutional uncertainty.)

Some municipalities and provinces try to regulate or tax such non-Indian land interests or uses, and in supporting this, some courts have tried to distinguish between regulation of a land user and regulation of a land use. Such a fine distinction has led to results making no practical sense, such as finding that municipal zoning bylaws did not apply but that municipal building permit bylaws did apply in the same situation. The law remains highly unsettled, with provincial courts of appeal expressing opposite opinions. This is quite unsatisfactory since major economic development is now taking place on leased reserve land.

The point may become less controversial with the taxation issue. Since 1985, First Nations have had the explicit power to tax interests in land on the reserve, including designated lands. British Columbia has responded to this by taking steps to vacate the field to the extent required to prevent double taxation. (See chapter 9 for a more detailed discussion of First Nations and taxation.)

2. Statutory interpretation of the Indian Act

Once the municipal or provincial legislation passes the division-of-powers hurdle, it must still be determined if federal legislation covers the same subject. First Nations bylaws passed under the Indian Act would be paramount and would prevail over inconsistent municipal bylaws.

A further twist is that provincial legislation of general application affecting "Indianness," and therefore inapplicable to First Nations members of its own force, is made applicable to them with federal force by section 88 of the Indian Act. However, according to section 88, this *incorporation by reference* does not apply if the law in question —

(a) is inconsistent with any terms of a treaty,

(b) is inconsistent with any other act of parliament,

(c) is inconsistent with any order, rule, regulation, or bylaw made under the Indian Act, or

(d) makes provision for any matter dealt with by or under the Indian Act.

Because of the nature of municipal bylaws, it is extremely rare for them to meet the conditions required by section 88 to be given federal force.

3. Constitutional guarantee of treaty and Aboriginal rights

On top of the limits imposed by the division of powers come the limits imposed by the constitutional guarantee for treaty and Aboriginal rights. These rights are recognized and affirmed in section 35 of the Constitution Act, 1982. Any law — federal, provincial, or municipal — that otherwise had force, either of its own or via section 88 of the Indian Act, to Indians or Indian lands could not prevail over a treaty or Aboriginal right unless the infringement of the right was justified.

Courts have placed a heavy onus of proof on anyone seeking to show justification. A provincial law regulating hunting, for example, was held, in *Dick v. R.*, not to apply to Indians of its own force but to be given force by section 88 of the Indian Act. However, such incorporated federal legislation is inapplicable by virtue of section 35 of the constitution, unless it passes the justification test.

d. JURISDICTION

1. Boundary issues

Relatively ordinary jurisdictional questions arise in boundary issues. For example, there may be a road allowance or a travelled road on the boundary of a municipality and a First Nation reserve. Questions may arise about who has the right or obligation to deal with the road. If the road lies entirely on the First Nation's side of the boundary, the First Nation would, in the absence of any other arrangement, seem to be entitled to treat it as a private road. If the road straddles the boundary, joint jurisdiction and responsibility would seem to be in order. Even if none of the road lies on the reserve, however, the First Nation might have some say about the road, depending on the circumstances.

In Ontario, for instance, if this situation were to occur between two municipalities, the two municipalities would have joint jurisdiction. In light of the Statement of Political Relationship (SPR), a 1991 formal agreement between Ontario and the Chiefs of Ontario recognizing a government-to-government relationship between First Nations and Ontario, it would hardly be appropriate for a municipality to treat a First Nation as having *fewer* rights than a neighboring municipality. Although the SPR is a political commitment not intended to create or define rights, it amounts to provincial policy, and municipalities disregard it at their peril. A First Nation, by invoking the SPR as a provincial policy, may be able to prevent a municipality from proceeding with plans for a boundary road to which a First Nation objects.

2. Traditional lands

"Traditional lands" are historic territory a First Nation aboriginally occupied. Profound types of jurisdictional questions arise over off-reserve traditional lands, lands which First Nations members often continue to use for traditional pursuits such as hunting, fishing, trapping, or gathering. Such uses are the exercise of Aboriginal rights and possibly treaty rights as well, which, of course, have constitutional protection. Thus, the exercise of these rights prevails over laws that might infringe them, unless the infringement can be justified. For example, bylaws prohibiting hunting, discharging firearms, or smoking fish are overridden by Aboriginal or treaty rights, unless, for example, such bylaws are required for public safety.

It is also possible that First Nations have the jurisdiction to regulate the exercise of treaty and Aboriginal rights by their members, including the exercise of these rights off reserve. For example, First Nations may regulate the harvesting of fish and game on reserve, including harvesting by non-members, since this is an explicit power under the Indian Act. First Nations bylaws for such matters prevail over inconsistent federal and provincial legislation. As well, while the Indian Act does not grant such jurisdiction, it may well be within the inherent powers of a First Nation to regulate its members' renewable resource harvesting activities off reserve. It has also been argued that inherent jurisdiction for First Nations should extend to regulation of activities of non-Indians off reserve, if doing so is necessary to conserve the resources required to exercise Aboriginal rights.

An interesting interaction between the assertion of First Nations' interests in traditional land and a municipality seeking to extend its boundaries occurred in *Re Geraldton Annexation*. The town of Geraldton was seeking to annex seven townships in which First Nations exercised traditional harvesting activities. The First Nations were engaged in negotiations with Ontario over these harvesting activities. Largely because of the impact on the negotiations and the current land use practices of the First Nations, the Ontario Municipal Board granted only the annexation of a much smaller area of land than that which Geraldton had sought.

3. Negotiations and settlements

The jurisdiction or recognition of First Nations' jurisdiction may increase in a number of ways. Naturally, this may affect the jurisdiction of municipalities.

First, there may be a court decision recognizing the jurisdiction of a First Nation. This is brought into sharp relief by *Skerryvore*. In this case, the court found that a road passing through an Indian reserve, which was the only land access to Skerryvore, on Georgian Bay, was a private Indian reserve road. Although the case had been before the courts for 13 years, the municipality and residents were totally unprepared for the decision, had no contingency plan, and had trouble accepting that the road was not public.

Second, as part of a land claims settlement — or for other reasons — not only the title to lands but the jurisdiction over the lands may change. Canada has an elaborate policy for the creation of new Indian reserves or the addition of lands to existing reserves. A significant part of this policy is devoted to ensuring that arrangements with municipalities are made for loss of tax base and for providing municipal services, applying and enforcing bylaws, and consulting on land-use planning. The policy is very restrictive and may be — or soon become — inconsistent with the current legal and political context (i.e., negotiations based on First Nations' inherent right of self-government.)

Third, there may be agreements recognizing or creating additional jurisdiction for First Nations. It is important to realize that these negotiations may take place at different conceptual levels. Negotiations under Canada's 1986 Community Based Self Government Policy would result in Canada delegating greater authority to First Nations. Some provinces have also implemented arrangements amounting to a delegation of provincial authority to First Nations institutions, such as Aboriginal Child Welfare Agencies.

The most fundamental conceptual level of negotiations are those on the level of inherent right. It is entirely conceivable that such negotiations could recognize First Nation authority over certain matters off reserve or recognize some kind of Aboriginal authority in urban centres.

Courts have been open to the idea that First Nations have an inherent right of self-government. For example, one particular form of Aboriginal self-government was recognized by the court when Aboriginal custom adoptions were recognized as valid and constitutionally protected by the

British Columbia Court of Appeal in *Casimel v. Insurance Corp. of B.C.*. The Supreme Court of Canada was also prepared, in *R. v. Pamajewon*, to "assume, without deciding," that the constitutional rights of Aboriginal people include rights to self-government, although it went on to find that the particular right being asserted, the right to regulate gambling, was not an Aboriginal right for the particular First Nation in question. It is clear that courts will not approach the subject as a matter of there being or not being a right of self-government in general. Instead, they will want to look at rights of specific First Nations to regulate specific activities on the basis of the particular customs and history of the relevant Aboriginal people.

Canada and a number of provinces are proceeding on the basis that the inherent right of Aboriginal self-government exists and is constitutionally protected. Ontario's commitment to this is contained in the SPR, and Canada released a formal Aboriginal self-government policy, *Aboriginal Self-Government: Federal Policy Guide*, in 1995.

Negotiations under the 1986 Memorandum of Understanding with the Nishnawbe-Aski Nation (NAN) are one example of negotiations based on the inherent right of Aboriginal self-government. These negotiations began some time ago and anticipated more recent developments. NAN is an association of 48 First Nations with traditional territory covering much of northern Ontario. The Memorandum of Understanding was an undertaking by Canada and Ontario to enter negotiations on various matters, including Aboriginal government and resource management sharing.

e. LAND TITLE

Various issues of land title affect First Nations and municipalities, including protection of First Nations' interests pending resolution of a land claim and effects on municipalities of a land claims settlement.

1. Protection of First Nations interest

Standard legal remedies — a certificate of pending litigation or an injunction — are available to First Nations pending resolution of a land claim. For both of these remedies, First Nations would need to litigate, a relatively uncommon avenue of asserting an Aboriginal land claim.

However, there are also specific matters of municipal law that may provide remedies to First Nations. For example, if a municipality's actions prejudice the interests of a First Nation asserting a land claim, the actions may be subject to court review. Since a municipality must ordinarily act by bylaw, the bylaw might be challenged on grounds of particular procedural requirements, jurisdictional requirements, or the general ground of bad faith.

An example of this is the case *Chippewas of Saugeen* where bylaws of the Township of Keppel, which dealt with shore road allowances, were challenged by the Chippewas who were asserting land claims to the land in question. The land owners had been suing Keppel for the road allowances, but dropped the suit after the court ruled that the Chippewas should be parties to the proceeding. After the suit was dropped, Keppel passed bylaws authorizing the issuing of quit-claims to the allowances. The court granted the Chippewas' application, inferring bad faith from the timing of the passage of the bylaws and also from the fact that Keppel had not fulfilled its previous undertaking to inform the First Nations of transfers of road allowances.

2. Effects of land claims settlements

A constitutional dilemma lies at the heart of any Aboriginal land claims settlement. The Constitution Act, 1867, allocates to Canada jurisdiction for Indians and land reserved for the Indians but allocates to the provinces jurisdiction over and ownership of lands. The dilemma was created by the *St. Catharine's* line of cases that found that, because of the particular nature of the Aboriginal interest in traditional lands, after a treaty in which First Nations released their interest in land to Canada, it was the province, not Canada, that ended up with the land. Since it had been the practice for Canada to sell and grant the lands, these decisions caused considerable difficulties for everyone concerned.

To try and fix up the mess, Canada made various agreements with the provinces over the years. One of the most recent, a 1986 Indian Lands Agreement with Ontario, enables Canada and Ontario to reach specific agreements with First Nations on land or natural resource matters.

There are many unsettled questions of law surrounding these issues. For example, numerous commentators dispute the correctness of the *St. Catharine's* line of cases altogether. It should also be noted that a province's ownership of the land is explicitly subject, under the constitution, to any interest other than its own. While questions of provincial obligations to Canada on Aboriginal issues have been extensively litigated, the question of a province's obligations to First Nations for lands surrendered by treaty has never been squarely before a court. Given all this uncertainty surrounding a *valid* land surrender, negotiations over First Nations land claims *disputing* a land surrender can be very complex.

The issue of a land title transfer as a land claims settlement is distinct from the jurisdictional question of whether that land would become Indian reserve land. However, First Nations frequently want both title and jurisdiction, and the non-Aboriginal public frequently views these matters as overlapping. Probably for this reason, most provinces undertake public consultation about land claims settlement negotiations. While Canada's policy for some years has been to involve municipalities if lands are to be set aside as reserve lands, Canada has only recently begun to undertake public consultations about title transfers as well. (Some of the dynamics of these issues, and a number of examples, are set out in D. Forrest, "Our Home and Native Land," *Cottage Life*, Nov/Dec 1994.)

f. ENVIRONMENTAL AND PLANNING ISSUES

1. On-reserve developments

All of the above issues of title and jurisdiction have environmental and planning aspects. In fact, it is likely environmental and planning concerns about *how* Aboriginal jurisdiction may be exercised that cause some of the public interest in title or jurisdiction issues. Non-Aboriginal people may be concerned about resources they are in the habit of using, although without an enforceable right to do so, such as sport hunting or fishing in a certain area. If they fear that they may not be able to continue these practices, they will often object to a First Nation's having title or jurisdiction.

Non-Aboriginal people may also have concerns about the impact economic developments on First Nations' lands will have on the local economy or environment, or about the municipality losing part of its tax base if lands under municipal jurisdiction are set aside as reserved lands. The coordination of municipal services may also be an issue.

Of course, sometimes public concern is more philosophically based, with philosophies ranging from formal equality notions to outright racism. What the philosophically based concerns fail to recognize is the historic, social, and legal uniqueness of First Nations. The pragmatic concerns are typically given more than adequate attention by provinces and involve public consultation.

The applicability of environmental legislation to on-reserve projects needs to be considered as well. While it is not First Nations who historically have been environmentally insensitive or unwilling to share resources, a municipality might be concerned about the environmental impacts of on-reserve developments. While the municipality has little chance of invoking planning legislation or exercising its own jurisdiction for on-reserve projects, it may be able to invoke environmental legislation. It is an open question whether or not — and to what extent — provincial environmental legislation applies if an on-reserve development has environmental effects off-reserve. I know of no province presently attempting to apply its environmental laws to reserves. However, the Canadian Environmental Assessment Act (CEAA) applies if there are environmental effects on or off reserve.

2. Off-reserve developments

On the other side of the coin, First Nations may have environmental or planning concerns about off-reserve developments. If the development affects the exercise of Aboriginal rights, First Nations have a powerful and constitutionally guaranteed right at stake. First Nations regularly raise issues of treaty and Aboriginal rights at environmental hearings and litigation and include environmental matters in land claims settlements. First Nations have had reasonable success in prohibiting, temporarily, development projects threatening to affect the exercise of their Aboriginal rights. In comprehensive land claims settlements, provisions for Aboriginal involvement in environmental assessment and resource management are typical.

First Nations have access, of course, to the same recourses on environmental or planning matters as other affected parties. For example, the Aboriginal and non-Aboriginal public alike has the right to make submissions at hearings about zoning changes or development approvals. First Nations can carefully study environmental or planning legislation for opportunities to raise concerns either on the basis of interference with a treaty or Aboriginal right or simply because of an environmental or planning concern. First Nations may appeal to provincial environmental laws concerning off-reserve developments with on-reserve effects, and it should not be overlooked that, recently, the Ontario Environmental Assessment Act was extended to apply generally to private sector developments meeting certain requirements. (Before 1993, the act applied only to public sector developments unless a specific regulation was passed making the act applicable to a particular private sector development.)

Some provincial acts may give First Nations particular procedural rights. For instance, the Ontario Cemeteries Act gives First Nations certain rights when an Aboriginal burial site is discovered. The Ontario Planning Act gives First Nations some rights of notification and appeal for planning matters. And again, the CEAA will also apply if there is an environmental effect on-reserve, even if the development in question is located off-reserve.

First nations and municipalities should keep in mind that they can affect each other on planning and environmental issues. Information sharing, in both directions, is beneficial to both First Nations and municipalities. Keeping each other informed may lead to better planning decisions and avoid legal challenges to particular developments.

Although waiting to be ratified, a land use notification agreement-in-principle has been reached between First Nations, municipalities, a conservation authority, Ontario, and Canada over Ontario's Grand River area. This agreement-in-principle provides for the various governments or agencies to notify each other of developments that might affect each other. It may also be efficient and appropriate in certain circumstances for First Nations and municipalities to contract with each other to provide particular types of services.

None of these suggestions should prejudice any jurisdictional claims, but both First Nations and municipalities may be more comfortable reaching arrangements with each other if those arrangements were made explicitly without prejudice to any such claims.

Municipalities, for their part, need to keep in mind that First Nations are fundamentally different in nature and in powers from municipalities. Therefore, municipalities should treat First Nations with respect and be aware of the differences.

9

FIRST NATIONS AND TAXATION

by Chief Manny Jules

There are few, if any, Aboriginal issues in Canada today generating as much controversy as taxation. Why is a tax exemption available to First Nation peoples? What are some of the problems with the current tax exemption? What are the challenges facing a First Nation seeking to raise necessary revenues by enacting tax laws of its own? What is the First Nations' perspective on these issues? These are some of the questions I want to answer in this chapter.

The views expressed in this chapter are mine. However, I owe much to the many sources I consulted. I would like to acknowledge the extremely valuable perspective Tony Mandamin provided of the First Nations' view of reserves. Mr. Mandamin is a First Nation lawyer from Alberta who has dedicated his practice to First Nations law. Other material I relied on was produced by a prolific writer on Indian taxation issues, Richard Bartlett. His analysis is always concise and informative. The easiest way to obtain any of Mr. Bartlett's work is to contact the Native Law Centre at the University of Saskatchewan.

I have spoken to thousands of Aboriginal people in hundreds of communities over the eight years that I have been involved in taxation issues. I have been strengthened, and at the same time humbled, by the determination of these people. First Nations peoples are committed to changing their lives for the better and they have the courage, strength of spirit, and resolve to see these changes through to realization. I resolutely believe that the key to some of these changes is in the power of First Nations to assert tax jurisdiction over users of their land.

a. THE INDIAN EXEMPTION FROM TAXATION

In 1899, the treaty commissioner of the day, referring to Treaty 8 and the Indian bands of British Columbia with which the treaty was made, reported that,"...we assured them that the Treaty would not lead to any forced interference with their mode of life, that it did not open the way to the imposition of any tax, and there was no fear of enforced military service." This assurance did not form the written text of the treaty but is an official part of the record.

The Indian exemption from taxation was recognized in legislation predating the commissioner's statement by nearly 50 years. In 1850, the Province of Canada enacted a law stating that no taxes would be levied or assessed on any Indian or any person married to an Indian for any Indian land. It also stated that no taxes or assessments would be imposed on any Indian or any person married to an Indian if that person resided on Indian lands not ceded to the Crown, or if the lands had been ceded and were set apart by the Crown for Indians to occupy.

In 1876, Canadian Indian legislation was consolidated in the Indian Act. The tax exemption for the real and personal property of an Indian found in the 1850 statute was maintained. Modern treaties such as the 1975 James Bay Agreement and the 1984 Western Arctic Agreement preserve this tax exemption. So, to this day, does the Indian Act.

The personal property of an Indian or a band on a reserve is exempt from taxation under section 87 of the Indian Act. The courts have ruled that this means that income an Indian earns on reserve is tax exempt. The exemption has been held to apply in certain cases even where the work itself was done off reserve. As we will see, the courts have developed some complicated rules for deciding exactly where, in law, income should be said to have been earned.

With *Nowegijick*, decided by the Supreme Court of Canada in 1983, the rules seemed quite simple. If the head office of the employer was on reserve and the pay cheques were issued from that office, the Indian's income was considered earned on reserve and therefore exempt from income tax, even if the work was physically done off reserve.

But with *Williams*, the Supreme Court has declared that the rules are not simple. The circumstances and connecting factors between the Indian and the employment income must be examined in each case. Residence, location of the employer, the kind of employer, whether the employer has a profit motive, and where the work is performed — all these factors must be considered. The issue has now reached almost a mystical dimension.

To try to clarify matters, Revenue Canada has issued controversial guidelines setting out its view of the appropriate connecting factors for income to be tax exempt. It is clear that these will be challenged in the courts and, unfortunately, further litigation will result.

However, there are a few things that are beyond debate. The courts have held that the Indian Act exemption applies to "Indians" as defined by the Indian Act and does not apply to other people of Aboriginal descent. Also, Canadian courts have ruled that even Indians resident on reserves are subject to sales tax, unemployment insurance premiums, and other charges levied for transactions occurring off reserve or relating to property not destined for use on reserve. (However, the law here is confusing, and specific questions should be directed to a lawyer.)

There is considerable room for argument about the scope of the Aboriginal tax exemption. One problem is that the words used in the Indian Act relating to taxation are ambiguous. I do not intend an exhaustive etymology here, but I will mention several examples as illustration.

The use of the word "exempt" itself fails to convey the understanding First Nations have of the issue. Some First Nations have argued that a more appropriate word is "immune," since an exemption requires a decision to modify a condition where a tax would otherwise be applicable. The use of the word "immune" would underscore that the right to tax Indians did not exist in the first place.

The use of the word "Indian" has also raised questions. Canadian courts have interpreted the word to mean a natural person and not a corporation (even if the latter is 100% owned by Indians). This court interpretation obviously has huge economic implications for businesses on reserve. But even this interpretation is subject to exceptions. It seems that if the corporation is considered as a bare trustee for Indians, the tax exemption applies.

The word "taxation" is also unclear. Taxation includes a shifting host of circumstances, forms, and varieties ranging from income tax to customs duties. Each situation, often with its own group of administrators, offers an opportunity for intrusion into the life of First Nations peoples.

From First Nations' perspective, a more fundamental problem with the exemption is that it is placed in the Indian Act. First Nations view tax exemption as a right integral to the historic fabric of this country, a fundamental part of the understanding reached between the Aboriginal and non-Aboriginal people of this land when Aboriginal people were asked to share the land and its resources. The treaty commissioner's assurances leading up to Treaty 8 are an example of this understanding. Unfortunately, government bureaucrats and politicians with short memories still treat the exemption as statute-based only, subject to change or even elimination. Government officials explain that the tax exemption is merely a feature of the scheme of protection set out in the federal government's historical Indian policy. Underlying that policy was the view that as Indians became "civilized" and assimilated, the need for protection (including tax exemption) would disappear.

Court cases involving Aboriginal tax exemption have limited themselves to interpretations of the wording in the Indian Act, even though, as we have seen, the tax exemption has its source outside current federal and provincial legislation. From an Aboriginal perspective, this is unfortunate and unfair. Thus, as long as the tax exemption is focused within the Indian Act, First Nations and other Canadians are forced into a false history.

b. TAXATION BY FIRST NATIONS

1. Fiscal challenges for First Nations

Taxation must be considered in context. Suppose you are the leader of a First Nation government on the first day on the job. Imagine opening a blank book. On the left side of the page you will write a list of investments you must make. You will have help filling in this part of the book by direction given to you by your electors. Resources will need to be committed to quality-of-life issues; housing and related capital expenditures are key investments here. At the same time, investment must be made to ensure health and safety. Policing will be a big cost. Health care and education will also figure prominently on the left side of the page.

Other investment decisions must also be made. Jobs, economic development, culture, youth, the elderly, and the operation of your government itself all require investment. Investment must also be made to attract new business investments to your reserve. Provisions must be made to make life comfortable for investors you hope will find a home for their businesses on your reserve. A further investment is required to support activities that preserve the integrity of your territory and the wholeness of your environment. Provision must be made for spiritual life. Property and other rights must be protected. All of these require substantial investment.

On the right side of the page, you now must list how you will pay for these investments. The obvious methods are not available to you. It will be very difficult to sell reserve lands, because this land represents the community's assets to be held in perpetuity. Much of your resources will come from federal programs. Yet they will not be enough. Other revenue might be generated from leases or the sale of subsurface rights. You must, of course, pay for the infrastructure associated with the leases from the lease revenues.

At the same time, you are aware that other governments are extracting, through taxes, the wealth of your reserve. Every incorporated business and non-exempt person earning income on your reserve must pay to these other governments. Your people working off reserve or buying most services off reserve also pay taxes that go off reserve. Yet you cannot raise your lease or business licence fees or investors will move elsewhere.

When you are required to buy services, whether social services, education, health, or policing, you must be willing to pay the full price. Others control the standards and arrangements existing between the federal and provincial governments.

Frequently, others negotiate for you. You may want to build your own schools, and you do. You may want to create your own police force, and you do. You may want to take care of your own children, and you do. Each time you do, however, you become increasingly vulnerable to changes in funding. You think of risk management — should you lease more?

You re-examine your situation. The reserve that you occupy is small but it is all you and your people have left. Most of your investment is siphoned off reserve, either through required service arrangements or taxes by other governments. The reserve is that part of the world where First Nations members are supposed to have complete control. The reserve is there for the use and benefit of First Nations as their own customs and practices dictate. Reserve lands are a special place where social and cultural values are preserved. At the same time, the reserve is a source of economic and legal advantage. It is a place to live and a place in which to be buried. As such, reserve lands are not just real estate.

Reserve lands are, sadly, the last refuge for a people who had possessed significantly more. For First Nations, reserves have a value beyond price. Reserves are rarely added to. On the other hand, surrenders, expropriation, and other activities rendering Indian lands unusable, such as their use as military bases and ranges, have tended to reduce the size of reserves and the opportunities available there. The Indian population itself is growing at a rate significantly higher than the Canadian norm. There is little room for growth and a significant need for protection. A full exercise of taxation jurisdiction by First Nations could assure this.

2. First Nations and the power to tax

True protection of Aboriginal rights will only occur when we have our own means to preserve our priorities. This movement must begin on reserves. I believe that First Nations must act as governments with full tax powers. The 1988 amendment to the Indian Act broadening First Nations' real property taxation power to extend over non-Indians located on reserve is a clear example of this movement. Section 83 provides, in part:

> (1)...the council of a band may, subject to the approval of the Minister, make by-laws for any or all of the following purposes, namely:

> (a)...taxation for local purposes of land, or interests in land, in the reserve, including rights to occupy, possess or use land in the reserve

It is only in this way, I believe, that First Nations can take necessary measures to prevent incursions by other governments into our territories. I have spent most of my political life affirming this view.

My involvement with taxation was, in all honesty, rooted in frustration. As chief of the Kamloops Band, I became responsible for an industrial park on a part of our reserve that had been, under the pre-1988 Indian Act, conditionally surrendered. When land was surrendered in this way, Her Majesty gained rights to the land that allowed the Crown to grant possession of it by lease to non-Indians. The Indians on the reserve, of course, must pay the costs of developing the land and providing services such as roads, water, sanitation, and all of the other things that tenants expect to receive for their investment. This, in itself, was not disturbing. However, the British Columbia government insisted on asserting its full taxation power over these non-Indians on what, because of the surrender, was no longer considered to be part of the reserve.

We were faced with a crisis. If the province claimed jurisdiction to tax on reserve, and the First Nation used its power to tax, overburdened tenants would be faced with a double tax bill. The economics of the situation would be disastrous for the reserve. After much soul-searching, the Kamloops Band decided that it had to assert its own powers of taxation. This was an extremely difficult undertaking. The Indian Act then acknowledged only a very limited power to levy taxes. Such power was available only to "advanced" bands and, because of the definition of "reserve," it did not extend to conditionally surrendered lands — the very land we wanted to tax!

We even went to court on the issue, arguing that leased lands should be considered part of the reserve and that we should therefore be allowed to tax those lands. In 1984, in *Leonard v. R. in the Right of British Columbia*, the British Columbia Court of Appeal held otherwise. We found ourselves in a very difficult situation. I wrote to all the chiefs in Canada asking them to support an amendment to the Indian Act that would change the Indian Act definition of "reserve" to include conditionally surrendered lands. With the support of the chiefs, I approached the federal government in 1985 and proposed the change. After three years of consultation and development, the Indian Act was amended through Bill C-115.

Besides clarifying the legal status of conditionally surrendered lands to ensure that these lands (now called "designated lands") fell within the ambit of band-council power, the reach of taxation bylaw powers was considerably extended.

Before the amendment, people could argue that the only taxation authority in the Indian Act related to a First Nation's ability to tax the land interests of its own members. Section 83 of the Indian Act was amended to make explicit the power of a band to tax non-Indian interests in reserve lands. This power was made available to all First Nations. Importantly, the archaic and frankly offensive requirement that First Nations be declared by the minister to be in an advanced stage of development before they could exercise their tax power was removed. The Minister of Indian Affairs retained the power, however, to review and approve all First Nations bylaws, including tax bylaws. The Indian Taxation Advisory Board was established to assist the minister in carrying out his or her responsibilities and to help First Nations develop their own taxation systems.

Since the 1988 amendments, more than 50 First Nations have now enacted taxation laws (see Figure #2). In doing so they have been able to encourage and reap some benefit from economic development on reserve (see Figure #3). At the same time, the exercise of First Nations taxation powers has served as an effective way to oust provincial real property taxation from the reserve.

3. Taxation as an instrument of Aboriginal self-government

While I am not sure what the federal government means in its policy when it talks about the "inherent right of self-government," I know what this idea of inherency means to

FIGURE #2
FIRST NATIONS WITH PROPERTY TAX BYLAWS

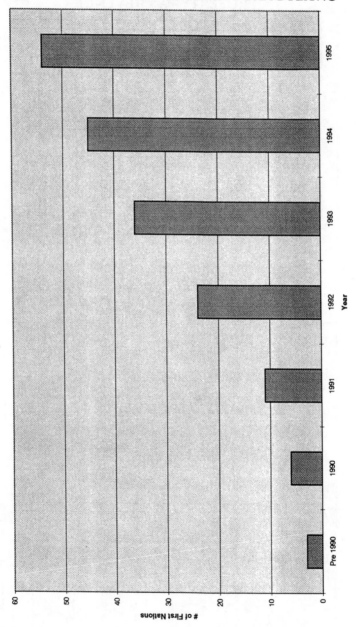

FIGURE #3
THE GROWTH IN FIRST NATION
PROPERTY TAX REVENUE

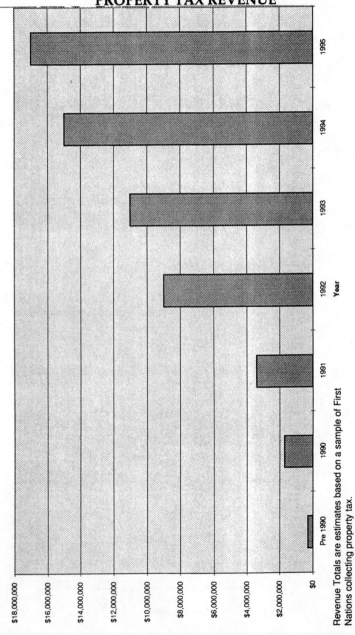

Revenue Totals are estimates based on a sample of First Nations collecting property tax.

me. It means that we, as Aboriginal peoples, must know what we want and must express this knowledge in our own laws, based on the fact that we exist because of the goodwill of the Creator. Our laws, however, must be direct and unambiguous, and this may mean seeking changes to existing laws that affect us. It may mean drawn-out discussions with people who would rather not be talking to us. It may mean dealing in an environment where all the public polls are against us. This may mean exhaustion and frustration and politics, but it must be done.

Be prepared to plan. Be prepared to have your purposes questioned. Be prepared to explain and explain again. Listen and temper your anger. You'll have occasions for both. Most of all, understand the issue and what your people want. Know what taxation can do and what taxation can undo. Seek your own jurisdiction. Be prepared to deal with the hardest issues.

Let me give you an example of the sort of self-questioning rigor you should apply to your decision to seek taxation jurisdiction. Suppose a First Nation government decides to pass a law, but within the law there is a provision distinguishing between an Indian and a non-Indian interest. The law might state, for example, that "any interest held by the band, a band member, or a corporation established for the benefit of the band is exempt." Is such a provision legal? Or would it be struck down as discriminatory? The Indian Act already exempts Indians from taxation. This establishes a legitimate legislative purpose for singling out Indians as a separate group and continuing the historic exemption. If federal law can rely on this, then surely a First Nation law can make the same distinction if the legislative purpose is similar.

Separate treatment of non-residents for voting, taxation, and permits can be justified to maintain community identity and distinctiveness: you may want to tax to regulate entry by outsiders or you may want to protect the income and property of Indians whose traditional pursuits leave them without money to pay the taxes.

In the interest of development, we will continue to seek ways to attract non-member investment on reserve. We should always be aware, however, that these non-members may be paying taxes to other jurisdictions. Perhaps the implementation of tax treaties allowing the co-existence of different tax systems will need to be considered.

Clear drafting of First Nation taxation bylaws is imperative. Let us look at land taxation, for example. The Indian Taxation Advisory Board has developed a model bylaw for taxation of land on reserve. In developing this model bylaw, we defined land as meaning "having the extensive meaning of the common law." We then went on to include *buildings* and *improvements* in the model.

Yet even this apparent clarity in meaning became the subject of controversy. We have since come to understand that land is traditionally distinguished from buildings in standard legal usage. Land is sometimes simply "the material of the earth." We thought we could rely on the 1988 amendment to the Indian Act that clearly extended First Nations' taxation power to both lands and improvements on these lands.

In fact, the public discussion paper I helped prepare that led to the 1988 amendment ("Proposed Amendments to the Indian Act Concerning Conditionally Surrendered Land and Band Taxation Powers," Ottawa, DIAND, 1988) clearly indicated that section 83, which until then defined the money-related bylaw powers including the power to tax "interests in land in the reserve of persons lawfully in possession thereof" (presumably only Indians), was clearly intended to indicate that any use, occupancy, or interest in land, including improvements on the land, of all persons could be subject to taxation bylaws. This intent was subsequently written in the Indian Act.

We thought the meaning was clear until our legal advisers admonished us, as we developed the model bylaw, that we should always be explicit, even if we felt that the Indian Act was unambiguous. Ambiguous language only encourages legal challenges. We decided that, regardless of the apparent clarity in the Indian Act, we would explicitly refer to *lands* and *buildings* whenever we spoke of land in the bylaw.

Unless First Nations are careful in drafting taxation laws, ambiguity will permit others to determine what we may have meant. At the same time, however, we could let things become too complicated. Taxation is an art that has for too long been the domain of experts. Tax laws should be readable and clear.

I have tried here, in this short chapter, to outline what I think is the basic and most important consideration in First Nations taxation — the need for First Nation jurisdiction. I have barely scratched the surface. We must continue to explore and discuss a wide range of taxation issues. These will surely include the following: opportunities to share tax jurisdiction on our traditional lands in areas beyond reserve boundaries; the taxation of utilities and railways crossing reserve lands which have an impact in the community but which often oppose or resist accepting our jurisdiction; the training of the staffs we will need as we mature in our treatment of fiscal policy; taxation under the new federal inherent right policy and what it means in the context of modern treaty discussions; the taxation of natural resources and its relationship to royalty regimes; and the enforcement of First Nations tax laws.

In the end, I believe there is a need to establish a First Nations institute that could, on an ongoing basis, consider all these matters and support the fight of First Nations coming to grips with the reality of taxation controlled by others. I have written here about the need for a forward-looking agenda that seeks to establish First Nation governments as a player in the field. It is large and it is worth the effort.

10

RESOURCE AND ENVIRONMENT ISSUES

by Jerry Fontaine, Joseph Gilbert, Ian Jackson, and Dean Jacobs

a. CORE ISSUES

Resource and environment issues are of central importance to Aboriginal people throughout Canada. Resources and the environment are not just another group of issues related to self-government, nor are they simply another area where there are differences of opinion or priorities between Natives and non-Natives. The environment and the natural resource base are vital to the culture and traditions that Aboriginal peoples are fighting to protect.

Although they need considerable elaboration, and their relationship to each other needs explanation, the key features of the Aboriginal position on resources and environment can be stated as three straightforward propositions:

(a) Resources and the environment are not separate issues. In Aboriginal eyes, the environment *is* the resource base.

(b) At the heart of Aboriginal cultural tradition (Inuit and Métis as well as Indian) is the belief — and practice — that humans should live in harmony with the natural world of which they are a part. Environmental resources are therefore held and used in trust for the generations to come.

(c) The consensus principle which dominates Aboriginal decision making is a vital part of their attitude to resources and environment, and derives in large part from the belief that land and other environmental elements exist for the common use of the community.

To explain the significance of these propositions in more detail, let us take them in reverse order, beginning with the consensus principle and the attitude to land.

1. Consensus principle

When the Indian treaties were signed, a major objective of the Canadian government was to establish a legal basis for immigrant land settlement, based on individual ownership. But for hundreds and thousands of years, Aboriginal peoples had occupied those lands without seeing the need for, or even the relevance of, individual ownership. As Michael Whittington wrote in "Political and Constitutional Development in the N.W.T. and Yukon," an essay published in *The North* in 1985:

> The concept of individual possession, which is such an important cornerstone of liberal societies, is replaced by the principle of communal sharing of wealth or effort. Individuals are thus not seen to own things, rather, they simply use them; and when not using something, it automatically reverts to the community again to be put to use by some other member of the group. Nowhere is this concept more prominent than in the native concept of the land.

Clearly, there are practical limits to this notion of communal sharing: Aboriginal people count things such as cars and television sets as their personal possessions, and probably their distant forefathers felt the same way about their tools and weapons. That said, in the Indian tradition, a person's wealth was measured mainly in terms of how much he or she gave away. The guiding principle remains important, and so therefore does the principle of consensus decision making. Although the community is more important than the individual, the attitudes and interests of each member of that community matter, and the community should not ride roughshod over individual objections, even in the name of majority rule.

One consequence of the consensus principle is that First Nations or other Aboriginal groups may find it difficult or impossible to adopt comprehensive development plans for their community. Although such plans are designed to bring net overall benefits to a community and therefore may seem to fit well with the Aboriginal emphasis on community values, the typical plan usually limits the freedom of action (now or in the future) of some members of the community. Zoning, for example, provides that some uses may be permitted in this place but not in that place. Objections to such plans are common in both Native and non-Native communities, but whereas the will of the majority tends to carry in non-Native settings, a strong attachment to the consensus principle may make an Aboriginal group unwilling to impose a plan on its members. (However, the consensus principle should not be regarded as a prescription for inaction. At the level of international diplomacy, for example, it may sometimes be the only basis on which progress is possible.)

2. Environmental conservation

The proposition that environmental resources should be conserved so they are available for future generations suggests that what non-Aboriginal people have recently recognized as "sustainable development" is something Aboriginal people have practised since time immemorial. There are, however, some significant differences between Aboriginal tradition and sustainable development as it is envisaged by the non-Aboriginal majority.

The differences can perhaps best be explained by an example. The Walpole Island First Nation, the most southerly First Nation in Canada, is located on a wetland area beside Lake St. Clair in southwestern Ontario. Part of its territory has been drained for agriculture, but it also contains, within its relatively small total area of about 91 square kilometres, substantial areas of undrained marsh, tallgrass prairie, and on higher ground, relics of the broadleaved Carolinian forest type that once characterized the whole of southwest Ontario. Indeed, of 36 such sites examined by a Carolinian-Canada task force some years ago, Walpole Island Prairie, Savannah, and Marsh was the area that best preserved the landscape of the past. Its plants and animals include many species rare in Canada, and some that are found nowhere else in Canada.

Meanwhile, the landscape of the rest of southwestern Ontario has been transformed. Forests have been cleared, more than 90% of the extensive wetlands have been drained for intensive agriculture, and Canada's largest concentration of heavy chemical industries has been established between Lake Huron and Lake St. Clair.

There is therefore a vast difference between the environmental resource conservation Walpole Islanders have practised over the centuries and sustainable development as it is envisaged elsewhere in southwestern Ontario. Sustainable development is seen as cleaning up past pollution and ensuring that chemicals, agricultural pesticides, and other contaminants do not destroy more species or damage the health of humans and wildlife. It may mean efforts to re-introduce some plants and animals that have disappeared from the area and an end to further wetland loss. It does not, however, mean an end to development.

What particularly annoys Walpole Island about the present non-Aboriginal concern for sustainable development and protection of threatened environments is the unthinking, if sincerely meant, pressure from scientists and others for special measures to protect Walpole Island's distinctive environment, simply because the pace of development has led to the disappearance of threatened environments practically everywhere else. As Ian Jackson said some time ago: "I resent very much when outsiders tell us we now have an obligation to preserve these plants for the benefit of humankind. This kind of attitude ignores our contributions and traditional management legacy. At its worst it is racism. It implies that underdeveloped Native communities, those who can least afford it, must bear the burden of previous uncontrolled and unsound development."

3.   Indivision of resource and environment issues

The contrast between the Aboriginal tradition of resource use and the dominant pattern in southwestern Ontario illustrates the first proposition: for Aboriginal people, the environment is the resource base. In the rest of the region, the immigrants found forest and marshland. These they transformed into a highly productive agricultural landscape. The environmental impacts of soil erosion, pesticide use, and some other elements of the agricultural economy are recognized nowadays as problems needing to be addressed, but the value of the overall landscape transformation is scarcely questioned. Rather it is a matter of pride: an unproductive wilderness has been drained and made fruitful.

But how unproductive is that "wilderness," even when measured in present-day terms of dollars and cents? Walpole Island has about 6 800 hectares of wetland. Two-thirds of this area is leased during duck-hunting season to six hunt clubs. Some of these leases have been renewed for more than a century, which is one measure of sustainability. The First Nation also manages a substantial sport fishery. In the mid-1980s, an environmental audit by Cherod Ltd. estimated that annual income to the community from both leased and non-leased wetland was about $1.5 million (from things such as leases, duck-hunting and fishing permits, trapping income, and employment as guides). Valuable maybe, but surely the wetland that could be drained would be even more productive in agriculture? Not necessarily. A 1990 economic study undertaken by a University of Waterloo student concluded that marshland is just as profitable as agriculture land.

It can be argued that such comparisons are over-simplifications. The value of Walpole Island's marshlands to a non-Aboriginal duck hunter is due in no small part to the ducks' scarcity value; if surrounding areas had not been drained for agriculture, the hunt clubs would not need to come to Walpole Island. The economic return from the marshlands has declined in recent years, at least temporarily, as anti-fur campaigns reduced demand for the sustainable yield of muskrat pelts. Publicity of chemical pollution of the St. Clair River has also led to smaller numbers of duck hunters. Nevertheless, the central point remains valid: the Aboriginal tradition of using, instead of attempting to transform, the natural environment is in sharp contrast to non-Aboriginal attitudes to development, and it is a tradition that can be justified using economic as well as cultural and environmental criteria.

Ways in which these fundamental differences in attitude to resources and environment between Aboriginal and non-Aboriginal groups arise and can be resolved are described in the following sections. However, there is one further factor that is crucially important to understanding the Aboriginal position. There is no way, from an Aboriginal standpoint, that environmental or resource issues can be separated from sovereignty and self-government, since Aboriginal society, culture, and economy are all intimately linked to the environment.

This inseparable relationship is, however, something non-Aboriginal institutions and organizations are reluctant to recognize and are usually ill-equipped to handle. In a typical situation, a company may want to carry out activities that directly affect reserve lands or that have indirect implications for a First Nation's use of environmental resources. In the world of the 1990s, the company anticipates objections to its proposals and stands ready to work out acceptable solutions. From its point of view, however, such an objection lodged by a First Nation is likely to be regarded as just one of a collection of environmental objections made by a number of persons or groups. The company likely sees the matter as primarily involving scientific evidence and either alternate strategies or compensation. The company has the expertise to respond.

That, however, is not how a First Nation is likely to view the situation. The First Nation is not a stakeholder or interest group. The development is likely to be seen as a threat to the cultural, economic, or spiritual basis of the First Nation. In legal terms, the proposed development may appear to infringe the First Nation's jurisdiction or it may conflict with treaty or other rights negotiated a century ago or embodied in the Royal Proclamation of a century earlier. Even more typically in the 1990s, the First Nation is likely to see the proposal in terms of land claims or ongoing negotiations with federal and provincial governments, the outcome of which may see a major change in the power of the First Nation to authorize or prevent similar developments. Understandably, the company does not wish to become involved in such issues, seeing them as matters for governments or judicial interpretation. It can separate them from its proposal, but the First Nation cannot.

Again, Walpole Island provides a vivid example of this difference in outlook, which is not limited to private corporations and individuals but is evident also in the attitudes of federal, provincial, and municipal governments and their agencies. Unlike many other First Nations, Walpole Island is unceded territory and its boundaries have never been defined. In 1989, Canada, Ontario, and Walpole Island began negotiations to settle the boundaries of the reserve. It was agreed that the negotiations should simultaneously cover the ownership and management of sub-surface resources, wildlife harvesting rights, wildlife management, water quality and environmental protection, navigation and shoreline erosion, as well as other issues.

The negotiations on these resource and environmental issues made excellent progress, leading to sub-agreements initialled by all parties. The basis was laid, among other things, for a rational and more productive management system for the Lake St. Clair fishery, which depends heavily on the nursery areas represented by the Walpole Island marshlands. The negotiations, however, ground to a halt as the senior levels of government finally realized that these sub-agreements were not matters of specialized and technical concern but had important implications for Aboriginal sovereignty, jurisdiction, and reserve boundaries.

b. RESOURCE-USE CONFLICTS AND RESOLUTION

1. Adverse effects of development on the Sagkeeng First Nation

Most of the examples discussed in this section are taken from the experience of the Sagkeeng First Nation in Manitoba, while those in the following section, focusing on environmental issues, are from Walpole Island First Nation. It is, however, necessary to emphasize that this separation is for ease of understanding only. As will be seen in both sections, resource and environmental issues constantly interact at both locations.

The Fort Alexander Reserve of the Sagkeeng First Nation is on both sides of the mouth of the Winnipeg River where it enters Lake Winnipeg. The reserve is about 100 kilometres northeast of the city of Winnipeg, which is home to half of Manitoba's population; the reserve contains close to 3 000 residents. One-third live on the north shore of the river, and northward again is the boreal forest of the Canadian Shield. To the south of those on the south shore, the land is mainly agricultural prairie, though the reserve itself is largely unproductive bog and forest away from the settled areas. Except in winter, when there is a road across the river ice, the only link between the north and south shores is a road crossing a hydro dam, several kilometres upstream from the reserve boundary. On both shores, the reserve settlement is concentrated along the riverbanks.

Major elements, and associated environmental problems, of the resource development in the Winnipeg River Basin since Treaty 1 was signed in 1871 are outlined in the *Winnipeg River Task Force Report*, a 1995 report prepared by a task force established by the federal government and the Sagkeeng First Nation:

(a) Between 1906 and 1955, seven dams and hydro-electric generating facilities were constructed across the river to serve the electricity needs of Manitoba; six of these are currently operating.

(b) A newsprint mill was constructed in 1927 on the south shore, adjacent to the upstream boundary of the reserve. The mill and the town of Pine Falls that is dependent on the mill continue to generate the principal economic activity in the area and are the main focus of non-Aboriginal settlement and development.

(c) The Whiteshell Laboratories of Atomic Energy of Canada and the community of Pinawa were established in the mid-1960s, approximately 60 kilometres upstream from Sagkeeng.

(d) Since 1979, Manitoba Hydro has regulated the level of Lake Winnipeg with the objective of maintaining high water levels in the fall so that winter electricity peaks can be served by major new generating facilities on the Nelson River.

The task force report set out in detail the adverse affects to the Sagkeeng First Nation of each of these developments, although they found that activities at Whiteshell Laboratories were unlikely to have posed a significant threat.

Probably the most serious problem caused by these developments is erosion of the riverbanks — the most valuable areas of the reserve. There is disagreement about the relative importance of the various erosion processes involved and about whether the erosion is solely a result of the damming of the Winnipeg River, or whether lake regulation has also played a significant role. What seems to be undisputed is that the reserve has lost approximately 3.3 square kilometres of its best land since the reserve was surveyed in 1874; in some places the riverbank has retreated more than 750 metres.

However, the incident that brought Sagkeeng's resource use and environmental concerns to a head and led to the creation of the federal-First Nation task force was not riverbank erosion but a public health crisis involving the newsprint mill and its effluent. Though not all of the reserve's housing and other buildings are connected to a piped supply, the First Nation has constructed and operates state-of-the-art water treatment facilities, using river water, on both shores. Meanwhile, from its opening until the end of 1995, the newsprint mill discharged its effluent untreated into the river approximately eight kilometres above Sagkeeng's water intakes. It was believed by the mill and regulatory authorities, if not by many Sagkeeng residents, that no public health problems arose from the situation, and tests of raw and treated water at the intakes appeared to confirm this.

That confidence, however, has been diminished by several recent events. In March 1994, the mill spilled almost a tonne of pesticide (Busan 52) through its outfall into the Winnipeg River, but did not report the spill to anyone except the pesticide suppliers for more than 48 hours. The travel time between the mill's effluent outlet and the reserve's intakes is approximately two hours.

As well, fisheries research since 1993 has shown that the mill effluent is not immediately diluted to undetectable concentrations in the massive flow of the Winnipeg River, as had been thought, but persists as an identifiable plume for several kilometres downstream. Although neither the chemical spill nor the presence of the plume appears to have affected the quality of Sagkeeng's drinking water, tests of water in the mill and at recreational beaches on the reserve's shoreline downstream from the mill have indicated the presence of elevated levels of *E. coli* bacteria, the source or sources of which have not yet been identified.

It is scarcely surprising that many Sagkeeng residents are convinced that their drinking water is contaminated. The task force acknowledged that the same concerns would surely be felt by any other community in the same circumstances and it recognized that measures such as routine testing or special studies — no matter how many were conducted — were not likely to provide reassurance.

The effect of these major resource developments on Sagkeeng goes well beyond the principal issues of riverbank erosion and threats to public health. Damming the river has changed its physical character, flooded many sites used by Sagkeeng residents, and changed irreversibly the aquatic ecosystem and fishery resources. Use of the river to transport logs to the mill ended only in 1993, and no expert is prepared to forecast the date when the riverbed organisms vital to fish will return to their pre-mill character. The mill controls and manages substantial areas of forest in the region, and Sagkeeng residents report numerous barriers to the exercise of their treaty rights to hunt and fish in the forest area.

A significant roadblock to resolve such problems has been the attitude of the Manitoba government, which has taken the view that First Nations are essentially within federal jurisdiction and so has been unwilling to join in round-table discussions. It did not participate in the work of the task force, despite strong invitations to do so, and its proposal to establish a co-management agreement with Sagkeeng First Nation on fisheries resources foundered when Sagkeeng discovered that the "agreement" had to be on terms dictated by the provincial government.

From a First Nations perspective, the provincial government's aloofness appears to be based on criteria other than a desire to respect the federal government's jurisdiction over Aboriginal peoples. Sagkeeng is well aware that the provincial government has a strong financial and political interest in the continued prosperity of the Pine Falls mill and community and is also well aware that the organization with which it must negotiate for compensation for riverbank erosion is a provincially owned Crown corporation.

2. Sagkeeng's response

How has Sagkeeng tackled these problems and others related to them? The following is only a partial answer, not least because the process is an ongoing one, and Sagkeeng's attitude and strategy depend to a considerable extent on the willingness of the other parties involved to reach swift, effective, and equitable solutions.

(a) Negotiations with Manitoba Hydro

The First Nation is engaged in negotiations with Manitoba Hydro aimed at finding, and quickly implementing, engineering measures that will prevent or substantially reduce further riverbank erosion. Over the past several years, Sagkeeng has also been negotiating compensation for past erosion. It is almost inevitable that these negotiations influence and delay a satisfactory solution to remedial measures, since the nature of the measures necessary may have implications for Manitoba Hydro's overall liability. That is, Manitoba Hydro probably would not wish to accept the view that Lake Winnipeg regulation has accelerated the rate of riverbank erosion, since acceptance or proof of this could open the way for compensation demands from many other communities on the lakeshore that might have similar claims. The task force urged, however, that it was in both parties' interests not to wait until a comprehensive settlement was reached to implement measures.

(b) Claim for compensation for mill land

There is a *prima facie* case that the land on which the newsprint mill stands was formerly part of the Fort Alexander Reserve and was sold to the mill's original owners without the proper consent of the First Nation. Sagkeeng is preparing a claim for compensation. If successful, the compensation would be paid by the federal government and the title to land possessed by the mill would not be affected.

(c) Claim for compensation for pesticide spill

The Busan-52 spill at the mill provoked a strong public reaction on the reserve, covered extensively by the media, to which the mill's owners (at that time, Abitibi-Price) were forced to respond. Abitibi-Price paid $156 000 in compensation to the First Nation. A criminal prosecution resulted in a fine of $15 000 and Abitibi-Price was also required to pay an additional $35 000, administered by Environment Canada, to fund projects to promote the conservation of fish or fish habitat in the Winnipeg River system. Subsequently, Abitibi-Price pleaded guilty and paid a fine of $12 990 in a private prosecution in which Sagkeeng alleged that the company had operated the mill without a provincial water licence from 1987 until the transfer of ownership.

(d) Changes to discharge regulations affecting Sagkeeng

The longstanding practice of discharging untreated mill effluent into the river ended late in 1995, when the mill brought into operation a secondary treatment plant complying with the 1992 amendments to the federal Pulp and Paper Mill Effluent Regulations. However, this was not a specific response to the Winnipeg River situation but a coincidental requirement imposed on all such mills throughout Canada, and the federal regulations are aimed at protecting fish, not drinking water quality. As well, there is little indication as yet that Sagkeeng residents recognize the significant change that the secondary treatment plant will cause in effluent quality. To them, the mill continues to discharge its effluent through a visible pipe on the edge of the reserve.

(e) Withdrawal of participation in Manitoba Model Forest

Sagkeeng is invited to participate in the Manitoba Model Forest, a federal initiative close to the reserve, intended to produce a forest management system much more in tune with Aboriginal attitudes toward the resource. However, Sagkeeng and other First Nations in the area withdrew their participation at an early stage, partly because they objected to aspects of the organization and management of the program, but also because they believed their participation might endanger their treaty rights in the area of the Model Forest.

(f) Direction to task force

More positively, Sagkeeng has insisted that the work of the task force be structured as far as possible on a basis of mutual respect and cooperation. This was made evident at a series of public forums and also in the task force's report, where a deliberate attempt was made to express the attitudes and concerns of the various parties. The non-confrontational tone of the task force's report has provided the basis for a series of meetings involving (at present) Sagkeeng First Nation, Pine Falls Paper Company, Manitoba Hydro, and Whiteshell Laboratories, aimed at the long-term future of the Winnipeg River Basin. Walpole Island is seeking similar mutual respect and cooperation to achieve long-term objectives in its negotiations with Canada and Ontario.

c. ENVIRONMENTAL CONFLICTS AND RESOLUTION

1. River pollution near Walpole Island

Though the actual reserve boundaries are yet to be determined, Walpole Island has a smaller on-reserve population than Sagkeeng (rather more than 2 000 people), drawn from three nations: Ojibwa, Ottawa, and Potawatomi, who since 1940 have united under a single chief and council, the Council of Three Fires. In 1965, Walpole Island was the first Indian band in Canada to cast off the agency system. Since that time, the First Nation has taken a strongly proactive role in land claims, sovereignty, environmental protection, and other issues. For more than a decade this proactive role has been supported, and has perhaps even been made possible, by the work of a research and documentation facility, the Walpole Island Heritage Centre.

Most, though not all, of the environmental issues encountered by Walpole Island are rooted in the presence upstream of Sarnia's "Chemical Valley," the main chemical manufacturing complex in Canada. Its location from Sarnia southward owes something to the presence of local oil and salt deposits, but more to a transcontinental oil pipeline's reaching the area from Alberta about mid-century. Pollution of the adjacent river was, as elsewhere at the time, not a major consideration. Toxic chemicals routinely entered the river through drains and other means, and by 1957, according to a report by the Lambton Industrial Society in Sarnia, there was virtually no life on the northern 17 kilometres of the river bottom. Many species, tolerant now to the pollution, filled the remaining 27 kilometres.

That situation has changed substantially in recent decades. In particular, pollution normally occurs in the form of accidental spills, though daily loadings, including urban sewage from Sarnia, remain a problem. The Remedial Action Plan for the St. Clair River anticipates that the chemical plants, Dow in particular, will be completely separated from the river by the end of the century.

If that is the hope, the reality is that spills are declining in number, but are much too frequent. Geometrics International, in its *Final Report of the Emergency Spills Task Force*, has reported that from 1986 through 1991 the total number of spills decreased by half. There were more than 100 spills in all but one of the four years prior to 1990.

2. Walpole Island's response

Because the problem of chemical spills is of long standing, Walpole Island's response has been more diverse than was possible for Sagkeeng's reaction to the Busan-52 spill. Like Sagkeeng, Walpole Island has not hesitated to organize public protest, and media coverage has again helped influence the subsequent actions of the large multinational corporations involved. Most of the latter were already working to eliminate chronic leakages of toxic materials to the river and to reduce the incidence of spills, but the pressure exerted by Walpole Island has probably accelerated their action and helped to move their strategies toward creating firm barriers between the plants and the river.

An effective notification procedure in the event of spills gives Walpole Island and adjacent municipalities perhaps up to 20 hours to decide whether to close their water intakes in the river. Walpole Island has recently provided substantial storage capacity by building a water tower on the reserve. The First Nation has also encouraged dialogue with individual chemical companies and has brought these companies' representatives to Walpole Island to give them a better understanding of the importance of unpolluted water to the First Nation's health, economy, and environment. Walpole Island has participated actively in the development and implementation of the Remedial Action Plan for the St. Clair River, under the auspices of the Canada-USA 1978 Great Lakes Water Quality Agreement.

In one important respect, Walpole Island's strategy has differed from that of Sagkeeng. Whereas many in the Sagkeeng community and leadership would like to see its water intakes moved upstream of the mill effluent discharge, Walpole Island has firmly rejected opportunities to create a regional water supply system using water from Lake Huron. Its reasoning is that to use an alternate source for drinking water might reduce the pressure on the chemical companies to improve the St. Clair River. Perhaps more important, it would do nothing for the aquatic ecosystem on which a large part of the First Nation's economy and culture is based.

In 1989, Walpole Island found itself in the bizarre situation of seeking an injunction in the Federal Court of Canada to prevent three branches of the federal government — Environment Canada, Public Works, and the Coast Guard — from actions that, in the First Nation's view, were liable to pollute Lake St. Clair, the only connecting channel in the Great Lakes system that is not an Area of Concern under the Water Quality Agreement.

This situation arose because of the need for periodic dredging of the seaway channel through the delta on which Walpole Island is located. Walpole Island had previously permitted the creation of a cut through its territory, eliminating some tortuous bends in the ship channel; it had also made an area available for confined disposal of the dredged material because of its possible contamination. (Material dredged from the area by U.S. agencies is similarly routinely placed in a Confined Disposal Facility on nearby Dickinson Island, Michigan.)

In 1989, however, the Canadian government agencies notified Walpole Island that they had done a number of tests of the sediment to be dredged, had concluded that there was no significant contamination, and therefore intended to adopt the simpler and cheaper method of open water disposal in Lake St. Clair. In seeking the injunction, Walpole Island pointed out that the tests undertaken had been for a limited number of pollutants only. Yet only two or three years previously, the four senior governments (Canada, United States, Ontario, and Michigan) had completed a lengthy pollution study of the St. Clair River, listing many toxic chemicals likely to be found in such sediments. These included hexachlorobenzene (HCB) and octachlorostyrene (OCS), neither of which had been included in the 1989 sampling.

Walpole Island lost the battle, but it won the war. The injunction was not granted, and the open water disposal took place. Subsequently, however, further testing of the sediments revealed the presence of a suite of pollutants including HCB and OCS, and the federal agencies pledged that dredging and disposal in future would be determined through consultation with Walpole Island in a joint dredging committee.

Because of its proactive overall strategy, linked to the unresolved question of Walpole Island's boundaries and environmental resource management authority, the First Nation continues to intervene in any development proposal that appears likely to ignore or infringe its claims to territory and jurisdiction, or that threatens the environment of the area used by the First Nation in the past. In principle, it is willing to reach agreement with developers, provided that the fact of its claims is recognized and that it can be satisfied about environmental protection.

Such an agreement was negotiated on a directional drill beneath the St. Clair River. Other proposals have been withdrawn after (though not necessarily because of) objections by Walpole Island, or they have been defeated at hearing. Examples include a proposal to site a hazardous waste incinerator near Chemical Valley, Ontario Hydro's plan to upgrade electricity transmission lines between London and Windsor, and a directionally drilled pipeline crossing the St. Clair River.

In one very recent situation, however, Walpole Island First Nation has made it clear that environmental protection, and the health of its inhabitants are a paramount concern, for which neither reassurance nor substantial compensation can be substituted. A major chemical company, ICI Canada, is no longer a producer in Chemical Valley but retains responsibility for the safe disposal of liquid contaminants stored in a series of open lagoons at its former site. For several years, the company sought a technically and financially feasible method of emptying these lagoons. It involved external interests, including representatives from Walpole Island, in the work and claims to have spent about $11 million in the search.

In 1995, however, ICI Canada abandoned both the search for a solution and the consultative process that supported it. Claiming that tests now indicated that the toxicity of the liquids had diminished significantly over time, and also that rainwater was threatening the overflow of the lagoons, the company applied to the Ontario government for a licence to discharge the lagoons into the St. Clair River, with careful monitoring of both effluent and effects.

After the downstream Ontario municipality of Wallaceburg was satisfied that there was no threat to its drinking water supplies, Walpole Island remained the only major objector, supported by the municipality of Algonac, Michigan. A series of negotiations led to a draft agreement between the company and the First Nation, providing for additional monitoring of water and ecosystem quality in the area of Walpole Island and immediate cessation of the discharge if this monitoring showed unexpected results. ICI Canada was prepared to fund Walpole Island's monitoring program and associated activities, at a cost of approximately $750 000.

Despite the substantial economic benefit to the First Nation, and the improvement in its environmental knowledge base, the draft agreement was eventually rejected by Walpole Island's chief and council, without community objection. The

First Nation believed that ICI Canada should not solve its problem by creating another. Walpole Island adopted the position of the International Joint Commission that zero discharge of persistent toxic chemicals — a principal objective of the Great Lakes Water Quality Agreement — means just that: zero discharge. At the time of writing, the application for a controlled discharge awaits a hearing before provincial authorities, where it will be opposed by the Walpole Island First Nation.

d. PROSPECTIVE CHANGES IN FEDERAL LEGISLATION

1. Proposed changes to the Canadian Environmental Protection Act

In June 1955, the House of Commons Standing Committee on Environment and Sustainable Development issued a lengthy report on the Canadian Environmental Protection Act (CEPA) called *It's About Our Health! Towards Pollution Prevention, CEPA Revisited*. CEPA was enacted in 1988 and was an attempt to replace the 1975 Environmental Contaminants Act with more effective federal legislation. The House of Commons Committee, however, found that the CEPA did not effectively address Canada's urgent environmental problems, a view widely shared beyond the committee. For example, part IV of the act, dealing with federal departments, agencies, crown corporations, works, undertakings, and lands, was intended to fill the regulatory gap that had existed because federal works, lands, and undertakings were not, for the most part, subject to provincial environmental laws. The committee found, however, that there had been very little activity under part IV. In seven years, only one set of regulations had been passed and only one set of guidelines issued. Neither of these was relevant to Aboriginal groups, although one objective of part IV was to address the regulatory gap on Indian lands. The committee endorsed the view that part IV had failed because of a "combination of low resources, inadequate legal drafting, minimum political will and almost no regulations."

This is directly relevant to Aboriginal peoples, since neither the Indian Act nor CEPA has proved a useful mechanism for environmental improvement for Aboriginal people, as reserves are normally considered federal lands. The committee acknowledged that Aboriginal peoples do not have even the basic levels of environmental protection enjoyed and taken for granted by other Canadians, and it devoted a separate chapter, and several specific recommendations, to the subject of Aboriginal peoples and environment protection. The committee clearly recognized the link between sovereignty and self-government on the one hand, and environmental resources on the other, recommending that self-government and land claim settlement agreements negotiated between the federal government and Aboriginal peoples include terms to establish environmental protection systems and adequate authority and resources to implement them.

The committee similarly urged that a revised CEPA recognize the value of the environmental knowledge possessed by Aboriginal people.

Unlike many other reports from standing committees and similar organizations, the parliamentary committee's review of CEPA did not get only a token response from the federal government. Although the process still has a long way to go, and may ultimately fail or be squeezed out by other priorities, the committee's report now appears to have been a first major stage in a process leading to a new and effective CEPA. The government's response was published in December 1995, and its title, though as convoluted as that of the report itself, states clearly the government's intent: *Environmental Protection Legislation Designed for the Future — A Renewed CEPA, A Proposal.*

The government's positive attitude was reflected in the text of the proposal, which adopted many of the committee's recommendations and endeavoured to show how these could be transformed into effective legislation. The federal government agreed that a renewed CEPA should provide for effective environmental protection on Aboriginal lands. It recognized the need for adequate consultation with Aboriginal peoples and also accepted that flexible arrangements would be necessary. Earlier legislation had tended to assume that there would be a single Procrustean bed of environmental regulation, managed from Ottawa, into which all Indian reserves would be fitted. As noted already, no bed of any kind emerged from Part IV.

A renewed CEPA, however would recognize a wide spectrum of situations extending from self-government regimes that included environmental laws and enforcement powers to Aboriginal groups that rejected self-government and were content to leave environmental management to the federal government.

The federal government's proposals left no doubt that Aboriginal groups would have the power to establish measures to protect their environment, including enforcement, if they wish to do so. Where that stage has not been reached, a renewed CEPA is intended to provide for Aboriginal peoples what has been lacking in CEPA's present version — namely, the same level of environmental protection enjoyed by other Canadians.

2. Advantages to First Nations

From a First Nation standpoint, the government's proposals (provided always that they are swiftly transformed into effective legislation) appear to have the following, essentially new, advantages.

(a) The underlying philosophy recognizes the central role of environmental resources in Aboriginal life and also the major role that these play in sovereignty and self-government.

(b) The amount of environmental authority a First Nation may exercise is a matter for negotiation, with the implied assumption that a First Nation (or other Aboriginal group) will be able to exercise as much legitimate jurisdiction as it can handle.

(c) Aboriginal peoples' environmental knowledge is recognized and is implicit in the proposed right to consultation.

(d) The difficult questions of monitoring and enforcement are recognized and addressed.

From the standpoint of the individual, company, or other organization interacting with First Nations or other Aboriginal groups, the future is likely to see a more clearly defined tripartite set of rules and procedures. It seems likely that the environmental regime will differ, at least in detail, from one reserve to the next. If this sounds impossibly complex in principle, it is not likely to be so in practice. Each municipality, after all, has its own set of bylaws and other ordinances, tailored to its specific situation. If the underlying philosophy is understood, dealing with Aboriginal groups on environmental protection should be no more onerous than similar dealings with municipalities.

e. THREE RULES FOR NON-ABORIGINAL GROUPS

(a) *Remember that environmental resources are not just sets of issues for First Nations in the way they tend to be considered by non-Aboriginal society.* These resources are at the core of the culture that Aboriginal peoples are determined to maintain and protect. What is crucial is how the non-Aboriginal company or organization approaches such issues. They must be treated as matters of central significance to whatever is proposed or negotiated, not as matters to be hived off to the company's environmental expert or department to handle.

(b) *From the standpoint of First Nations and other Aboriginal groups, resource and environment issues are often indissolubly linked to unresolved problems of sovereignty and self-government.* The Aboriginal group does not expect companies or individuals to resolve such issues, or to wait until they have been resolved. But the group has a position to protect, just as a company may have on matters such as trademark protection, taxation, or other issues that may seem extraneous to the other party in a negotiation. It is important that the Aboriginal group's position be recognized, so that ways can be found for agreements to be reached that protect their legal or negotiating position.

(c) *Recognize that the consensus principle may require a very different approach to negotiation and agreement than is typical in the non-Aboriginal world.* Broadly speaking, it is better to focus initially on small projects that may over time develop into expanding and long-term relationships. If the whole community is to provide at least tacit approval for an agreement between the Aboriginal group and an outside individual or organization, the approval is more likely if the benefits to the Aboriginal group are obvious, the initial commitment is small, and that commitment has a limited life. More time than usual may be required to achieve such an initial commitment, but experience with a small project may be the key to building confidence in the community on which a continuing relationship can be based.

11

RESOURCE DEVELOPMENT ON TRADITIONAL ABORIGINAL LANDS

by Hans Matthews and Donald Wakefield

The recent discoveries of diamonds at Lac de Gras in the Northwest Territories and of a huge body of nickel and copper at Voisey's Bay in Labrador underline the need for a greater understanding between Aboriginal communities and developers. At the time of the discovery at Voisey's Bay, the Labrador Inuit Association, the Innu Nation, and the federal and Newfoundland governments had made little progress in the settlement of Aboriginal land claims. Within months of the discovery, hundreds of mining crews arrived on the site, even though the land was subject to an outstanding land claim. The result was a standoff lasting 16 days in which approximately 100 angry Innu faced RCMP constables sent to protect the interests of the developer.

The business pressure for development of natural resources and tourism in traditional Aboriginal territories has had a profound impact on Aboriginal communities. Indians, Inuit, and Métis peoples form the majority of the residents in vast areas that are increasingly attracting mining, logging, and tourism developers from the south. These lands include areas that are now held by the provinces or federal government as Crown lands, but were used by Aboriginal people at the time of European contact. Activities by developers intrude on the traditional uses that Aboriginal peoples have made (and continue to make) of these lands, such as trapping,

fishing, harvesting, and hunting. Indiscriminate development can also interfere with spiritual, cultural, and special
values by intruding on important spiritual, community, or
burial sites. The influx of non-Aboriginal developers, bent on
realizing a profit from the land, continues to strain the cultural values of the Aboriginal communities, sometimes pit-
ting younger members against their elders' beliefs, as a
resource-based wage economy competes with the traditional
ways of the communities. At the same time, resource activities, if not conducted responsibly, may also cause significant
environmental damage.

For generations, resource development has been carried
out in Canada with little or no regard to the concerns of the
Aboriginal occupants of the land. In fact, the energies of
successive governments that obtained surrender of Aboriginal territories by treaty were aimed at getting lands out of
Aboriginal hands so that a great portion of Canada's land
mass could be "opened up" for resource development and
European settlement.

The need to address Aboriginal concerns justly in the
economic development of Canada has changed this. Aboriginal rights, which include rights to hunt, fish, trap, and harvest
on traditional lands, are now recognized constitutional rights
that developers must respect. It is also becoming clear to
resource development companies that building a harmoni-
ous relationship between Aboriginal and non-Aboriginal
communities is a desirable goal, well worth the initial additional costs for the long-term success of their ventures. Most
Aboriginal communities are anxious to share not only in the
use of traditional lands but also in the economic benefits
associated with the development of these lands. In addition,
Aboriginal people and non-Aboriginal environmentalists are
rightly concerned about the effects of new developments on
animal habitats, renewal of forests, and the quality of water,
fish, and air.

This chapter concentrates on the effect of mining activities on Aboriginal communities. Some different considerations apply to the involvement of Aboriginal peoples with forestry or hydro development. However, many of the challenges are the same and mining activities will be used here to illustrate these challenges.

Mineral explorers and developers need to find approaches that promise benefits to Aboriginal peoples and provide answers to their concerns. To date, Aboriginal people have not had significant involvement in the management of the mining industry. However, a number of impact and benefit agreements have been signed between Aboriginal groups and mining companies to minimize the effects and maximize the benefits of mining to local communities. This chapter is intended to assist the resource developer to understand the challenges and some solutions for those looking to do business in traditional Aboriginal territories.

A final note: For the purposes of this chapter, the phrase "traditional lands" is used to refer to lands outside an Indian reserve.

a. UNDERSTANDING THE INTERACTION

1. Aboriginal communities' concerns

Generally, Aboriginal communities in Canada are concerned that they receive advance notice of and have significant input into proposed changes to the lands on which they depend for their traditional way of life. They wish to participate in mineral and other developments on their traditional lands; they seek to obtain quality benefits from development projects and seek assurance that the developer's activities will be carried out in a way that shows respect for Aboriginal cultural values and causes minimum damage to the natural environment. Aboriginal people wish to preserve the land for future generations.

In contrast to some environmental organizations that are concerned only with long-term effects and are mainly anti-development, Aboriginal communities understand that even initial exploration operations cannot be carried out without some damage to the land. In effect, most development operations involve a cost benefit analysis: how significant is the impact on the environment in relation to long-term benefits? Generally, Aboriginal communities want to participate in the process of balancing environmental issues with the perceived economic benefits to their communities.

2. Developers' objectives

The purpose of initial mineral exploration is to explain a geological or a geophysical fact quickly and inexpensively. But before exploration — for example, diamond drilling — begins, mineral developers want to know what they will be faced with. For example, an investment is at risk if the mining companies are uncertain as to who holds title and what the regulatory regime will look like after a land claim settlement. This has encouraged several mining companies and other developers to seek Aboriginal support for their activities at an early stage. Sometimes the developer and the local Aboriginal community have signed a memorandum of understanding (see section f. below) setting out the main objectives of each party. If development later seems feasible, an impact and benefit agreement will be negotiated. The contents of such an agreement, as set out, for example, in the Nunavut land claims agreement, are discussed later in this chapter.

3. The role of governments

Governments have always played a significant role in resource development. Whether minerals are under the administration and control of a province (such as at Voisey's Bay) or of the federal government (as in the Northwest Territories and Yukon), the mining recorder, the government's land-use officer for mineral exploration, can serve as a go-between for mining companies and Aboriginal groups. To date, such a role has not been mandated for the recorder. However, mineral developers must obtain work permits even for initial activities on Crown land, and notice provisions must be followed. The result is that, depending on the area, certain permits will simply not be granted without formal notice to designated Aboriginal organizations. The government official may not issue a permit for a proposed activity that is likely to have a significant effect on a neighboring Aboriginal community without prior notice to the affected community. While this is a judgment call, the tendency of government officials has often been to err on the side of giving more notices to Aboriginal communities rather than fewer. (In some areas, notices of proposed development that may affect First Nations are formally required by an agreement between government and First Nations, as in the Nishnawbe-Aski territory in northern Ontario.) Although there have been some misunderstandings of the effect of these notices, by and large they have given Aboriginal community leaders and the companies involved an opportunity to enter into discussions at an early stage of development and negotiate beneficial arrangements for both groups.

As well as ensuring Aboriginal input before granting permits and facilitating communications between developers and Aboriginal communities, governments can play a role in providing skills training to Aboriginal communities wanting to participate in development. In mineral development these skills will involve training in prospecting, staking, mineral identification, project management, camp support, and environmental baseline studies, to name a few. More Aboriginal communities are requesting training in management-related areas to provide skills for their own community projects and administration. While there are examples of successful Aboriginal businesses in the forestry field (for example, sawmill operations), the number of Aboriginal people in management positions in the mining field is still dismally low.

4. Communication issues

Most Aboriginal communities are understandably sceptical about the potential benefits of mining operations in their traditional territory. There have been some noticeable megaprojects in the recent history of Canada, such as the James Bay hydro-electric development, where the affected Aboriginal communities were not consulted before development was approved by the government. As well, Aboriginal people have not had much of an opportunity to gain a detailed understanding of the minerals industry or of the corporate requirements and structures of a mining company, and senior management of mining companies often lacks cultural understanding of Aboriginal communities' decision-making processes. In a traditional Aboriginal community, the chief does not make decisions alone but generally accepts and carries into effect decisions made by the community. It goes without saying that an Aboriginal community cannot make informed decisions about mineral development unless information about the project is communicated to all levels of the community.

Corporate executives often do not show an appreciation for Aboriginal economic development needs or understand that reaching a consensus among the community is a time-consuming process. Developers need to communicate with Aboriginal communities in ways that respect the education level and language skills of community members. Some of the elders, though fluent in an Aboriginal language, are unable to read and write in English. Thus, visits to the site of the proposed activity and oral presentations may be required to communicate with some members of the Aboriginal community. At the same time, corporate executives may benefit greatly from the input they receive from the Aboriginal community about the proposed development. The Aboriginal community members, particularly the elders, live as part of the earth, know the earth as it was, as well as the way it may change tomorrow.

5. Possible solutions

Aboriginal communities may wish to prepare an inventory of community skills, trades, and businesses to be in a position to respond quickly to opportunities from outside developers. As well as long-range plans for economic development and land use, they may also wish to develop plans for training, skills up-grading, and methods of transporting their members to and from work sites. While community members may initially express interest in catering, expediting, camp set-up, and demobilization, community participation will increase with training and community members will understandably expect higher paying work such as positions in mine-mill management. Employment and training issues may be dealt with in a written agreement between the community and the resource company. Careful planning will see community members placed in a trained work force and, hopefully, see those skills transferred to future projects in the community.

In order that development not have serious effects on hunting, trapping, fishing, and harvesting, the Aboriginal community may choose to prepare a calendar of its seasonal events so that, to the extent possible, developers can create work timetables that do not interfere with important activities in the Aboriginal calendar. For the developer and the Aboriginal group to decide what issues are vital to each of them, it is often helpful for each to prepare an internal list of their negotiable and non-negotiable issues.

b. BUSINESS CHALLENGES

1. Community income and land-use issues

Aboriginal communities naturally expect that mechanisms will be developed to ensure that significant income and other benefits from mining, forestry, and tourism go to the community. They would also like to be involved in land-use planning and in protecting burial sites and areas where hunting, trapping, and harvesting are centred.

The availability of appropriate housing for local residents is an important issue in the development of a project. Aboriginal residents may be interested in upgrading their housing as part of the benefits from the development and may be resentful if all the improved housing goes to non-Aboriginal developers. They may expect opportunities for the community work force in terms of jobs in the construction trades at the mine site or sawmill.

2. Practical methods of increasing income to Aboriginal communities

In recent years, more and more Aboriginal communities are seeking to share in the taxes or royalties paid by resource development companies to the government. Their view is that this is a simple way to direct some of the economic benefits back to the Aboriginal community from whose traditional lands the resources are now being harvested. After all, Aboriginal communities are the groups most likely to feel the negative effects of resource development near their homes. It is worth noting that some major resource development companies have recently agreed to negotiate this issue with local First Nations. In such cases, of course, resource companies will wish to seek agreements from the relevant governments (provincial or federal) so that they do not pay royalties twice.

Sometimes developers cannot carry out their activities without interference with traditional land uses. In these situations, the developer should make efforts to minimize damage and reach a consensus on appropriate compensation. Here it is important that a mineral developer make contact with, for example, the local trappers' association, rather than simply paying persons whose traplines may be affected.

Local Aboriginal communities want to be able to provide the work force to construct and maintain any roads that are to be established for forestry or mineral development work.

They may be interested in, for example, security services, land clearing, road building, and the supply and operation of construction equipment. If an atmosphere of understanding and trust can be created between the developer and the local community, there are few developers that would not seek to use local labor rather than pay transportation and ferrying costs for outside contractors and their equipment.

3. The role of governments

Governments can be helpful by providing financial support and encouragement to Aboriginal communities interested in working in the resource industry. For example, governments might provide funding for Aboriginal communities to develop local land-use plans that allow for mining and forestry. Governments can also develop methods for Aboriginal peoples to have input into the selection and management of protected areas and parkland and develop a data base of traditional land-use information. The Aboriginal community might share in royalties, whether or not a land claims settlement agreement is being negotiated. Governments should encourage Aboriginal communities to provide developers with contact persons who can communicate proposed developments to the local Aboriginal community members.

4. The role of developers

Resource developers can and should determine the availability of local Aboriginal suppliers of products and give them preference if those suppliers have available workers with appropriate skills. Mining and forestry companies can show their commitment to the local community by providing scholarships and summer employment as well as technical training to community members. Such skills may range from staking, line cutting, technical equipment operation, administration, expediting, camp set-up, demobilization, and reforestry practices to project management. Among the broader issues confronting many Aboriginal communities is the absence of a long-term community development plan. Since having such a plan is a crucial aspect of community development, the developer might offer expertise to the Aboriginal community and, perhaps, form strategies with the community on how the development activities can be integrated to become part of the community's plan.

c. COMMUNITY ENVIRONMENTAL CONCERNS

1. Lack of Aboriginal involvement in planning

At present, unless a public information session is held, Aboriginal communities are usually not asked for their input in the preparation of impact assessment studies or progressive rehabilitation measures for proposed forestry or mineral operations. Where the proposed development lands are the Aboriginal community's "backyard," it would be prudent and fair for the developer to involve the community in baseline studies and long-range planning. Developers can also benefit from Aboriginal expertise, such as ecological knowledge acquired over generations.

2. Roles for governments, developers, and Aboriginal communities

To limit environmental damage, Aboriginal communities and governments may wish to consider working together to develop long-term land-use plans incorporating reporting and other procedures. A system of government reporting to community and community reporting to government is not now in place, other than through the comprehensive land claim agreements. All kinds of information can be reported to either party, such as the location of exploration projects, sacred sites, and spiritual areas. This process would allow the Aboriginal community to play a key role in decision making.

Aboriginal elders and community members should also be invited to attend and have meaningful input in developers' planning sessions. Aboriginal communities can train residents for environmental monitoring roles (i.e., conservation officers and inspectors) to ensure developers comply with conditions in their work permits. The emphasis here is not on land-use plans but on whether the developer has constructed the road or completed the stream crossing according to conditions of the permit.

If resource development causes environmental damage and rehabilitation measures are required, preference might be given to Aboriginal employers with workers skilled in averting soil erosion, reforestation, leaching, pollution containment, and clean-up of spills. Several Aboriginal communities already have experience in these areas.

d. LAND CLAIMS AND SELF-GOVERNMENT

We have seen that there are many reasons for a resource development company to approach local Aboriginal communities early in the planning stages of potential resource development on traditional lands. If a land claim has already been accepted for negotiation by the federal or provincial government, or if a land claim is in the research or pre-negotiation stage, the economic reasons for consultation are obvious. Even if it appears that no particular land claim is on the horizon, there may still be good business reasons for consultation. As we have noted, Aboriginal communities are often the ones most directly affected by the environmental impact of resource developments on their traditional lands. They also have a working knowledge of the local ecosystem and, sometimes, access to capital that makes them natural partners in development on their traditional lands. More and more in recent years, major resource companies have negotiated specific agreements with affected Aboriginal communities and, where appropriate, with the federal and provincial governments, to ensure Aboriginal input into the development. The agreement on the Golden Patricia mine in northwestern Ontario, which appears to have functioned quite well, is only one of several examples of such agreements.

Governments are also signing agreements with Aboriginal groups for resource development in their traditional lands. In 1990, for example, the federal and provincial governments negotiated an interim measures agreement with the Nishnawbe-Aski Nation (NAN) in northern Ontario. This agreement gives the more than 40 First Nations of NAN the right to be notified of pending government approvals of resource developments on their traditional lands. The intention is to promote consultation and cooperation with the First Nations.

Aboriginal communities are already among the largest land holders in Canada. With further land settlements on the way, Aboriginal land holdings will continue to increase and it is estimated that First Nations will own or control one-third of the total land mass of Canada by the year 2000. As there are now over 100 000 Aboriginal people with post-secondary school training and as the total value of all land claims to be decided by 2000 has been estimated at between five and six billion dollars, there is a young, vibrant Aboriginal population concerned with opening up business in traditional land settlement areas.

Finally, in large areas of Canada where historical treaties were not signed, comprehensive land claims settlements have now been reached that affect resource use. Such comprehensive claims settlements now cover portions of the Northwest Territories, Yukon, and northern Québec. These settlements contain detailed provisions about resource development.

e. COMPREHENSIVE LAND CLAIMS SETTLEMENTS

A comprehensive land claims agreement is negotiated between the government and the Aboriginal group once the federal government has accepted Aboriginal title for negotiation. The Aboriginal group will receive defined rights and benefits in exchange for giving up Aboriginal title. In contrast to the treaty procedure, a modern comprehensive land claims agreement involves not only confirmation of ownership of defined lands and the payment of cash over time but also provisions for how the lands and adjoining lands will be managed. A complete system includes the procedures for granting land-use permits; access and entry rights to the lands; and rules for environmental review, wildlife management, economic development, and royalty sharing. Such agreements may also provide for the formation of local governments.

In 1993, for example, the Tungavik Federation of Nunavut (TFN) concluded a comprehensive land claims settlement covering an area of more than 350 000 square kilometres, with aggregate payments of $1.2 billion. The Inuit population of this area (which comprises the eastern portion of the present Northwest Territories) is approximately 18 000 persons. The area will become a new territory in 1999, with its own legislative assembly and government. In 1984, under an earlier comprehensive claims settlement, the largely Inuit population of the Inuvialuit Settlement Region (comprising approximately 91 000 square kilometres) was awarded $170 million on behalf of a population of 2 500. To cite another well known example, under the James Bay and Northern Québec Agreement of 1975 and the Northeastern Québec Agreement of 1978, the Cree and Inuit of Québec and the Naskapi of Schefferville (on behalf of an aggregate population of approximately 17 000) were awarded access rights over approximately 150 000 square kilometres for resource management and traditional pursuits and cash payments totalling $231 million.

Although not, strictly speaking, a comprehensive claims settlement, the 1990 Alberta Métis Settlement Legislation is worth noting here because of its scope. According to this legislation, over 4 856 square kilometres of land, accompanied by a $310 million financial commitment, will be transferred to Alberta Métis control over 17 years. Alberta retains a right of management of roads, certain fixtures and improvements, and subsurface ownership of the land, including royalties from the disposition — through sale, assignment, or transfer — of mineral rights. However, the Métis Settlement Access Committee has the power to deny the disposition of mineral rights on patented lands (lands previously disposed of to a private owner, who is about to further dispose, probably to a mineral developer) or to settle the terms and conditions for any such disposition. In the oil and gas area, the committee has the right to approve the bids awarded by the Minister of Energy and to negotiate with the successful bidder for a royalty override and up to 25% equity participation.

1. Existing rights and access for development

All comprehensive land settlement agreements have recognized existing third-party surface and mineral rights, or will at least until they expire under applicable mining legislation. These rights are identified in each agreement and administration of these rights continues to be the responsibility of the appropriate provincial or federal government agency. Invariably, however, mining companies have access to new mineral rights only after notification of the designated Aboriginal organization. Some agreements require consent from the Aboriginal organization to access the lands and the Aboriginal organization is entitled to attach certain conditions to its consent.

2. Environmental considerations

In many comprehensive claims settlement areas, environmental impact review boards have been established that include Aboriginal representatives. For example, the Nunavut Impact Review Board has the power to screen project proposals to determine whether a review is required, to gauge and define the extent of regional impacts, and to review the environmental and socio-economic impacts of development proposals. In approving proposals, these impact review boards take into account the measures proposed to minimize adverse affects, measures to be put into effect in the event of an accident or spill, and provisions for shutdown and rehabilitation when the mine closes.

Some agreements also provide for the establishment of institutions to manage resources such as land and water. For example, the Nunavut Planning Commission is charged with conducting land-use planning in the settlement area and the Nunavut Water Board will take over the functions of the Northwest Territories Water Board in permitting water uses for that area. Therefore, mining and other resource developers will need to obtain authorizations from a regulator controlled by Aboriginal peoples.

3. Royalty payments to the Aboriginal community

Except for the settlement agreements negotiated for the northern parts of Québec, Aboriginal communities within the settlement area will, according to the comprehensive claims settlement agreements, receive a share of royalty payments made to the Crown governments with jurisdiction over the area. For example, in Nunavut the federal government must pay the Inuit 50% of the first $2 million and 5% thereafter of royalties that the government receives from the production of minerals on Crown land according to the Canada Mining Regulations. However, if mineral production occurs on any of the 36 000 square kilometres of subsurface mineral rights awarded to Nunavut Tungavik, then, under the lease to mining companies proposed by the Nunavut Tungavik Lands Administration, the proposed royalty is 12.5% of net proceeds of production, with a minimum annual royalty of $50 000.

f. IMPACT AND BENEFIT AGREEMENTS

To date, one of the most extensive impact and benefit agreements negotiated in Canada is for the Raglan project developed by Falconbridge Limited in northern Québec. The agreement was initiated under the James Bay Land Claim

Agreement which required the developer to notify the Aboriginal community of its plans. The parties were not obligated to enter into any business negotiations. However, after many meetings and negotiations they did. The Raglan Agreement is approximately 70 pages without annexes. Like similar agreements, it states that its terms are not to derogate or abrogate, or not to be interpreted to do so, from any Aboriginal rights, titles, claims, and interests of the Inuit beneficiaries in and to the offshore areas surrounding Québec.

Under the Raglan Agreement, the Makivik Corporation and four other Inuit corporations contracted for benefits from part of the mineral land holdings of a Falconbridge operating company in northern Québec. The environmental provisions were specifically tied to the impact assessment completed at the time of the agreement, and provision was made for later review of the measures initially proposed. The section on Inuit enterprises is noteworthy. After listing the type of goods and services required during the development phase, the parties agreed that a substantial portion of these would be done off-site and would require specialized contractors and suppliers. Since those goods and services needed to be acquired and constructed on a tight time schedule, the developer reserved the right to invite tenders from contractors and suppliers of its choice but agreed to include qualified Inuit enterprises in the group of invited tenders.

For goods and services required during the operations phase, the agreement requires the developer to negotiate in good faith for an extended period with qualified Inuit enterprises before inviting any third-party tenders. Also, under all invitations to tender, contractors are required to identify the number of Inuit and Inuit enterprises that would be engaged as subcontractors or suppliers.

From the perspective of providing resources to the Inuit residents, perhaps the most important sections of the Raglan Agreement are its monetary provisions. In very general terms, the Raglan Agreement calls for three kinds of payment for the benefit of the Inuit: a guaranteed first allocation of $10 million, a guaranteed second allocation in the aggregate of $4 million, and a profit-sharing allocation of 4.5% of the annual operating cash flow from the project after the recoupment of certain portions of the developer's investment. Most of these payments went to the Raglan Trust, except for a $50 000 per annum payment to the Makivik Corporation for ten years. According to the agreement, all payments were to ensure that Inuit beneficiaries received direct economic benefits from the project and to compensate them for the foreseen impacts of the project.

g. CONCLUSIONS

Aboriginal peoples are no longer content to have resources developed on their traditional lands without substantial participation in the economic benefits. They wish to be involved at all stages of resource development and to be kept informed and have input to and decision-making power over the land-use and environmental planning connected with each project. Aboriginal peoples wish to have their enterprises given the opportunity to contract for the supply of goods and services at all stages of developments and they are seeking the opportunity to participate in the profits derived from the development. Often, they would also like a share in government revenues from resource developments in their traditional territories. In light of the history of resource development in Canada, these objectives of Aboriginal peoples are understandable. It will be best if the developer's commitment to these objectives is seen as an initiative which has been willingly undertaken rather than a process forced on the developer by government regulation or other action.

12

THE CHALLENGE OF FINANCING FIRST NATIONS SMALL BUSINESSES

by Elizabeth Jordan

Aboriginal Canadians have identified economic self-sufficiency as the key to successful self-government. To this end, more and more First Nations have been negotiating for control over natural resources in and near their communities, developing comprehensive training strategies for community members, and developing comprehensive economic development strategies for their communities. Key to developing a robust economy is fostering businesses owned and operated by Aboriginal people.

Canadians have also begun to realize the importance of a healthy Aboriginal economy for Aboriginal self-government. Canadians are generally supportive of initiatives toward Aboriginal self-government, and not simply for altruistic reasons. Part of what seems to motivate this support is the belief that with self-government will come economic self-sufficiency of Aboriginal people and a subsequent end to Canadians' financial obligations to First Nations.

Whatever the reason, the government has long recognized that First Nations' economies are underdeveloped. The federal and provincial governments have sponsored numerous programs aimed at fostering establishment and growth of Aboriginal businesses and increasing employment in Aboriginal communities. Over the years, these programs have met with varying degrees of success. They have had a higher success rate in recent years, as federal and provincial agencies recognized the realities of operating businesses in Aboriginal communities and adapted programs accordingly.

a. DEMOGRAPHIC FACTORS

The remoteness of many reserves limits employment opportunities for Indians living on them. Lack of education, training, and daycare are all major barriers to Aboriginal people's economic advancement; although Aboriginal people are interested in upgrading their education and employment skills, the expense of higher education, the need to relocate to obtain training, and family responsibilities are prohibitive. There are few employment opportunities on reserve apart from working for the band council. This lack of job opportunities within First Nations communities often leads educated young people to move to urban centres, where jobs are more readily available.

However, unemployment of Aboriginal people is still about 25% (compared to 10% for the total population) and climbs to 31% for Aboriginal people living on a reserve or in an Indian settlement. These figures account only for Aboriginal people actively seeking employment and are therefore conservative estimates; unemployment rates can be misleading because they do not indicate the number of Aboriginal people who have stopped looking for work. Labor force participation rates are also much lower for Aboriginal people: fewer Aboriginal people are employed or actively seeking employment than Canadians as a whole. As well, employment income among Aboriginal people is significantly lower than the national average. Aboriginal people are well aware of the detrimental impact of unemployment and the need to address this problem. In many surveys, Aboriginal people themselves have identified unemployment as *the* major problem facing Aboriginal people.

b. PROFILE OF ABORIGINAL-OWNED BUSINESSES

Low incomes, high unemployment rates, and family responsibilities all provide compelling reasons for Aboriginal people to start their own businesses.

Despite the obvious benefits of starting a business, estimates indicate that only 7.8% of Aboriginal people are self-employed, compared to 13.3% of the total Canadian population. However, Aboriginal businesspeople face numerous challenges, many common to all entrepreneurs, such as financing, business planning, marketing, and networking. Other problems Aboriginal businesspeople encounter are unique to them and require innovative solutions.

Estimates of the number of Aboriginal-owned businesses in Canada range from 5 500 to 20 000. The vast majority of Aboriginal-owned businesses are service oriented, providing services such as construction, transportation, gas bars, and groceries. Aboriginal-owned businesses tend to be both smaller and younger than businesses owned by Canadians as a whole. The majority are located in rural communities or small towns. There are some outstanding examples of Aboriginal-owned businesses in large urban areas, although because it is easier for Aboriginal people to find employment in larger cities than on reserve or in remote locations, those who move to urban areas generally look for employment rather than starting their own business.

Aboriginal entrepreneurs are more likely to operate their businesses from their homes than non-Aboriginal entrepreneurs. While this is partially attributable to the convenience of operating a business out of the home, the lack of readily available capital has, at times, necessitated doing so.

c. ADVANTAGES TO STARTING A BUSINESS ON RESERVE

1. Tax exemptions

Although there are many challenges to starting a business on reserve, there are also some unique advantages. First, there are potentially significant tax benefits for on-reserve businesses. Section 87 of the Indian Act exempts property of a status Indian from taxation if that property is on a reserve. Accordingly, income taxable off reserve may be tax exempt if it meets the criteria of being on reserve. This could potentially include income generated from a business, if it is on a reserve, as well as employment income and pensions benefits. (For a detailed discussion of the taxation issue, see chapter 9.)

Unfortunately, there are not clear rules about when income earned from a business is considered to be on a reserve. In 1995, Revenue Canada changed the rules and guidelines it uses to determine whether or not property is on reserve. This change merely aggravates the problem, since the new rules are no less confusing (and no more publicized) than the old ones.

The great majority of Aboriginal-owned businesses are organized as sole proprietorships. The preference for sole proprietorships over other forms of business organization is the result of multiple factors. First, because a business located on reserve tends to be small, often run by only one person, a sole proprietorship makes good sense. The time and expense of incorporating often is not worthwhile. The chief advantage of organizing a business as a corporation is that the liability of the owners and shareholders is limited to the amount they've invested in the business. The threat of being sued with unlimited personal liability, as is the case with a sole proprietorship, frequently doesn't outweigh the costs of incorporating or the loss of the tax exemption.

Second, it is easier to determine whether income from a business organized as a sole proprietorship is exempt from taxes under section 87 of the Indian Act. Because there is only one owner, it is much easier to determine whether the business is located on reserve and whether the owner lives on reserve. As well, the tax exemption does not apply to corporations, regardless of where they are located or where the shareholders live.

A third factor is that willing and able partners, particularly in smaller communities, are difficult to come by.

2. Partnerships and joint ventures

Recent partnerships between First Nations and natural resource development companies have included agreements with provisions for Aboriginal business development, employment of Aboriginal people, and a share of profits. Some companies have also developed policies to encourage the purchase of goods and services from Aboriginal businesses.

The incentive for natural resource development companies is to ensure access to resources on First Nations land or on land to which there is an outstanding claim. First Nations are partners in these sorts of agreements to ensure that their communities are self-reliant and share in the benefits of harvesting natural resources. These partnerships are not without their problems. For example, partnership agreements limited to revenue sharing create communities dependent on resource extraction. Nonetheless, carefully negotiated agreements potentially give Aboriginal people a variety of business and employment opportunities.

The more sophisticated organization of Aboriginal businesses by way of corporations, partnerships, and joint ventures also creates a great deal of confusion about tax implications. This is unfortunate because the costs associated with structuring such businesses to avoid tax liability may deter much-needed partnerships between non-Aboriginal business ventures and Aboriginal Canadians. Such partnerships have occurred in the past with some success. A clear tax policy from Revenue Canada recognizing the need for tax incentives to attract these partnerships to First Nations would certainly help to achieve economic self-sufficiency in Aboriginal communities.

3. Keeping money on reserve

Small businesses also help keep money within the First Nations' communities. The largest source of money on reserve is transfer funds from the federal government, but often, the communities surrounding and servicing reserves are the ultimate beneficiaries of this money. Because few reserves produce their own goods and services, money leaves First Nations communities relatively quickly.

The potential to create employment within a First Nation community also carries a certain appeal for Aboriginal entrepreneurs. Many Aboriginal entrepreneurs cite employment of family and community members as a major factor in their decision to start a business in their communities.

d. CHALLENGES TO ABORIGINAL-OWNED BUSINESSES ON RESERVE

1. Education

Aboriginal people today are attending post-secondary institutions in record numbers. Nonetheless, Aboriginal people still tend to have less formal education than Canadians as a whole, putting them at a disadvantage.

It is interesting to note that Canadian entrepreneurs, particularly women, tend to have more formal education than the average Canadian. This additional education, combined with business experience, gives these entrepreneurs both the business skills and self-confidence they need.

2. Market

The small population on many reserves often means a small market for whatever goods or services a business may offer, unless entrepreneurs are able to sell in other markets. However, the long distance from urban areas of many First Nations communities makes marketing in these areas difficult.

Access to outside markets is often complicated by a lack of knowledge of other (urban) markets and few, if any, business contacts in these markets. Aboriginal people in remote areas frequently lack the business networks that would enable them to more easily develop new and bigger markets for their products.

3. Financing

The greatest challenge for Aboriginal entrepreneurs starting a business is financing — raising the money needed to start the business. Not so surprisingly, this is also a monumental problem for non-Aboriginal entrepreneurs. The difficulty of accessing credit through banks is also a problem all small entrepreneurs share. However, Aboriginal people wishing to start their own business face unusual financing challenges if their collateral is located on reserve. Provisions of the Indian Act prevent the seizure by a non-Indian of reserve land and assets located on reserve, making it difficult for Indians on reserve to do basic things many Canadians take for granted, such as getting a home mortgage. While from a legal perspective it *is* possible for the bank to get security for a loan, the perceived inability to do so — and the very practical difficulties in seizing assets — has made banks reluctant to lend on reserve until fairly recently.

Another potential problem is the lack of credit history or the poor credit history of many Indians on reserve. Although banks have made recent efforts to facilitate access to credit for Indians living on reserve, obtaining loans through banks remains challenging for the average Aboriginal person, as meeting the legal technicalities of ensuring that there is requisite security for a loan is both expensive and time consuming. This is particularly true in remote communities where the economy is primarily a cash or barter economy.

Many Aboriginal-owned businesses are quite young and this too makes obtaining credit difficult. To receive credit from many institutions, businesses must be able to show that they have a solid earnings record, substantial assets, and a high probability of future earnings growth. The youth and small size of many Aboriginal-owned businesses makes this difficult. Very often, the loan amount sought by an entrepreneur is smaller than a bank can afford to process.

e. ALTERNATIVE SOURCES OF FINANCING

While the chartered banks are the most obvious source of financing for a business endeavour, many other sources of financing are available to the small business, such as credit unions and loan circles. As well, there are government initiatives specific to Aboriginal people.

1. Private sources

Personal savings and help from family or friends are two ways to finance a small business and the most common source of capital for entrepreneurs just starting their business. Friends and family have the advantage of being an easily accessed source of capital. However, if the business should fail, the inability to pay back the loan may create a strain in family relations. For Aboriginal people, it may be difficult to obtain any substantial sum of money from family and friends simply because Aboriginal people generally don't have the financial resources to invest in fledgling businesses.

2. Credit unions

Credit unions are grass-roots savings and loan institutions which commonly offer personal and business accounts, consumer loans, project financing, residential mortgages, and RRSPs. Credit unions may offer some viable financing services for Aboriginal entrepreneurs and so are worth investigating as a financing option.

3. Loan circles

Loan circles are community-based sources of financing, ideal for microenterprises — small, home-based businesses. In a loan circle, a group of borrowers pool financial resources and lend money to one another. These loans are modest — under $1 000 — compared to the typical bank loan. As well as providing needed loans, loan circles potentially provide entrepreneurs with the support of their peers and an opportunity to network. Because future loans to other circle members depend on the prompt repayment of existing loans, circle members choose who will receive loans from the fund cautiously. Peer pressure helps ensure that loans are paid on time. Funds for loan circles can be raised through a variety of sources; in recent years, there have been a number of loans offered specifically to Aboriginal entrepreneurs with capital raised from corporations.

4. Credit cards

Credit-card financing is another method frequently used to finance small businesses. Although potentially the most expensive way to finance a business, financing through credit cards is frequently the only option for smaller businesses.

5. Business Development Bank of Canada

The Business Development Bank of Canada (BDC) provides business training programs and loans to small businesses. Once again, geography is an issue: members of First Nations in remote areas have difficulty accessing programs offered by the BDC.

6. Aboriginal Capital Corporations

Aboriginal Capital Corporations (ACCs) are Aboriginal-owned and controlled lending organizations that provide lending services, loan guarantees, and business advisory services to Aboriginal people. ACCs operate on a regional basis, offering services to several First Nations in a geographical area. Loans granted to Aboriginal entrepreneurs through ACCs usually have more flexible terms and conditions than loans offered through banks: ACCs are more focused on the needs of the Aboriginal communities they serve, and the terms of the loans more likely reflect the reality of these communities. Advisory and support services are frequently available to ACC clientele that are not available at more conventional financial institutions. These services might include critiquing an entrepreneur's business plan so that it can be revised and made suitable for presentation to financial institutions and investors, helping entrepreneurs fill out loan applications, and suggesting other potential sources of financing. These additional services offered by ACCs, when delivered effectively, can mean the difference between success and failure for many Aboriginal-owned businesses.

7. First Nation guarantor

In addition to ACCs, some First Nations may be willing to provide loans to band members or guarantee the loans of band members starting small businesses. When a First Nation agrees to act as a guarantor, it agrees to pay off the loan if the borrower fails to do so. The willingness to act as a guarantor will vary from First Nation to First Nation. Some First Nations are reluctant to risk their money in this manner, since all band members will pay if there is a default on the loan and the money used to cover the default might otherwise be allocated to education or health expenses. Additionally, it is an unsettled legal question whether a band council has the legal authority to guarantee loans for its members under the powers granted to band councils in the Indian Act.

8. Government-sponsored programs

Government-sponsored programs have been the biggest supporter of Aboriginal-owned businesses. Relatively frequent changes and closures of these programs require a great deal of patience and diligence on the part of entrepreneurs in finding an existing program that is appropriate for the business in which he or she is engaged. Some Aboriginal entrepreneurs, particularly those in the earliest stages of business start-up, have criticized some of these government programs for being too complicated for their needs and too slow in providing feedback on the status of applications.

Notwithstanding these shortcomings, many successful Aboriginal-owned businesses received advisory services, grants, and loans under programs developed as part of the Canadian Aboriginal Economic Development Strategy (CAEDS). CAEDS, a cooperative effort of the Indian and Northern Affairs, Industry Science and Technology, and Human Resources departments of the federal government, was a comprehensive strategy for economic development in Aboriginal communities. The strategy included both entrepreneurial training and training more oriented toward labor force development, grants, and loans. The grant and loan programs encouraged seeking business advisory services and engaging in joint ventures with a non-Aboriginal partner.

The programs developed by the federal government in future will, ideally, build on the successes of CAEDS. (See the Appendix for a list of organizations and government departments that may be contacted for information on business programs.)

Despite all the hurdles facing Aboriginal entrepreneurs, there is some good news. There are more business opportunities for Aboriginal people, more business education, and more resource development occurring in partnership with Aboriginal people than ever before. Banks have begun to make efforts to make loans more accessible to Aboriginal people. Canadians, Aboriginal and non-Aboriginal, are beginning to realize the importance of encouraging entrepreneurship in Aboriginal communities.

13

ABORIGINAL GAMING —
LAW AND POLICY

by Paul K. Frits

Aboriginal communities have come to see gaming as a tremendous opportunity. Many regard the authority over gaming on Aboriginal lands, as well as the control of revenues from this gaming, as an exercise of inherent self-government rights. Many also strongly believe that gaming could generate the resources required to speed First Peoples to their goals of self-reliance. Aboriginal communities in Canada have seen great success stories emanate from their American counterparts; in the United States, exceedingly lucrative gambling casinos provide some Indian Nations with economic prosperity.

Aboriginal peoples in Canada have extreme difficulty taking advantage of the potential gaming has to offer. This chapter outlines current gaming legislation and some of the relevant issues affecting First Nations' efforts to become involved in this highly lucrative market. In this chapter, gaming and betting activities are referred to collectively as gaming, while casino gaming activities are referred to as lottery schemes.

a. LEGISLATION AFFECTING GAMING

Legalized gaming such as bingo, blackjack, lottery, and the operation of mindless devices like slot machines is a complex matter involving an intricate and often unclear network of federal and provincial legislation.

Generally, gaming is considered criminal and is prohibited by Canada's Criminal Code. A broad range of gaming activities is prohibited, including many forms of lottery schemes, book-making, gaming equipment, common gaming houses, and betting. There are a few exceptions: Aboriginal communities are most concerned with lottery schemes.

Legal lottery schemes are categorized into two classes: those that may be conducted and managed exclusively by provincial governments and those authorized by both the Criminal Code and a provincial government to be conducted and managed by non-governmental parties. An example of a provincially run gaming establishment is the government casino in Windsor, Ontario; an example of a non-governmentally run gaming operation is the charitable gaming operation run at Rat Portage, Ontario.

1. Provincial (commercial) government lottery schemes

Commercial in nature, provincial government lottery schemes are operated on or through a computer, video device, or slot machine and are often the principal source of revenues for large scale, permanent, destination resort casinos such as the one now being built at the Rama First Nation near Orillia, Ontario.

Commercial lottery schemes are subject to a number of constraints. For example, the federal government prohibits anyone but a provincial government (or as a number of provinces insist, its agent) from operating a commercial (non-charitable) lottery scheme. While a provincial government may launch a commercial lottery scheme in conjunction with another provincial government, it may not operate one in partnership with any other group, such as an Aboriginal government or a municipality.

Commercial lottery schemes must also heed relevant provincial legislation. However, licensing, regulating, and operating commercial lottery schemes is not merely subject to the day-to-day policies of a provincial cabinet; a majority of votes in the provincial legislature must approve measures or processes for commercial lottery schemes before they may be implemented. In fact, some provinces even require a majority of provincial voters (or, alternatively, a majority of locally affected citizens) to approve measures in a referendum before they may be implemented. Generally, the law in this area of legalized gaming does not specifically address the involvement of the Aboriginal community. In fact, it appears to exclude this community, except in the isolated instance where First Nations may share in revenues, as at Rama.

There have been some provincial government attempts to include Aboriginal participation, most notably the former Ontario NDP government's implementation of a commercial casino on First Nations land. In 1993, the government of then-premier Bob Rae decided to establish a commercial casino at the Rama Reserve as a counterpoint to the commercial casino it had created in Windsor. This one-for-one policy is based on similar policies of balance in U.S. federal gaming legislation. While the location of this Ontario casino will be at the Rama First Nation, the net revenues are to be shared with other First Nations in Ontario on a formula yet to be resolved.

2. Charitable lottery schemes

Lottery schemes not conducted by a provincial government must be conducted under a license issued by a provincial government or a specified authority such as a municipality or a First Nation. These schemes are often referred to as *charitable casino activities* or *charitable lottery schemes* because of the reasons for which they are exempted under the Criminal Code.

Under the code, a provincial government or an authority specified by a provincial government may permit a charitable or religious organization to conduct and manage a lottery scheme. The proceeds of the scheme *must* be used for a charitable or religious purpose.

Charitable lottery schemes are the most popular and accessible way for Aboriginal communities throughout Canada to become involved in gaming. In authorizing a charitable lottery scheme, a provincial government can delegate to an Aboriginal authority or organization the power to issue a licence to conduct and manage a charitable lottery scheme. The licensing power transferred is subject to the limitations of the Criminal Code, the document authorizing the delegation of power, and any relevant provincial legislative or regulations.

The right to conduct a charitable lottery scheme is usually delegated through an order-in-council. Some provinces have developed numerous categories of orders-in-council, some of which are designed specifically to empower Aboriginal persons or authorities.

For example, in Ontario, three classes of orders-in-council address Aboriginal licensing power, with progressively less significant levels of First Nation input into the scope of licensing and regulatory policy. The three classes in order of priority are the following —

(a) a permanent Aboriginal facility,

(b) a temporary or occasional Aboriginal gaming licence power, and

(c) a temporary or occasional non-Aboriginal gaming license power.

The first two orders specifically address Aboriginal communities: one gives First Nation band councils the authority to license a permanent charitable gaming facility; the other gives First Nation authorities the power to license impermanent charitable gaming activities. The third order-in-council is more general and gives authority for licensing occasional charitable gaming activities to all municipalities.

Each order-in-council specifies limits such as bet limits, hours of operation, and days of play per month. An order-in-council delegating authority to license an occasional or temporary charitable gaming event to First Nations band councils is less liberal and provides considerably fewer opportunities of yielding significant revenues than one delegating authority to license a permanent charitable gaming facility.

These gradations of scope for authority were calculated to recognize Ontario First Nations' inherent right of self-government and also comply with Ontario's 1991 commitment to deal with First Nations on a government-to-government basis. The tiering of levels in the orders provide an opportunity for individual First Nations to evolve at their own pace, from a municipal order of authority over gaming to a near-provincial order of sophistication, scale, and permanence.

While the tiered system is progressive, it does have a fundamental flaw: it is subject to the contingencies of day-to-day provincial cabinet policy, political expedience, and changes in government. Consequently, there is no guarantee this policy will remain intact.

b. CRIMINAL OFFENCES ARISING FROM LOTTERY SCHEMES

Anyone who does anything for the purposes of a lottery scheme (i.e., conducting, managing, operating, or participating) that is not authorized by or according to section 207(3) of the Criminal Code is guilty of a criminal offence. For example, a commercial lottery scheme might not meet the requirements of the code because it is not technically "conducted and managed" by a provincial government if too much control has been delegated to the operating agent. A charitable casino might not comply with the Criminal Code if the casino is operated outside the scope of the authorizing order-in-council, perhaps by exceeding authorized bet limits.

In terms of commercial lottery schemes, it would seem as if there is little, if any, opportunity for a First Nation to become involved in an illegal gaming situation. But a second glance reveals a very different scenario.

Although only a provincial government may conduct and manage a commercial lottery scheme, Ontario recently set the precedent for using a Crown corporation as an agent and an independent, professional casino manager/operator as a sub-agent to run the province's casinos. Other suppliers deliver gaming and non-gaming products, services, and premises to the Crown corporation.

Over time, and with sufficient management and training programs, a First Nation could conceivably take on the role of operator in a commercial casino. In addition, a First Nation could easily supply premises (as at Rama), goods, or services to an operator or a Crown corporation. If the lottery scheme does not meet the Criminal Code requirements, most of those involved in the lottery scheme may face criminal penalties (e.g., sentences).

Moreover, some provinces' recent legislation governing the licensing and regulation of operators and suppliers does not give much protection. Even those who have been properly registered as a supplier may face criminal charges if they are found to be operating, participating in, or involved in a scheme not properly conducted, managed, or operated.

It is also important to note that an operator's or supplier's failure to comply with licensing or regulatory requirements will expose it, again, to criminal charges. In a nutshell, non-compliance with provincial legislation is non-compliance with the section of the Criminal Code permitting commercial lottery schemes to be conducted and managed according only to the provincial legislation.

First Nations or Aboriginal peoples not operating gaming schemes but receiving revenues from an unauthorized lottery scheme could also face criminal prosecution. For example, the Nova Scotia government shares the gaming revenues with First Nations. This government uses a private-sector commercial operator for at least one casino. First Nations of Ontario are expected to share revenue from the Rama Casino. When it establishes four casinos across the province in the near future, the Saskatchewan government also intends to revenue share with the provincial Aboriginal community. Therefore, it is advisable for Aboriginal communities that will be revenue sharing to negotiate in the agreement with the provincial government a commitment, and an indemnity, in favor of the First Nation or community, that the commercial lottery scheme will be managed and operated in accordance with the Criminal Code.

An Aboriginal organization with a licence to conduct a charitable lottery scheme (a *licensee*) should be aware that criminal prosecution may still arise if the licensing authority or the licensee does not sufficiently control a person or organization hired by the community to operate the lottery scheme, as a lack of sufficient control over the lottery scheme's operation, if significant enough, will breach section 207(3) of the Criminal Code.

The test is whether the operator hired by the licensee is subject to so little control that the operator, rather than the Aboriginal licensee, is actually conducting and managing the lottery scheme. So far, Canadian courts have not had the opportunity to provide guidance for Aboriginal licensees. However, the Aboriginal licensee should be cautioned to maintain overall control of casino management, even when management is contracted out to another person.

c. NON-CRIMINAL OFFENCES ARISING FROM LOTTERY SCHEMES

Several provincial governments have implemented legislation, regulations, and orders-in-council for both charitable and commercial lottery schemes. Operators and suppliers of goods, services, and premises to provincial governments and licensees legally conducting and managing lottery schemes are registered and governed under these regulations. The governing of charitable lottery scheme licensees is also controlled by these regulations.

As previously mentioned, inadequate control over operators and suppliers could result in criminal charges. As well, non-compliance with the terms and conditions of a provincial order-in-council by a licensing authority, of a licence by a licensee, or of regulations by a gaming supplier could lead to non-criminal charges under provincial rules.

Although non-criminal penalties, which may include fines and imprisonment, tend to be less severe than criminal penalties, they should not be ignored. The Ontario Gaming Control Act, for example, allows fines of up to $50 000 and imprisonment for one year.

d. FIRST NATION CHALLENGES TO FEDERAL AND PROVINCIAL JURISDICTION OF LOTTERY SCHEMES

1. Federal-provincial agreement

In 1985, a federal-provincial agreement on lottery schemes was reached. The agreement stipulates that the federal government will not conduct or license gaming, will not re-enter the field of gaming, and will ensure that each of the provinces' rights in gaming are not reduced or restricted.

This agreement was reached because the governments realized that the gaming market is quickly emerging as one of the most competitive and crowded industries in North America. As well, they see gaming as being fundamentally tied to the important policy matters of peace and civil order, morality, social integrity, and regional economic development. The recognition of these factors led to the argument that one government policy per provincial territory was the solution to regulating the market wisely and effectively. As a result, provincial governments have emerged as central figures in control of all forms of gaming activities. No Aboriginal leaders or representatives, however, were consulted during the negotiation of the federal-provincial agreement, nor were any Aboriginal interests invited to be party to it.

First Nations are mindful of the political recognition by federal and many provincial governments of First Nations' inherent right to self-government. Some First Nations are deeply concerned that a matter potentially involving the use of reserve lands and subject to the federal criminal power has been transferred to the provinces for jurisdiction. Many First Nations take the position that the inherent right of self-government is a constitutionally entrenched Aboriginal right and includes the right to exercise jurisdiction over all matters, including gaming activities, conducted on First Nation reserve lands. This jurisdiction would take precedence over any jurisdiction asserted by other governments.

This position has led to the question of whether current gaming law is valid and whether there is a basis for First Nations' territorial and legislative jurisdiction over gaming. There have been many challenges to the legality of federal and provincial gaming laws. With one recent exception, however, none of these challenges has met with success in the courts.

2. Court challenges

The court challenges involved three types of arguments. In a 1991 case before the Supreme Court of Canada (*R. v. Furtney*) it was argued that the Criminal Code, by allowing a provincial power to pass laws on and to license gaming activities, improperly delegates such matters to the provinces, and that the federal government exceeded its constitutional powers by doing so.

The court held that the federal government is not delegating jurisdiction over the criminal aspects of gaming, but rather the provinces are regulating and administering only non-criminal, civil aspects of gaming, and are within provincial jurisdiction in doing so.

In another case before the Alberta Provincial Court (*R. v. Gladue and Kirby*) involving the Beaver Lake Indian Reserve, a defendant argued unsuccessfully that sections of the Indian Act supersede the application of the Criminal Code to gaming on a reserve. The defendant referred to provisions allowing federal power to regulate places of amusement on reserve and a band council power to make bylaws on the control and prohibition of public games and other amusements.

The third argument, involving the Shawanaga First Nation, was heard in the Ontario Court of Appeal in 1995 in the companion cases of *R. v. Jones* and *R. v. Gardner*. The argument was based on the idea that it is the constitutional right of a First Nation to exercise inherent and exclusive or absolute jurisdiction over gaming matters on a reserve.

The court turned down this argument for three reasons: gaming on the reserve involved members of the public who did not live on the reserve; there was no evidence to support that gaming of the sort at issue was part of the First Nations' historic culture and traditions, or an aspect of their use of the land; and there was no evidence that any traditional form of gaming was ever regulated under traditional law.

In contrast, in the 1994 case of *R. v. Bear Claw Casino Ltd.*, the one successful Aboriginal defence involved a similar argument, but in this instance the Saskatchewan Provincial Court found it unnecessary to rule on the issue of First Nation self-government. Instead, the court held that the accused honestly and reasonably believed that it had the right to carry on unlicensed (or Aboriginally self-licensed) gaming on the White Bear reserve.

The accused has appealed to the Supreme Court of Canada and argued the self-government issue in that court. It is most significant that the Supreme Court held that the Aboriginal inherent right of self-government is not affected by the current system of federal and provincial gaming laws. Accordingly, it was necessary for the court to consider the question of whether any impact on such rights was justified, further to the test in *R. v. Sparrow* (see chapter 2 for a detailed discussion of this test).

The strict enforcement of the Criminal Code and provincial legislation and regulation of lottery schemes on First Nations reserves will continue to prevail unless changes are introduced by way of new legislation to the Criminal Code. The current position of the federal government reveals nothing to indicate that such changes might be in the process. The present government has stated that it will continue to monitor developments in Ontario and the rest of Canada, but that, generally, it is not interested in exercising jurisdiction or delegating administrative authority to Aboriginal governments in this area.

e. INTERGOVERNMENTAL COOPERATION

The success of licensing, regulating, and operating lottery schemes ultimately depends on intergovernmental cooperation; the success of dealing with issues raised between Aboriginal and provincial governments appears to hinge on balancing the powers over these three components. It is helpful to break these components down and identify the specific issues of each. The examples given are of the Ontario regime because, at the time of writing, it was the most detailed one in Canada and one of the most advanced examples of provincial-Aboriginal cooperation in gaming.

1. Licensing

The pilot Aboriginal selection process in Ontario has resulted in one cooperative intergovernmental decision to license a commercial casino located on a specific First Nation reserve. However, many First Nations see the need for additional Aboriginal casino licences, including an Aboriginal casino in a major urban setting, for greater market share and greater Aboriginal revenues. This model has seen some support in Saskatchewan, but the extent of Aboriginal involvement in the choice of locations or the development of a policy framework for implementing commercial casinos is unclear.

2. Regulating

In 1993, Ontario's newly elected NDP government expressed an interest in establishing a government-to-government arrangement with Ontario First Nations. The arrangement was to address special concerns about regulating First Nations casinos by including some Aboriginal representation on the Ontario's Gaming Control Commission.

It is doubtful that this arrangement would have resulted in meaningful regulatory power sharing. While it has been argued that such an arrangement would both accommodate First Nations' consultation rights and avoid unnecessary regulatory duplication, it would also limit First Nations' representation to the role of a minor participant.

3. Operating

The current ambiguity over operating lottery schemes, and the rigidity and narrowness of the Criminal Code, expose any participant — including Aboriginal participants — to criminal charges. The Code also shepherds provincial governments along a restrictive policy path, even when a provincial government wishes to liberalize.

Accordingly, in my view, there is a definite need to create federal legislation that would more clearly define the roles of all those participating in the gaming market:

provincial governments, Aboriginal governments, operators, and suppliers. In particular, legislation is badly needed to legalize and recognize the right of Aboriginal First Nations to directly conduct and manage commercial casinos.

f. CONCLUSION

The need for a new framework for legalized gaming is prompted by the tension between existing provincial domination of lottery schemes and the Aboriginal hope that a basis for self-reliance will be achieved by exercising both authority over lottery schemes and the right to conduct and manage, as principals, lottery schemes on Aboriginal lands. Even if the complex of gaming issues could be reduced to the single issue of jurisdiction, and Aboriginal governments enjoyed exclusive authority over gaming activities in their territories, intergovernmental cooperation would be necessary to avoid the cannibalization of two unharmonized markets by competitive forces.

There are different ways an Aboriginal community can become involved in gambling and gaming today:

(a) Aboriginal communities can apply to the appropriate government authority to conduct a charitable lottery scheme.

(b) Aboriginal communities can participate in revenue sharing from gaming activities off reserve, subject to the concerns discussed above.

(c) Aboriginal leaders can seek to negotiate with a provincial government to establish a commercial casino, as was done at the Rama Reserve.

(d) Aboriginal communities can conduct self-licensed gaming activities under the rule of self-government.

The first three options include working within the existing federal and provincial regulations largely developed without participation or regard to the needs of Aboriginal communities. The fourth option involves the assertion of Aboriginal rights not yet supported at law and exposes Aboriginal people to criminal prosecution. A fifth option is for all the parties involved to totally review the legislative schemes (including the Criminal Code, provincial legislation that would authorize a provincial authority to conduct and manage commercial gaming, and provincial licensing policies governing charitable gaming) to determine if more creative schemes might emerge.

The shared challenge for all players is to balance licensing, regulation, and ownership to ensure a fair distribution of opportunity in legalized gaming. The Aboriginal community is at a disadvantage in meeting this challenge because current law does not recognize an Aboriginal jurisdictional right in gaming. Therefore, the challenges ahead for Aboriginal people are to develop an internal consensus within Aboriginal, provincial, and territorial organizations through consultation, community planning, research, and development of a knowledge base that respects social, cultural, and economic risks and benefits, and to implement a consensus-oriented policy.

14

BUILDING A NEW RELATIONSHIP WITH ABORIGINAL PEOPLE IN NORTHERN CANADA

*by Anne B. McAllister**

Land claims. Aboriginal self-government versus public government. Treaties. Devolution. Division. Nunavut. Constitutional development. Provincial status for the territories. All are pieces of a larger puzzle of vital concern to both Aboriginal and non-Aboriginal people living in Canada's northern regions. As the century draws to a close, the North is working out arrangements by which all northerners can live together with respect for each other's history and traditions. This is a daunting task, but it represents a unique opportunity to create processes and institutions that, perhaps more than anywhere else in the country, can be responsive to cultural and other differences and to local circumstances. Aboriginal people are at the centre of this change and will have a critical voice in its outcomes.

a. THE CONTEXT

Aboriginal people have lived in the north of what is now Canada for 25 000 to 30 000 years. Non-Natives arrived only within the last 200 to 300 years. At Confederation, the vast lands to the north and west of the new Dominion of Canada — known as Rupert's Land and the North-Western Territory

---

* *Anne B. McAllister is a lawyer with the Department of Justice, Government of Canada. The views expressed are those of the author and not of the Government of Canada.*

— were controlled by the Hudson's Bay Company, whose immense fur-trading empire stretched north to the Arctic Ocean and west to the Rocky Mountains. Fearing American expansionism and sharing the entrepreneurial dreams of the railway companies, Sir John A. Macdonald asked Britain to buy the land from the Hudson's Bay Company and transfer it to Canada. Aboriginal and non-Aboriginal residents of these vast territories were neither consulted nor informed in advance about this enormous land transfer. Once it became known, reactions varied. In what is now Manitoba, the Métis, fearing loss of their way of life, culture, and freedom, reacted with open hostility in a rebellion led by Louis Riel.

It was a different story in other parts of Rupert's Land and the North-Western Territory. Wanting to encourage farmers and settlers to the "last, best West," the new Canada signed a series of numbered treaties with Indians in parts of what are now Manitoba, Saskatchewan, Alberta, and the Northwest Territories, requiring Aboriginal groups to extinguish their claims to the area in exchange for land and cash. No such agreements were negotiated with the Inuit.

Soon more and more non-Natives began to explore and settle in the North. Unlike other parts of the country, where provincial governments ran their own affairs, administration of the territories remained directly under the control of the federal government. With the 1898 gold rush to the Klondike, the Yukon Territory was created, but it too remained an extension of the federal government. Between 1905 and 1954, not much attention was paid to political development in the territories. Although discovery of oil at Norman Wells in 1921 served as an impetus for the federal government to sign Treaty 11 with Aboriginal people living along the Mackenzie River, it was not until the 1940s that northern oil and minerals started to become more important. And it was not until the early 1950s when the United States, as part of its North American defence strategy, began building Distant Early

Warning (DEW) sites across the Arctic that the Canadian government renewed its interest in the North.

Key court decisions and pressures for resource development combined to trigger even more significant changes in the 1970s and 1980s. Native organizations began to form and be funded, the federal government started to negotiate comprehensive and specific claims, recognition was given to Aboriginal and treaty rights in the constitution, and governments began to show some willingness to consider Aboriginal self-government.

To a large degree, the federal government has historically taken an on-again off-again approach to political development in the North and, as in other parts of the country, has adopted an either-or approach to Aboriginal peoples and to Aboriginal rights generally. This either-or approach has been characterized by two contradictory themes: one emphasizing isolation of Aboriginal peoples on reserves; the other promoting assimilation of Aboriginal peoples into the larger non-Aboriginal society, with the consequent loss of their distinct culture.

The government's unsettled approach to Aboriginal peoples has encouraged the vast majority of Aboriginal people — whether on or off reserve — to continue to live outside the mainstream of political and economic life. This pattern has been exacerbated by governments' failure to develop policies fostering acceptance of Aboriginal values and traditions within public political and economic institutions. Indeed, many Aboriginal people question whether public institutions can accommodate their aspirations. Distinct Aboriginal institutions are viewed by many as essential if traditional values, practices, and lifestyles are to be maintained and if Aboriginal peoples are to have decision-making authority over matters necessary to their survival as distinct entities. Nowhere are these questions being asked with more urgency — and articulated with more clarity — than in the North.

To say that the North is a complex environment — physically, socially, politically, economically, linguistically, and culturally — is a profound understatement. The variation in circumstances and conditions between the two territories and within each territory is immense. Sweeping generalizations simply don't apply from one region to another.

1. Yukon

From a demographic perspective alone, Yukon differs from the Northwest Territories in a number of important ways. Aboriginal people in Yukon are in a minority (approximately 27% of the total population) and are more homogeneous, without the Inuit/Dene/Métis divisions characteristic of the Northwest Territories. Approximately two-thirds of the Aboriginal population are members of particular First Nations and are beneficiaries under the Council of Yukon Indians (CYI) Umbrella Final Agreement. The Yukon is home to 14 First Nations in different linguistic groups and with different cultural, political, and social priorities.

The Yukon government, like its counterpart in the Northwest Territories, has evolved in recent decades from a limited government under Ottawa's direction to a province-like entity with a high level of political autonomy. An atmosphere of general political stability, coupled with significant progress in settlement of land claims, provides a context for continued devolution of federal programs and services to the territorial government and the development of more province-like powers. For years the central political issues of Yukon have been economic development and greater independence from Ottawa; less important were Aboriginal issues. More recently the situation has changed. Today the relationship between the Aboriginal and non-Aboriginal population — focused in large measure on the land claims settlement and self-government arrangements — is probably the single most important feature of Yukon political and social life.

237

2. The Northwest Territories

The Northwest Territories has within its borders a greater array of cultural, social, and political complexities. The non-Aboriginal population of the Northwest Territories, 24 025 people, represents just over one third of the total population of some 65 000 people. The 18 000 Inuit who form the majority in the eastern and central Arctic are linguistically and culturally different from the Inuvialuit of the northwestern region. They in turn differ from the other Aboriginal peoples of the western Northwest Territories — the Dene and the Métis. Within the Dene community are further regional groups including the Gwich'in, Sahtu, and Dogrib. The Inuvialuit of the northwest (in 1984) and the Inuit of the eastern Arctic (in 1993) have concluded land claims settlements, as have the Gwich'in (in 1992) and the Sahtu (in 1993) of the west. Other groups are at various stages of negotiations.

By the late 1970s, Aboriginal peoples in the Northwest Territories, faced with federal refusal to negotiate northern political development through land claims, began to participate more actively in the political life of the territory. With the election of an Aboriginal majority in the legislative assembly, the government of the Northwest Territories became more sympathetic to Aboriginal aspirations — and to the notion of division of the Northwest Territories, a key element of the self-government aspirations of the Inuit of the central and eastern Arctic.

With the creation of Nunavut in the eastern Arctic on April 1, 1999, the Northwest Territories will be divided into two territories: a relatively homogeneous eastern territory with a large Aboriginal majority, and a western territory in which Aboriginal people are a minority. In the western territory, moreover, there is less certainty and stability and, accordingly, a serious threat of political fragmentation. The focus continues to be on settling outstanding land claims and determining political and constitutional arrangements in the post-division western territory. Aboriginal expectations for self-government continue to mount and debate continues on how Aboriginal government and public government — governmental processes and structures applicable to all residents, and in which all residents participate — can work together.

b. LAND CLAIMS

Two main types of claims are negotiated by the federal government. Comprehensive land claims are based on the concept of continuing Aboriginal rights and title over a territory that had not been dealt with by treaty or other legal means. In settling a comprehensive claim, the Aboriginal group, in effect, exchanges undefined Aboriginal rights for defined benefits or entitlements (such as cash compensation, land rights, harvesting rights, and so on).

Specific claims arise from alleged non-fulfillment of lawful obligations arising from treaties, legislation (such as the improper administration of lands and other assets under the Indian Act or formal agreements), or other formal agreements.

The federal government's comprehensive land claims policy, adopted in the early 1970s, was designed to deal with outstanding claims of Aboriginal groups who had not concluded treaties with the Crown and who were faced with the loss of traditional use and occupancy of their lands. The policy provided that in exchange for giving up Aboriginal interests arising out of traditional use and occupancy of land, Aboriginal groups would receive a combination of —

(a) cash;

(b) hunting, fishing, and trapping rights;

(c) resource revenue sharing;

(d) participation in local and regional government;

(e) economic opportunities; and

(f) fee simple absolute ownership of certain lands.

In subsequent policy statements, the federal government stipulated that structures and functions of government were not negotiable as part of land claims settlements. Thus, while supporting increased participation by Aboriginal peoples in public government, the federal government was not prepared to negotiate Aboriginal self-government. This changed in August 1995 with the launching of the new federal Approach to Implementation of the Inherent Right and the Negotiation of Aboriginal Self-Government. For the first time, the federal government conceded that self-government and land claims could be negotiated together and that certain rights related to self-government could receive constitutional protection in much the same way as do rights in land claims agreements (i.e., as treaty rights protected by section 35 of the Constitution Act, 1982).

The substantive results of land claims settlements and the timing of their resolution are important first and foremost to the Aboriginal beneficiaries. They are also an important element in the overall political, economic, and social development of the territories. Not to be overlooked, of course, are the implications for third parties, such as resource developers, who have operated in an atmosphere of uncertainty and volatility for many years.

1. Yukon: Umbrella Final Agreement

After over 20 years of tough negotiations, the Council for Yukon Indians (CYI) reached a land claims settlement in 1991 with the federal and territorial governments (the lands included in this and other settlements mentioned in this chapter are shown on the map in Figure #4). An Umbrella Final Agreement was concluded, providing a general framework to guide negotiations with 14 individual First Nations. The vehicle of an umbrella agreement allowed individual First Nations to address their needs and priorities in specific agreements without undermining the fundamental principles of the overall agreement available to all First Nations. (At the time the land claim was concluded, the 14 Yukon First Nations were represented by CYI. Since then, a new organization, the Council of Yukon First Nations (CYFN) has been created, representing 13 of the 14 First Nations. For the purposes of the following discussion, reference will be made to CYI, the corporate entity that is a signatory to the Umbrella Final Agreement.)

Of the 14 First Nations covered by the Umbrella Final Agreement, four have finalized individual land claims agreements (Vuntut Gwichin, Teslin Tlingit, Champagne Aishihik, and Nacho Nyak Dun). Negotiations are at various stages with the other ten Yukon First Nations.

In overall terms, the CYI claim involves Aboriginal fee simple title to 41 439 square kilometres of land and payments over five years of $242.6 million (in 1989 dollars). The exact amount of land (including land with and without subsurface rights) and the financial compensation involved in specific First Nation claims vary and are subject to negotiations depending on the priorities and circumstances of individual First Nations.

Perhaps most important, the land claims settlement guarantees First Nations a role in land management and resource development in Yukon, not only on settlement lands but also throughout the territory. The public boards, councils, and committees that will control the overall management regime will usually include 50% Aboriginal participation. These organizations include Surface Rights Board; Yukon Land Use Planning Council, to which the CYI nominates one-third of the members; Yukon Development Assessment Board; Yukon Heritage Resources Board; Water Board (one-third CYI nominees); and Renewable Resources Council. The creation of such a comprehensive co-management regime in the Yukon is a significant feature of the Yukon land claims settlements. It ensures Aboriginal participation in decision making in land and resource management.

FIGURE #4
COMPREHENSIVE LAND CLAIMS IN
NORTHERN CANADA

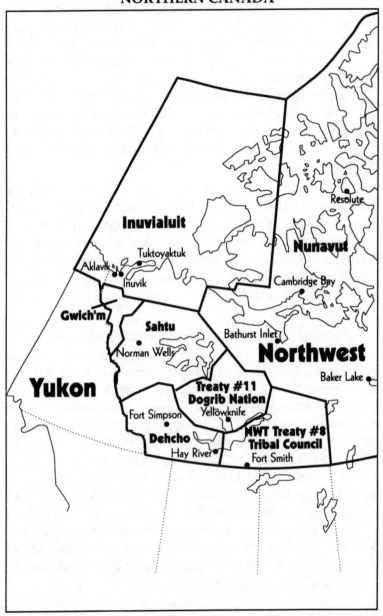

FIGURE #4 — Continued

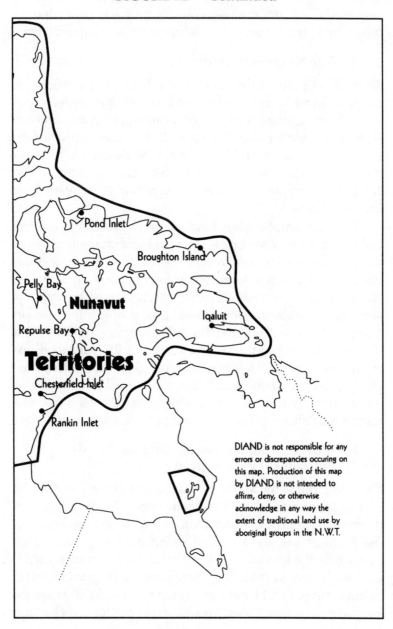

DIAND is not responsible for any
errors or discrepancies occuring on
this map. Production of this map
by DIAND is not intended to
affirm, deny, or otherwise
acknowledge in any way the
extent of traditional land use by
aboriginal groups in the N.W.T.

The Umbrella Final Agreement also provided that individual self-government agreements could be negotiated subsequently within the general framework provided in individual First Nation land claims settlement agreements.

2. The Northwest Territories

As in other parts of the country, the land claims process in the Northwest Territories has until recently proceeded separately from negotiation of self-government. Four comprehensive land claims (with the Inuvialuit of the northwestern Arctic, the Gwich'in and the Sahtu of the western Arctic, and the Inuit of the eastern Arctic) have been finalized in the Northwest Territories. Success in the area of self-government has been limited.

Each comprehensive land claims agreement reflects unique features according to priorities and characteristics of the various Aboriginal groups, the context of the negotiations, and the lessons learned from previous agreements. Nonetheless, all include essential features found in all claims settlements: financial compensation, fee simple title to certain tracts of land (with ownership of subsurface rights over a limited portion), and participation in wildlife and environmental management boards, in exchange for the Native peoples' agreement to extinguish their Aboriginal title to the land included in the claims. A commitment to future self-government negotiations is also common to these agreements.

3. Inuvialuit Committee for Original Peoples' Entitlement Final Agreement

The Inuvialuit of the Mackenzie Delta and Victoria and Banks islands were first to finalize a comprehensive land claim in the North. Against the backdrop of the oil and gas boom in the Beaufort Sea and the need to ensure control over their own lands, the Inuvialuit of the Western Arctic coast signed a final settlement in 1984. The Committee for Original Peoples' Entitlement (COPE) Final Agreement covered 312 000 square kilometres and established a series of corporations, such as the

Inuvialuit Development Corporation, to administer the land and money from the claim and to foster and channel economic development for the benefit of the Inuvialuit. It also provides for several public government boards through which the Inuvialuit participate in co-management of resources and in environmental protection across the settlement area.

4. Nunavut Final Agreement

The Nunavut Final Agreement was signed in 1993 by the Inuit of the Central Arctic, Baffin, and Keewatin regions. Over 20 years in the making, its land and financial components are broadly similar to those concluded elsewhere in that it provides for a substantial land base, monetary payments, and a significant role in resource management. The agreement establishes an Inuit settlement region of some two million square kilometres in the central and eastern Arctic with direct Inuit ownership of 350 000 square kilometres with sub-surface rights to 36 000 square kilometres. The cash settlement for the 17 500 beneficiaries is $1.14 billion to be paid over 14 years, with an additional $13 million in the form of a training trust fund. The agreement guarantees Inuit involvement in a range of resource management boards (land, water, wildlife, and environment) that will render decisions throughout the settlement region and the new territory of Nunavut once it is established.

What is truly unique about the Nunavut Final Agreement is the federal commitment to establish a separate territory called Nunavut ("our land"). The new territory will have effective Inuit control over the full range of provincial-type responsibilities. Other land claims settlements, such as the Yukon settlement, have included general commitments to the separate negotiation of self-government within a broad framework but none incorporated a commitment like the creation of Nunavut.

The carving out of a separate territory in the central and eastern Arctic was the fundamental cornerstone of the Inuit land claim since the late 1960s and early 1970s. Preservation of Inuit identity and traditional way of life was inextricably linked to the establishment of a separate territory with an Inuit majority. Accordingly, the Inuit never wavered from the fundamental premise that settling their land claim required establishing a separate territory reflecting Inuit values and perspectives.

5. Gwich'in and Sahtu Final Agreements

In 1988, an agreement-in-principle was reached between the federal government and the Dene and Métis of the western Northwest Territories. Concerns about the federal requirement that Aboriginal title be extinguished and about the absence of self-government provisions in the Final Agreement led to its rejection in 1990 by groups in the southern part of the settlement area (particularly the Dene from the Deh Cho and Treaty 8 areas). Faced with an irreconcilable split among the Aboriginal groups, the federal government agreed to entertain regional claims modelled on the overall Dene/Métis Final Agreement.

The Gwich'in reached a Final Agreement with Canada and the Northwest Territories quickly. Settlement legislation was passed in Parliament in 1992. The settlement covers 57 200 square kilometres and provides for compensation of $140 million over 15 years, administered by the Gwich'in Development Corporation.

The Sahtu Dene and Métis of the Great Bear region reached a Final Agreement in September of 1993 and federal legislation was passed in Parliament in 1994. The settlement covers some 285 480 square kilometres and provides for compensation of $130 million over 15 years and shares in royalties (to be shared with the Gwich'in) from resource development such as Esso Resources' Norman Wells oil fields.

In general terms, the Gwich'in and Sahtu Final Agreements are similar to the Inuvialuit settlement. Significantly, however, these two claims settlements include commitments by governments to negotiate self-government appropriate to the unique circumstances of each and consistent with their desire to have self-government exercised as close to the community level as possible. Self-government framework agreements reflecting a predisposition to regional public government models are appended to the land claims settlement agreement. Although clearly anticipating that exclusively Aboriginal institutions may be required in areas such as culture, language, and custom adoption, the general direction appears to be adaptation of public government institutions to accommodate Aboriginal representation. A wide range of subjects are listed as potentially within the scope of such institutions, including culture and language, housing, taxation, education, social services, health, and the administration of justice.

6. Ongoing negotiations

As noted above, after the breakdown of the 1990 Dene/Métis Final Agreement, the approach taken was based on negotiating regional claims that would be organized along cultural and linguistic lines. Two such claims — with the Gwich'in and with the Sahtu — have been concluded, leaving three outstanding.

In the fall of 1992, the Dogrib, including eligible Métis of Dogrib ancestry, in the North Slave region of the Mackenzie Valley submitted a regional claim. There are approximately 3 000 Dogrib living in four communities in the claim area. The size of the claim is 207 480 square kilometres in a territory that includes most of the major diamond activity in the western Northwest Territories, including BHP/Dia Met's Lac de Gras project, which promises to be one of the largest diamond deposits in the world.

Formal negotiations began in January 1994. Two interim agreements were signed by the chief negotiators. One provides the Dogrib with opportunities to participate in government organizations that assess and review development activities and regulate land and resource use in the North Slave regions. The other withdrew from disposition approximately 12 900 square kilometres of land around the four Dogrib communities and in a culturally sensitive area.

These agreements remain in effect pending settlement of the Dogrib claim. In November 1994, the parties agreed to a pause in negotiations to allow the appointment of a new chief federal negotiator and a review of the federal mandate in light of the then-impending inherent right policy. In April 1996, a framework agreement was initialled by the Dogrib, the government of the Northwest Territories, and Canada. Negotiations are expected to begin again soon.

The situation in the South Slave region is complicated and unresolved. The Treaty 8 Dene have rejected the regional claim approach in favor of pursuing satisfaction of their treaty land entitlements under the federal Treaty Land Entitlement policy. While negotiations are proceeding, it is difficult to predict the outcome. How the concerns of Métis in the South Slave region will be addressed is still being discussed between the Métis and federal government.

Discussions between the federal government and the fifth regional group, the Deh Cho Dene and Métis, have not led to establishment of a negotiating process.

c. SELF-GOVERNMENT IN YUKON

The Council for Yukon Indians' Umbrella Final Agreement committed Canada, the Yukon, and First Nations to negotiate self-government agreements. A Model Self-Government Agreement between Ottawa and Yukon First Nations was finalized in 1991, setting out an overall framework within which individual First Nations could work to develop detailed self-government arrangements. While providing common provisions applicable to all First Nations, it also offers flexibility in tailoring arrangements suitable to individual priorities and circumstances. First Nations may choose to negotiate assumption of jurisdiction in most areas now falling under the territorial government's authority, and at the rate conducive to local circumstances. Also, powers previously exercised by the federal government through the Indian Act may be taken up by a First Nation. These self-government agreements are implemented by federal legislation.

To date, the four First Nations that have settled individual land claims agreements have also concluded self-government agreements. One unique feature of these agreements is worth mentioning. Each First Nation government has jurisdiction over all its members, regardless of place of residence in Yukon. This is contrary to the usual situation in which a First Nation government will only have jurisdiction over its members while they reside on the land base. In the Yukon situation, for example, Vuntut Gwichin child welfare or adoption laws would apply to its members regardless of their place of residence in Yukon. How this will work in practice remains to be seen.

These agreements were negotiated before the government launched its Approach to Implementation of the Inherent Right and the Negotiation of Aboriginal Self-Government in August 1995. Before this, self-government agreements were treated differently from constitutionally protected land claims agreements. Jurisdiction or authority of First Nations is delegated from the federal government in federal legislation implementing the agreements. Future self-government negotiations in the Yukon, as elsewhere, will proceed under the new policy based on an inherent right of self-government, recognized in section 35 of the Constitution Act, 1982. Existing self-government agreements are being re-examined and the necessary adjustments made to make them consistent with the new policy, particularly for constitutional protection of certain aspects of self-government arrangements.

d. POLITICAL DEVELOPMENT IN THE NORTHWEST TERRITORIES

The Northwest Territories is a less homogeneous and thus more complex environment than the Yukon. Issues of devolution, enhancement of territorial powers, land claims, Aboriginal self-government, division, and regionalism all overlap in an often confusing and divisive atmosphere — an atmosphere that may become increasingly charged as April 1999, the date for division of the territories, comes closer.

In the 1960s and 1970s, largely as a result of federal refusal to negotiate self-government with land claims, two separate political development processes emerged in the Northwest Territories: one for non-Aboriginal peoples in the legislative assembly and one for Aboriginal peoples through their own organizations, focusing to a large degree on land claims. Both non-Aboriginal and Aboriginal peoples realized in the early 1980s that this would not produce results; it had become apparent that non-Aboriginal peoples could not develop a government without respecting the rights of the Aboriginal majority and Aboriginal peoples could not develop governments solely through claims negotiations.

This realization resulted in more Aboriginal participation in politics at the territorial level and in a more cooperative approach between Aboriginal and non-Aboriginal leaders. This cooperation, however, was based on the understanding that when a plebiscite on the issue of dividing the Northwest Territories was held, there would be a broad support for division by both groups. The plebiscite was held in April 1982; 56% of the voters favored division. Consequently, all future discussions on constitutional development were based on recognition that there would ultimately be two territories — Nunavut in the eastern Arctic following settlement of the Inuit land claim, and one in the western Arctic. How each territory would develop, and how both Aboriginal and non-Aboriginal interests could be reconciled and accommodated following division, emerged as key questions.

Public debate in the western Northwest Territories is today focused on building consensus around new processes and institutions that all residents — Aboriginal and non-Aboriginal — will view as legitimate. In the eastern territory, on the other hand, energies are devoted to getting Nunavut off the ground in 1999.

1. Nunavut

Creation of Nunavut has been consistently bound up with the Inuit land claim and is a direct consequence of the land claims settlement. The Inuit, of all the Aboriginal groups negotiating claims, have been most successful in linking settlement of their political aspirations to their claim to land ownership and control. Their success can be linked in large measure to their acceptance of a public government model, as opposed to Aboriginal government, as the vehicle for expressing their political objectives. This was a viable strategy for several reasons. There is a large Aboriginal majority (over 80% of the residents of the Nunavut territory are Aboriginal) and this is not likely to change in the foreseeable future; Inuit will likely be a clear majority for many years to come. The Inuit will probably have a number of years to develop a style and structure of government reflecting their values and traditions, even if at the time of division they adopt arrangements much like the present government of the Northwest Territories. Also, regional antagonisms characteristic of the western territory are much less pronounced in the Nunavut territory, resulting in social homogeneity and a political context that is less complex.

The Nunavut Act, which became law in 1993, sets out the basic framework for the new government and creates a process for managing the daunting task of making the transition to division. The Nunavut Implementation Commission oversees division planning. Although the new government will, from the beginning, have the same range of legislative and executive authority as the other territories, it may well be that during the transition stage it will contract with private sector organizations and other governments to deliver certain programs and services on its behalf. Issues related to matters such as division of assets and liabilities between the western territory and Nunavut, financing Nunavut, infrastructure requirements, administrative structures, training, and distribution of authority between the new territorial government and communities will need to be addressed. Questions related to the interface between the institutions set up under the land claim itself and the new territorial government will also require consideration. Costs may become a particularly challenging issue in light of the federal goal of deficit reduction through spending cuts.

Whether Nunavut will meet the self-government aspirations of the Inuit of the central and eastern Arctic remains an open question. Although the Inuit expect that Nunavut will meet their self-government objectives for the foreseeable future, in the event of a marked demographic shift (i.e., if the Inuit majority is significantly reduced or disappears), the Inuit may want to negotiate further elaboration of their inherent right of self-government, whether through Inuit-specific institutions or guaranteed participation in territorial-wide organizations.

2. The western territory

The western territory is a different situation. For a variety of reasons it may be more important, but perhaps also more difficult insofar as Aboriginal peoples and their interests are concerned, for new institutional arrangements to be in place at the time of division. Two key factors make reaching consensus difficult: the existence of a non-Aboriginal majority in the west and the important differences among the various Dene, Métis, Inuvialuit, and Inuit cultures and language. To further complicate matters, the non-Aboriginal majority is centred in Yellowknife, while the majority of Aboriginal people reside in the communities and regions outside of Yellowknife.

Division on its own will do nothing to achieve recognition of Aboriginal rights or to create structures for guaranteeing continued protection of Aboriginal interests. Indeed, in the west it may become more difficult after division to arrange for new forms of government that reconcile the competing and often contradictory interests of Aboriginal and non-Aboriginal residents. This may be exacerbated by the potential for rapid increase in the non-Aboriginal population after division.

Decisions will focus on a number of significant questions, including: How can a public government be created that protects both collective Aboriginal rights, as well as the individual rights of all residents? How can the pressures emanating from communities and regions be balanced against the need for a strong central government? How can the new territorial government continue to receive more powers from the federal government?

There is a growing demand for more powers to be vested in communities and regions Aboriginal peoples view as better placed to recognize their rights to control their own lands, resources, languages, and cultures. Historically, the territorial government has lacked legitimacy in the eyes of Aboriginal peoples. This perspective, coupled with the high expectations generated by the federal government's commitment to implement the inherent right of self-government, has re-invigorated Aboriginal demands for the establishment of governments that would replace the territorial government or at least reduce its authority over Aboriginal peoples.

While there is a general consensus that decision making should rest as closely as possible with those governed — and that every level of government must have the power, authority, and resources necessary to carry out its responsibilities

— there remains the question: who should legitimately get more power and who should not? There are potentially three levels of government in the North: communities, regions, and the territorial government. The impracticality and enormous cost of a multiplicity of governments is generally recognized. It would result only in diseconomies of scale and fragmentation of political authority, both significant impediments to economic development and effective resource management.

Special interests of Aboriginal peoples must be addressed in whatever governmental arrangements are instituted. In the south, Aboriginal self-government is mainly a question of separate development: an Aboriginal (i.e., ethnically based) government on an exclusive land base (i.e., reserves). In the north, however, the challenge is to create Aboriginal self-government within a public government system.

Political development in the west must take into account the self-government aspirations of Aboriginal peoples. Should this be done through exclusively Aboriginal institutions, through Aboriginal participation in public institutions, or a mix of both? Given that most communities in the west have a mix of Aboriginal and non-Aboriginal residents, it is likely that a mix of public and Aboriginal institutions and arrangements will emerge. Self-government, therefore, may find expression within a broader public government context. If so, should particular arrangements protect or guarantee the involvement of Aboriginal peoples in public government? This might include guaranteed Aboriginal seats, special language rights, or residency requirements for the community. On the other hand, are there particular subject matters, such as renewable resources or language and culture, that should be exclusively within Aboriginal jurisdiction? To what extent should authority, whether exercised by public or Aboriginal governments and institutions, be local or regional? How would regional boundaries be determined? Should they follow essentially racial or tribal boundaries to allow Aboriginal groups to establish balance vis-à-vis the non-Aboriginal majority?

Part of the task ahead will be the development of more appropriate structures and processes at the territorial level, as well as more flexibility for community and regional structures. What fits one region may not fit another. How much freedom can different regions and communities have to determine their own structures and still fit within the territorial framework? What powers should the territorial government keep for itself?

The challenge ahead is to develop a style of government that is Aboriginal as well as non-Aboriginal. This will include, for example, more use of Aboriginal languages in government and a continued commitment to consensus decision making (which has to date characterized the legislative assembly of the Northwest Territories) as part of the public government process. It may also weigh against the adoption of party politics in the western Northwest Territories and in favor of continuing the practice of not operating on the basis of party affiliation.

e. TOWARD PROVINCIAL STATUS

Although all northern residents agree that further powers must be transferred to the North and, indeed, that provincial status is inevitable for all three post-division territories, Aboriginal support for provincial status is conditional on legal recognition of ownership of Aboriginal lands and resources through the claims process and legal recognition of Aboriginal self-government within the broader framework of public government constitution.

Provincial status is not likely to occur in the near future. The federal government has been slow to transfer power to the North, particularly if it means the creation of new provinces. For one reason, it would shift the overall federal-provincial balance more in favor of the provinces. As well, the federal government is not keen to give up control over the rate and timing of resource exploitation. Control over non-renewable resource development is the source of much federal power to influence the energy policy of the country. In addition, the federal government would like to keep for itself the potential tax revenues from these non-renewable resources.

Another critical issue for the North is control over land. Provinces have the right to use, sell, manage, and tax most land within their boundaries; territories do not. This is a vital difference considering the non-renewable resources of the North. Both the federal government and Aboriginal peoples claim ownership of northern lands. It is critical that Aboriginal land claims be settled before transfers to the territorial government occur. In the Northwest Territories, for example, the federal government has transferred small areas of land around settlements to the territorial government. Even such small transfers have caused problems because they do not take into account Aboriginal interests in the land.

And, of course, the other obvious impediment to provincial status is the cost of creating three new provinces. In an era of deficit reduction, the financial burden associated with such changes are enormous, and the opportunities for revenue generation by the territories themselves are limited.

At the heart of what is going on in the North is the right of Aboriginal peoples to be distinct peoples and to enjoy unique systems of culture, language, and ways of life, not just as individuals but as a group. To maintain this identity there must be specific arrangements to ensure their ongoing collective survival. This is the real challenge being faced today in our northern regions, and indeed, throughout Canada.

15

INTERNATIONAL LAW AND ABORIGINAL DISPUTES

by Peter W. Hutchins and Carol Hilling

There is nothing radical in suggesting international law is applicable to many Aboriginal issues. Indeed, much of the Canadian law about Aboriginal people is based on international law. Francisco de Vitoria, one of the founders of modern international law, argued in the 16th century that indigenous peoples were the true owners of their lands, with full control in their public and private matters. Chief Justice Marshall of the U.S. Supreme Court in the early 19th century acknowledged the relevance of the law of nations when he attempted to extract the legal principles applicable to Aboriginal-European relations.

Marshall elaborated the law about the sovereignty of North American Indians, including what sovereignty they had left after they signed treaties surrendering their territory. The Indian Nations were considered limited in their external sovereignty but maintained sovereignty over their own people. Marshall characterized the Indian Nations as "dependent allies" and "domestic dependent nations." Yet he emphasized that their being domestic dependent nations did not involve their giving up their national character: "Protection does not imply the destruction of the protected."

In the 19th and early 20th centuries, international law began to legitimize the denial of Aboriginal sovereignty and Aboriginal rights. This approach unfortunately still conditions the thinking of far too many lawyers who perhaps have not bothered with the matter since law school (if then) and the majority of state politicians who take comfort for self-serving purposes in notions of European superiority and state sovereignty.

But recently, the direction of international law has shifted back to human values of the world community and away from the monopoly of state conduct, and the focus is increasingly on the rights of indigenous peoples in international law. International law is rediscovering its original path with the drafting of documents such as the U.N. Draft Declaration on the Rights of Indigenous Peoples and the adoption of treaties such as the I.L.O. Convention 169, as well as treaties on environmental protection.

a. INTERNATIONAL LAW AND ABORIGINAL DOMESTIC LITIGATION

Why should Canadian lawyers and courts involved in Aboriginal litigation consider international law? The simple answer is that international law is part of the law that applies to Aboriginal issues. Bluntly, it is not necessary to establish state sovereignty or international treaty status of Crown-First Nation treaties in order to use international law to support the legal positions being argued by First Nations.

1. International law as part of Canadian law

(a) International treaty law

International treaties are difficult to invoke before Canadian courts since Canada incorporates few treaties into Canadian law. These treaties must be incorporated by legislation to have legal effect in Canada, and the legislation must be enacted by the legislature with jurisdiction over the subject matter of the treaty. However, often the rules written in the treaties reflect *customary rules* of international law which may be invoked before the courts.

(b) Customary international law

Customary international law consists of rules deriving from state practice. When many states from various parts of the world adopt a certain practice and demonstrate that they feel obligated to act in this way, the practice results in customs that become compulsory for every state, even if they are not written in a treaty. Since Canada incorporates few of the international treaties it ratifies, customary law can provide a useful alternative.

Although there is some confusion and uncertainty in Canadian law about the application of customary international law, it can be argued that it applies as part of Canadian law to the extent that it does not conflict with statutory law. This argument is supported by a number of court decisions and has been adopted by the Supreme Court of Canada. Customary international law has been invoked on several occasions in Aboriginal litigation. For example, Aboriginal parties often refer to the rules of interpretation of international treaties in cases about Indian treaties. Although these rules are applied by the courts, judges do not feel bound by them.

2. Can international law help interpret statutes?

One principle of statutory construction is that parliament is presumed not to purposely violate international law when it creates statutes, even where international law does not apply directly in Canadian law. Therefore, if there is any ambiguity in the interpretation of a statute, the courts will favor an interpretation that respects Canada's international obligations. On the other hand, when a statute *clearly* contradicts international law, Canadian courts will follow the provisions of the statute, regardless of violating Canada's international obligations.

According to several court decisions, there is a rule that if legislation intends to override Canada's international obligations, it must do so very clearly and unambiguously. There is no reason this rule should not apply equally to the interpretation of common law — the law that recognizes the existence of Aboriginal rights.

b. HOW INTERNATIONAL LAW INFLUENCES CANADIAN LAW AND ABORIGINAL ISSUES

International law can be applied by analogy usefully to Aboriginal issues. In *Simon v. The Queen*, a 1985 case examining the 1752 Treaty of Peace and Friendship between the Mi'kmaq and the British, the Supreme Court of Canada broke the judicial ice on applying international law in Canadian Aboriginal domestic litigation.

In 1929, the County Court of Nova Scotia held that the treaties with the Indians of that province were not international since they were made between independent powers and the Indians were never considered one. Since only what the judge called "constituted authorities of nations" had authority to make treaties, he concluded that the Treaty of 1752 between the Mi'kmaq and the British was not a treaty.

In *Simon*, the Supreme Court of Canada rejected this conclusion, saying not only that such language was incompatible with Canada's growing awareness of Aboriginal rights but also was inappropriate in Canadian law. The court said that the Indians *did* have the capacity to enter into treaties: "An Indian treaty is unique, it is an agreement *sui generis* which is neither created nor terminated according to the rules of international law."

This statement by Chief Justice Dickson, now the law in Canada, has been taken to mean that Indian treaties are not international treaties and that international law does not apply to them. However, the criteria Dickson applied in reaching his conclusion are identical to those prevailing under international law. He recognized, for example, that under certain circumstances a treaty could be terminated if one of its fundamental provisions is breached. This is a rule of international law codified in the Vienna Convention on the Law of Treaties. It seems, therefore, that Canadian courts should not limit themselves to applying only one set of principles but should look to any pertinent source, including international law.

Australian law has recently been given this direction by the High Court of Australia. In *Mabo v. Queensland*, the court recognized the important influence of international law on the development of the common law.

Mabo has already found its way into Canadian case law through the decision of the British Columbia Court of Appeal in *Delgamuukw v. The Queen*. The Court of Appeal solicited oral and written submissions from all counsel on the significance of *Mabo*. Two of the judges quoted extensively from the judgment in their reasons.

The Crown-First Nation treaties were used to establish rights of access to territory and resources, military alliances, and commercial relationships. The language of these documents was not the language of domestic contracts between the Crown and its citizens but of treaties between independent peoples, albeit of uneven strength. As Chief Justice Marshall of the U.S. Supreme Court noted in *Worcester v. State of Georgia* in 1832, the words "treaty" and "nation" were given the same meaning by the European powers whether applied to Indian Nations or to any other nation in the world. Marshall referred specifically to international law in describing the treaty relationship, and the court noted that the parties did not need to be equal to apply international law:

> What is a treaty? The answer is, it is a compact formed between two nations or communities, having the right of self-government. Is it essential that each party shall possess the same attributes of sovereignty, to give force to the treaty? This will not be pretended: for, on this ground, very few valid treaties could

be formed. The only requisite is, that each of
the contracting parties shall possess the right
of self-government, and the power to per-
form the stipulations of the treaty.

International law from 1750 to 1850 did not emphasize
formal statehood. The British Crown made treaties with
many different kinds of parties, in many different circumstances. Almost 160 years later, a unanimous Supreme Court
of Canada echoed its 19th-century U.S. counterpart, confirming, in *Sioui*, that the Crown-First Nation treaties indicate that
the Crown considered Indian Nations independent nations.

c. USING INTERNATIONAL FORUMS TO RESOLVE ABORIGINAL DISPUTES

Although access to international forums to resolve Aboriginal disputes is limited, there are some avenues Aboriginal
peoples in Canada should consider.

1. International Court of Justice

The United Nations' court, the International Court of Justice
(ICJ), is in The Hague, Netherlands. Neither individuals nor
groups can bring a case before the court, only states. However,
the ICJ can advise on legal issues presented by the U.N.
General Assembly or the Security Council. Any other U.N.
organization, such as the U.N. Commission on Human
Rights (see below), may seek the opinion of the Court if
authorized by the General Assembly.

2. U.N. Commission on Human Rights and its subsidiaries

Created in 1946 by the Economic and Social Council of the
United Nations (ECOSOC), the Commission on Human
Rights is located in Geneva, Switzerland. It prepares reports,
proposals, and recommendations on human rights in general, minority rights, and the prevention of all forms of discrimination.

Its Sub-Commission on Prevention of Discrimination and Protection of Minorities investigates such flagrant violations of human rights as policies of racial discrimination, segregation, or apartheid. This procedure, commonly known as procedure 1235, is open to certain non-governmental organizations. Individuals may have access to it only through an authorized non-governmental organization.

The sub-commission also receives petitions, called communications, about massive violations of rights through procedure 1503, which authorizes it to investigate. However, unlike procedure 1235, this process is almost entirely confidential. The sub-commission may refer the most serious cases to the Commission on Human Rights which may, in turn, decide to study the human rights situation and government practices in the state concerned.

A related organization specifically concerned with Aboriginal peoples' issues is the United Nations' Working Group on Indigenous Populations, created in 1982. It examines developments in the promotion and protection of the rights of indigenous peoples, paying particular attention to the evolution of standards for these rights, in order to express opinions on ways to improve relations between indigenous peoples and governments. The Working Group meets annually in Geneva. Although it hears presentations on Aboriginal rights, it may not examine complaints.

3. International Labour Organisation

The International Labour Organisation (ILO), established in 1919 and made a specialized U.N. agency in 1945, is a trilateral organization representing governments, employers, and employees.

The ILO has adopted a number of conventions on various labor issues: freedom of association, protection of women and children, protection against forced labor, and discrimination in the workplace. It also adopted two conventions about indigenous peoples: the Indigenous and Tribal Peoples

Convention, 1957 (ILO Convention no. 107), and its update, the Indigenous and Tribal Peoples Convention, 1989 (ILO Convention no. 169). However, neither convention provides for any petition mechanism, nor has Canada ratified either of the conventions.

Four procedures of representation and complaint are possible before the ILO, but the procedure established to allege a violation of the freedom of association is most commonly used, since it is the only procedure not requiring prior ratification of any of the ILO conventions dealing with freedom of association. Two organizations examine the complaints: the Committee on Freedom of Association, which receives complaints from workers' and employers' organizations, and the Fact Finding and Conciliation Commission on Freedom of Association, which deals with complaints referred to it by the governing body of the ILO or by the state concerned. The procedure may lead to recommendations to the state concerned.

4. United Nations Educational, Scientific, and Cultural Organization

The United Nations Educational, Scientific, and Cultural Organization (UNESCO) is dedicated to the promotion of research and teaching of human rights. It receives petitions alleging the violation of rights of education, science, culture, and information, including the right to share in the cultural and religious life of the community, as well as the right to express oneself in the language of the community.

UNESCO declares inadmissible any petition based on political motives. It can be petitioned by an individual or a group of individuals who consider themselves victims of the alleged violations, or even by an individual or a group with knowledge of the violation, if they identify themselves. A simple letter to the general manager of UNESCO stating whether the author has brought the case before the national courts suffices.

UNESCO is not a court; it acts as a mediator for the parties and can only make recommendations to the government concerned. The procedure resembles the 1503 procedure mentioned above, however, it is less confidential since the author of a petition is informed of its outcome. Canada is a member of UNESCO.

5. U.N. Human Rights Committee

Established according to the International Covenant on Civil and Political Rights, the U.N. Human Rights Committee, located in Geneva, receives individual petitions against states that have ratified the Optional Protocol to the International Covenant on Civil and Political Rights.

The committee has already examined several petitions submitted by members of the First Nations of Canada, such as *Lovelace*, and the petition presented by the Lubicon Band.

In 1977, the U.N. Human Rights Committee found that Canada's Indian Act violated the right of Indian women married to non-Indians, and the right of the children of these women, to take part in the life of their community — a right guaranteed under the International Covenant on Civil and Political Rights. (At the time, marriage to a non-Indian led to the loss of Indian status for Native women and their children.) The recommendations of the U.N. Human Rights Committee were instrumental in the subsequent amendment of the Indian Act.

In 1990, the committee concluded that historical inequalities, as well as the treatment of the Lubicon Band (including Alberta's expropriation of band lands in order to lease them to private oil and gas companies), violated the International Covenant on Civil and Political Rights.

Petitions must be about violations of individual rights. Thus, the right to self-determination, deemed a collective right, cannot be petitioned for before the committee. However, a group of persons allegedly victims of the same individual prejudice may petition the committee collectively. All remedies before national courts must be exhausted (see section **d.1.** below), and the petition must be signed by its author.

The petition is lodged by the victim, his or her representative, or a third person who must explain why he or she is acting on behalf of the victim and why he or she believes the victim is incapable of petitioning the committee but would approve of the initiative taken on his or her behalf. The petition must identify the victim, the state allegedly responsible for the violation, as well as the provisions of the International Covenant on Civil and Political Rights allegedly violated. It must also contain a detailed account of the violation. If the petition is declared admissible, it may lead to recommendations to the government concerned.

6. Inter-American Human Rights Commission

When Canada ratified the Charter of the Organization of American States (OAS), it became subject to the jurisdiction of the Inter-American Human Rights Commission, which oversees the application of the American Declaration of the Rights and Duties of Man in all the state members of the OAS. Unlike the Universal Declaration of Human Rights, which it is similar to in content, the American Declaration of the Rights and Duties of Man legally binds Canada. It is a unique international document that does not have to be ratified to become compulsory and, according to the Inter-American Court of Human Rights, it contains the human rights obligations of all members of the OAS. This means that any person, group of persons, or non-governmental organization recognized in an OAS member state that alleges the violation of a right guaranteed under the American Declaration may petition the Inter-American Human Rights Commission in Washington, D.C.

The procedure to petition the commission is simple. The complaint does not need to be lodged by the victim; it may be submitted by any person or non-governmental organization.

The petition must clearly identify the petitioner and, if possible, the victim, and must include a detailed account of the act or situation denounced. As in any international procedure, all the remedies available before the national courts must be exhausted and the petition must be lodged within six months of notification of the final judgment. If the petition is declared admissible, the commission will make recommendations to the government concerned.

An additional legal work protecting human rights is the American Convention on Human Rights and its supervisory institution, the Inter-American Court of Human Rights. Petitioners do not have direct access to the court. Instead, the Inter-American Commission forwards the complaint when states do not comply with the commission's recommendations. The court's judgment, having the same legal force as a Canadian court judgment, carries more weight than the recommendations of the commission. However, governments are not bound by the convention unless the state has ratified it. As well, the Inter-American Court's jurisdiction is not compulsory: states must recognize it. Canada has not yet done so, meaning petitions from Canada can go no further than the commission.

The only sanction Canada exposes itself to by not following the recommendations of the commission is the inclusion of its name, the facts of the case, and the conclusions of the commission in the commission's annual report to the OAS General Assembly. Nonetheless, the report's wide distribution publicizes the case and may help to put pressure on the government.

The Inter-American Commission also promotes respect for human rights in OAS member states through investigations of human rights situations in certain countries, on-site visits, and recommendations to the governments of member states. If it deems it necessary, the commission may also dedicate a special report to a particular situation or state.

In 1992, in collaboration with the Inter-American Indian Institute, the commission conducted a first round of consultations to prepare a draft Inter-American paper on the rights of indigenous peoples. The commission now awaits the comments of governments, Aboriginal organizations, and other interested institutions and experts. This draft may be obtained from the Inter-American Commission at the address below (see section **f.**).

d. HOW TO CHOOSE THE RIGHT FORUM

Since, as a rule, the same facts cannot be the basis of simultaneous actions before different international institutions, you must choose the appropriate forum. In the following pages, we have chosen to concentrate on the avenues that, in our opinion, are the most promising because they are based on legal works that bind Canada and protect a wide range of human rights. These are the U.N. Human Rights Committee and the Inter-American Commission. These two organizations also have the most public processes and are more likely to put pressure on the federal and provincial governments than the other forums.

1. Exhausting local remedies

The first step in choosing the right forum is to ensure that all remedies available under Canadian law have been exhausted. This means that the case has been tried by domestic courts and a final judgment rendered, leaving no possibility of appeal.

However, there are some exceptions to the rule. If, for example, the Supreme Court has already decided a similar issue and the outcome in the domestic courts can be anticipated, direct access to international forums is allowed. This was the situation in *Lovelace*, which was submitted directly to the U.N. Human Rights Committee in 1977 because the Supreme Court of Canada had already decided on a similar issue in 1974 and one could expect an identical response.

As well, in the Inter-American system, if the claimant lacks sufficient funds to avail herself or himself of domestic remedies and cannot obtain state assistance, the petition may be declared admissible, if the other conditions are met.

2. Identifying the appropriate legal work and institution

You must also identify the right that was infringed and the international works protecting it, to which Canada is a party. Canada is bound by a number of international legal works protecting human rights, but not all allow for individual petitions. As well, Canada must recognize the jurisdiction of an institution authorized to hear individual petitions in order for you to petition that institution. A complete list of treaties in force in Canada may be obtained from the Treaty Registrar in Ottawa (Tel: 613-995-3130).

Usually, your choice is between the U.N. Human Rights Committee and the Inter-American Commission. However, this also depends on who is petitioning and the time involved. As well, your choice of forum to petition may be influenced by previous decisions of the institutions. Both the Inter-American Commission and the U.N. Human Rights Committee have heard petitions raising Aboriginal issues.

The U.N. Human Rights Committee hears petitions alleging violations of the International Covenant on Civil and Political Rights. The Committee Against Torture, a section of the U.N. Centre for Human Rights, hears communications about violations of the Convention against Torture and other Cruel, Inhuman or Degrading Treatment or Punishment. The Inter-American Commission, for the moment, hears petitions from Canada alleging violations only of the American Declaration of the Rights and Duties of Man.

3. The petitioner

If the petitioner is the victim, he or she can choose either the Inter-American Commission or the U.N. Human Rights

Committee. However, if the petitioner is someone other than the victim, the choice is limited. Any person or group of persons, whatever their age and nationality, may petition the Inter-American Commission whether they are themselves victims of the violations or whether they act on behalf of the victim or on their own behalf, if they have sufficient knowledge of the violation.

On the other hand, the U.N. Human Rights Committee will accept a complaint only if the petitioner is the victim or the victim's representative who can establish close ties with the victim. Mere knowledge of the violation is insufficient.

Of course, the victim's freedom of choice must be protected. If the victim decides to petition the U.N. Human Rights Committee, for example, the Inter-American Commission would refuse to hear a petition based on the same facts presented by a third party or a non-governmental organization because, as a rule, it does not hear petitions that are already being examined by another governmental organization. In other words, it is only if the victim is unable or unwilling to petition the Inter-American Commission and is not petitioning another institution that a third party may do so.

4. The time frame

A petition to the Inter-American Human Rights Commission must be made within six months of the date of the final judgment from a national court unless internal remedies cannot be exhausted, in which case the petition must be addressed within a reasonable period of time.

On the other hand, the U.N. Human Rights Committee requires only that it be petitioned within a "reasonable" period of time. There is no specific time frame, nor is there a precise definition of what is a reasonable period of time. We can only assume that the time period may vary according to factors such as the severity of the violation alleged, the availability of information on the international complaint procedures, or the difficulties in taking advantage of the available procedures, according to the circumstances of each specific case.

When choosing which forum you will petition, keep in mind that it is not possible to petition the Inter-American Commission after the U.N. Human Rights Committee has finished examining the case and made recommendations that prove unsatisfactory, principally because of the commission's six-month deadline. However, the U.N. Human Rights Committee has, in the past, agreed to examine cases already examined by the Inter-American Commission.

e. THE CONSEQUENCES OF THE ACTION TAKEN

As we mentioned earlier, the petitions most likely to put pressure on the Canadian government are those to the U.N. Human Rights Committee or the Inter-American Commission. Whatever the choice, all the avenues suggested above — including the U.N. Human Rights Commission, UNESCO, and the ILO — may lead to recommendations, but not judgments. The situation will be different when Canada ratifies the American Convention on Human Rights and recognizes the rights of the Inter-American Court of Human Rights to hear individual cases. Then individuals will receive a judgment which has binding force on Canada. Until the convention is ratified, however, the binding nature of the outcome should not be a deciding factor in your choice of forum.

Canada has a number of international obligations holding the Canadian government accountable to the international community. Canada is also actively participating in the drafting of specific international legal works recognizing and protecting Aboriginal peoples and rights. If negotiations or litigation do not lead to a satisfactory resolution, full use should be made of international recourses. It is important that the voices of Aboriginal peoples be heard, both at the United Nations and the OAS. The United Nations, through the Working Group on Indigenous Populations, as well as through the working group set up by the U.N. Commission on Human Rights to study the U.N. Draft Declaration on the Rights of Indigenous Peoples, encourages Aboriginal participation. Although participation at the OAS is more difficult in the absence of an equivalent of the Working Group and because non-governmental organizations have no status, written briefs may be submitted to the Inter-American Human Rights Commission.

f.   ADDRESSES

You may contact the agencies described above at the following addresses:

Commission on Human Rights

U.N. Human Rights Committee
U.N. Centre for Human Rights
United Nations Office in
  Geneva
Palais des Nations
CH-1211 Geneva 10
Switzerland
Tel.: (41)(22) 917-1234
Fax: (41)(22) 917-0123

Committee Against Torture

Secretary of the Committee
  against Torture
U.N. Centre for Human Rights
United Nations Office in
  Geneva
Palais des Nations
CH-1211 Geneva 10
Switzerland
Tel.: (41)(22) 917-1234
FAX: (41)(22) 917-0099

International Labour Organisation

ILO Governing Body
Committee on Freedom of
  Association
4, route des Morillons
CH-1211 Geneva 22
Switzerland
Tel.: (41)(22) 798-7707
Fax: (41)(22) 798-8685

UNESCO

Director of International Legal
  Standards and Legal Affairs
UNESCO
7, Place de Fontenoy
F-75700 Paris
France
Tel.: (33)(1) 45-68-10-00
Fax: (33)(1) 47-83-40-24

Inter-American Human Rights Commission

c/o Organization of
  American States
1889 F Street NW, 8th Floor
Washington D.C. 20006
Tel.: (202) 458-6002
Fax: (202) 458-3992

APPENDIX
NAVIGATING THE BUREAUCRACY

by Carol E. Etkin

Finding your way through the maze of government departments, ministries, and agencies administering programs and
policies that apply to Aboriginal peoples is a daunting task.
There is also a growing group of national and regional Aboriginal organizations representing various constituencies,
from on-reserve treaty organizations to off-reserve Métis.

When navigating your way through the wide variety of
organizations and programs, it always helps to have a starting point. This list, however, is by no means exhaustive. Keep
in mind that as governments change and evolve, so do their
departments, ministries, and agencies. Aboriginal organizations may also change over time.

The appendix is divided into two sections. Section one is
a national overview of federal government departments and
Aboriginal organizations, beginning with a national snap-
shot of Indian and Northern Affairs (also referred to as
Department of Indian and Northern Affairs), the primary
national government department responsible for Aboriginal
programs and policies. Other federal government departments also have programs geared toward Aboriginal peoples
and are included in the second part of section one. Section
two gives an overview of the provinces and looks at the
Aboriginal, provincial, and territorial ministries and agencies
in each province.

a. THE NATIONAL PICTURE

1. The federal government

Indian and Northern Affairs Canada

Minister's Office

House of Commons
Ottawa, ON   K1A 0A6
613-992-6418

Terrasses de la Chaudière
10 Wellington Street
Hull, QC   K1A 0H4
819-997-0002

Comprehensive Claims Branch

Hull, QC
819-053-4170

Specific Claims Branch

General Enquiries
Hull, QC
819-994-2323

Treaty Land Entitlement
sub-office
Vancouver, BC
604-666-5296

Self-Government Negotiations Branch

Hull, QC
819-953-4318

*Native Employment, Employment
Equity and Executive Group Services*

Hull, QC
819-994-2555

Publication Services: Kiosk

Hull, QC
819-997-0380

*Technical Services —
Public Works and Government
Services Canada*

Hull, QC
819-997-9787

Lands and Trust Services

Hull, QC
819-953-5577

Indian Taxation Advisory Board

Hull, QC
819-997-8210

*Environment and Natural Resources
Directorate*

Hull, QC
819-953-5971

*Indian Registration and Band Lists
Directorate*

Hull, QC
819-953-2249

Indian Oil and Gas Canada (Calgary)

9911 Chula Boulevard, Suite
100
Tsuu T'ina (Sarcee), AB   T2W
6H6
403-292-5628

Northern Affairs

Hull, QC
819-953-3761

Personnel Enquiries

Hull, QC
819-994-7422

Indian and Northern Affairs Regional Offices

Atlantic

P.O. Box 160
40 Havelock Street
Amherst, NS   B4H 3Z3
902-661-6200

Québec

P.O. Box 51127
Postal Outlet G. Roy
320 St. Joseph Street East
Québec, QC   G1K 8Z7
418-648-3270

Ontario

25 St. Clair Avenue E., 5th Floor
Toronto, ON   M4T 1M2
416-973-5282

Manitoba

275 Portage Avenue, Room
1100
Winnipeg, MB   R3B 3A3
204-983-2475

Saskatchewan

2110 Hamilton Street, 2nd
Floor
Regina, SK   S4P 4K4
306-780-5945

Alberta

630 Canada Place
9700 Jasper Avenue
Edmonton, AB   T5J 4G2
403-495-2834

British Columbia

1550 Alberni Street, Suite 300
Vancouver, BC   V6G 3C5
Box 11576
604-666-5201

Federal Treaty Negotiation Office

650 West Georgia Street, Suite
2700
Vancouver, BC   V6B 4N8
604-775-7144

Northwest Territories

P.O. Box 1500
Yellowknife, NT   X1A 2R3
403-920-8111

Yukon

345-300 Main Street
Whitehorse, YT   Y1A 2B5
403-667-3303

Other federal government departments delivering programs for Aboriginal people

Canadian Heritage

General Enquiries
Jules Léger Building
Terrasses de la Chaudière
15 Eddy Street
Hull, QC   K1A 0M5
819-997-0055

Parks Canada
Jules Léger Building
25 Eddy Street, 4th Floor
Hull, QC   K1A 0M5
819-994-2657

Department of Finance

General Enquiries
L'Esplanade Laurier
140 O'Connor Street
Ottawa, ON   K1A 0G5
613-992-1573

Tax Policy Branch
as above
613-992-1646

Department of Justice

General Enquiries
Justice Building
Kent and Wellington Streets
Ottawa, ON   K1A 0H8
613-957-4222

Native Law Section
as above
613-941-2238

Native Courtworker
as above
613-941-2268

Aboriginal Justice Directorate
130 Albert Street, 8th Floor
Varette Building
Ottawa, ON   K1A 0Z6
613-957-4704

Environment Canada

General Enquiries
Terrasses de la Chaudière
10 Wellington Street
Hull, QC   K1A 0H3
819-997-2800

Environmental Protection Service
Place Vincent Massey
351 St. Joseph Boulevard
Hull, QC   K1A 0H3
819-997-1575

Canadian Wildlife Service
as above
819-997-1301

Federal Environmental Assessment Review Office
Fontaine Building
Hull, QC   K1A 0H3
613-997-1000

James Bay and Northern Québec Agreement
as above
613-953-3008

Enquiries Canada
(if what you need isn't on this list, try here!)

47 Clarence, 3rd Floor
Ottawa, ON   K1A 0S5
613-941-4823

Business Development Bank of Canada

General Enquiries

Head Office
800 Victoria Square
Montréal, QC H4Z 1L4
1-800-361-2126

Fisheries and Oceans

General Enquiries:
Headquarters
Native Affairs Directorate

200 Kent Street
Ottawa, ON K1A 0E6
as above
613-993-0999
613-990-0181

Health Canada

Headquarters

Tunney's Pasture
Ottawa, ON K1A 0K9
613-957-2991

Indian and Northern Health
Services Directorate

Jeanne Mance Building, 11th
Floor
Tunney's Pasture
Ottawa, ON K1A 0L3
613-952-7178

Human Resources Development Canada

General Enquiries
(and for information on the
Pathways to Success program.)

Place du Portage, Phase IV
140 Promenade du Portage
Hull, QC K1A 0J9
819-994-6313

Industry Canada

General Information
235 Queen Street
Ottawa, ON K1A 0H5
613-941-0222

Aboriginal Business Canada
as above, 7th Floor East
613-952-5067

Natural Resources Canada

Note: As of November 1995
the Minister of Natural
Resources is also the Federal
Interlocutor for non-status and
Métis peoples.

Minister's Office
Room 323, West Block
House of Commons
Ottawa, ON K1A 0A6
613-992-4525

Minister's Office at
Headquarters
580 Booth Street
Ottawa, ON K1A 0E4
613-996-2007

General Enquiries

as above
613-995-0947

Northern Pipeline Agency Canada

Office of the Commissioner

Lester B. Pearson Building
125 Sussex Drive
Ottawa, ON K1A 0G2
613-993-7466

Public Service Commission
of Canada

Employment Enquiries
L'Esplanade Laurier Building
300 Laurier Avenue W., West
Tower
Ottawa, ON   K1A 0M7
613-996-8436

Training and Development
Canada
as above
613-953-5400

Solicitor General

Aboriginal Policing Branch
Headquarters
1200 Vanier Parkway
Ottawa, ON   K1A 0R2
613-993-6221

Correctional Service Canada:
Aboriginal Programs
340 Laurier Avenue W.
Ottawa, ON   K1A 0P9
613-995-2555

2.   National organizations

These organizations have a national perspective. For example, some organizations represent Aboriginal constituencies, such as the Assembly of First Nations and the Congress of Aboriginal Peoples. Others, such as the Canadian Council for Aboriginal Business and Canadian Executive Services Overseas (CESO), provide services to Aboriginal peoples across Canada.

Assembly of First Nations

55 Murray Street, 5th Floor
Ottawa, ON   K1N 5M3
613-236-0673

Canadian Council for Aboriginal
Business

204 St. George Street, 2nd
Floor
Toronto, ON   M5R 2N5
416-961-8663

Canadian Executive Services
Overseas (CESO)
Aboriginal Services

323 Sharpel Street, 2nd Floor
Ottawa, ON   K1N 7Z2
613-236-7763

Congress of Aboriginal Peoples
(formerly the Native Council of
Canada)

64 Bank Street, 4th Floor
Ottawa, ON   K1P 5N2
613-238-3511

Cree Naskapi Commission

222 Queen Street, Suite 305
Ottawa, ON   K1P 6V5
613-234-4288

Inuit Circumpolar Conference

170 Laurier Avenue W.,
Suite 504
Ottawa, ON   K1P 5V5
613-563-2642

Inuit Tapirisat of Canada

170 Laurier Avenue West,
Suite 510
Ottawa, ON   K1P 5V5
613-238-8181

Métis National Council

130 Slater Street, Suite 650
Ottawa, ON   K1P 6E2
613-232-3216

*National Association of Friendship
Centres*

396 Cooper Street, Suite 204
Ottawa, ON   K2P 2H7
613-563-4844

*Native Women's Association of
Canada*

9 Melrose Avenue
Ottawa, ON   K1Y 1T8
613-722-3033

United Aboriginal League of Nations

6803-78 Avenue
Edmonton, AB   T6B 2J5
403-468-5604

3. Independent commissions

Various independent commissions operate in Canada. Some
have a temporary mandate while others are ongoing. Commissions are often fact-finding organizations and the scope and
breadth of their work varies according to the particular focus
of the commission. Some organizations, such as the Indian
Commission of Ontario and the treaty commissions, serve as
neutral organizations to facilitate negotiations between First
Nations and governments.

B.C. Treaty Commission

(Facilitation of negotiations)

203-1155 West Pender Street
Vancouver, BC   V6E 2P4

Canadian Polar Commission

(Social and scientific research)

Constitution Square
360 Albert Street, Suite 1710
Ottawa, ON   K1R 7X7

Commission of inquiry

Indian Claims Commission

427 Laurier Avenue West,
Suite 400
Enterprise Building
P.O. Box 1750, Station B
Ottawa, ON   K1P 1A2
613-943-2737

Indian Commission of Ontario

(Facilitation of negotiations)

14 Prince Arthur Street, 3rd
Floor
Toronto, ON   M5R 1A9
416-973-6390

Saskatchewan Office of the Treaty Commission

(Facilitation of negotiations)
119-4 Avenue S.
Saskatoon, SK   S7K 5X2
306-695-2335

b. FROM SEA TO SEA TO SEA: THE PROVINCES AND TERRITORIES

The lists below represent a sampling of major government and Aboriginal organizations for each province or territory. For a complete listing, contact the regional office of Indian and Northern Affairs Canada (see above), which will be happy to help you out.

1. Atlantic region

Nova Scotia

Minister Responsible for Aboriginal Affairs
P.O. Box 726
Halifax, NS   B3J 2T3
902-424-6600

Director, Aboriginal Affairs (Priority and Planning)
as above
902-424-6918

Union of Nova Scotia Indians
P.O. Box 961
Sydney, NS   B1P 6J4
902-539-4107

Aboriginal Organizations:
Confederacy of Mainland Micmacs
P.O. Box 1590
Truro, NS   B2N 5V3
902-422-9120

New Brunswick

Department of Intergovernmental and Aboriginal Affairs
P.O. Box 6000
Fredericton, NB   E3B 5H1
506-453-2583

Director Aboriginal Affairs
as above
506-453-2671

Aboriginal Organizations:
Union of New Brunswick Indians
385 Wilsey Road
Compartment 44
Fredericton, NB   E3B 5N6
506-458-9444

Minister Responsible for
Native Affairs
P.O. Box 2000
Charlottetown, PEI   C1A 7N8
902-368-5290

Assistant Secretary to Cabinet
Native Policy
Province of Newfoundland
and Labrador
P.O.Box 8700
St. John's, NF   A1B 4J6
709-729-6062

2. Québec

Province du Québec

Secrétariat aux Affaires
Autochtones
875, Grande Allée Est
Québec, QC   G1R 4Y8
418-643-3166

Aboriginal Organizations:

Alliance Autochtone Du
Québec
21, rue Rodeur
Hull, QC   J8Y 2P6
819-770-7763

Association Des Métis et
Indiens Hors-Réserves
Du Québec
713, boulevard Saint-Joseph
Case postale 126
Roberval, QC   G8H 2L3
418-275-0198

Atikamekw Sepe-Conseil de
la Nation Atikamekw
317, rue Saint-Joseph
Case postale 848
La Tuque, QC   G9X 3P6
819-523-6153

Grand Council of the Crees of
Québec
1, Place Ville-Marie, Pièce
3438
Montréal, QC   H3B 3N9
514-861-5837
24 Bays Water Avenue
Ottawa, ON   K1Y 2E4
613-761-1655

Secretariat of the Assembly of
the First Nations of Québec
and Labrador
430 Koska
Village-Des-Hurons
Wendake, QC   G0A 4V0
418-842-5020

3. Ontario

As of July 1996, the province of Ontario was in the midst of a substantial restructuring of its bureaucracy. As some programs may be scheduled for elimination or downsizing, some of this information may not be valid at the time of publication.

Province of Ontario

Ministry of Agriculture, Food
& Rural Areas
801 Bay Street, 4th Floor
Toronto, ON   M7A 1B3
416-325-1149

Ministry of the Attorney
General
720 Bay Street
Toronto, ON   M5G 2K1
416-326-4687
(Aboriginal Law and Justice
Issue)

Ontario Native Affairs
Secretariat
Headquarters:
595 Bay Street, Suite 1009
Toronto, ON   M5G 2C2
416-326-2375
Thunder Bay Office
180 Park Avenue, Suite 120
Thunder Bay, ON   P7B 5G5
807-343-7545

Ministry of Citizenship,
Culture and Recreation
*Policy Advisor, Land Claims
Public Education*
77 Bloor Street West
Toronto, ON   M7A 2R9
416-325-6154

Land Negotiations
Ontario Government Building
199 Larch Street, 4th Floor
Sudbury, ON   P3E 5P9
705-688-3108
Heritage, Archaeology
10 Adelaide Street E., 1st Floor
Toronto, ON   M5C 1J5
416-314-4910

Ministry of Community and
Social Services
Aboriginal Social Services
Hepburn Block, 4th Floor
80 Grosvenor Street
Toronto, ON   M7A 1C9
416-327-4958

Ministry of Consumer and
Commercial Relations
250 Yonge Street
Toronto, ON   M5B 2N5
416-326-0272

Ministry of Economic
Development, Trade and
Tourism
Aboriginal Issues
Hearst Block
900 Bay Street
Toronto, ON   M7A 2E1
416-325-6485

Ministry of Education and Training:
Native Education Issues
900 Bay Street
Toronto, ON   M7A 1L2
416-325-2929

Ministry of Environment and Energy
Aboriginal Environmental Issues
135 St. Clair Avenue West, 8th Floor
Toronto, ON   M4V 1P5
416-323-4369

Ministry of Health
Aboriginal Health Office
5700 Yonge Street, Mezzanine Level
North York, ON   M2M 4K5
416-314-5515

Ministry of Municipal Affairs and Housing
Municipal Issues:
Self-Government, Land Claims
777 Bay Street, 13th Floor
Toronto, ON   M5G 2E5
416-585-6236

Ministry of Natural Resources, Northern
Development and Mines
Headquarters, Aboriginal Natural Resource Issues
P.O. Box 7000
380 Armour Road
Times Square
Peterborough, ON   K9J 8M5
705-740-1409

Aboriginal Policy Office
Whitney Block
99 Wellesley Street
Toronto, ON   M7A 1W3
416-314-1188
(For regional offices, check your
local telephone listings.)

Aboriginal Organizations

Association of Iroquois and Allied Indians
387 Princess Avenue
London, ON   N6B 2A7
519-434-2761

Chiefs of Ontario
22 College Street, 2nd Floor
Toronto, ON   M5G 1K2
416-972-0212

Grand Council Treaty No. 3
P.O. Box 1720
Kenora, ON   P9N 3X7
807-548-4214

Nishnawbe-Aski Nation
P.O. Box 755, Station F
Fort William Reserve
R.R.4 Mission Road
Thunder Bay, ON   P7C 4W6
807-623-8228

Union of Ontario Indians
P.O. Box 711
North Bay, ON   P1B 8J8
705-497-9127

4. Manitoba

Manitoba published a resource manual for the northern part of the province in 1992 entitled *Ota-Miska*. An updated, 1996 edition of this invaluable resource has recently been published by Manitoba's Industry, Trade and Tourism Ministry.

Province of Manitoba

Citizen's Enquiry Service
Manitoba Culture, Heritage and Recreation

511-401 York Avenue
Winnipeg, MB   R3C 0P8
1-800-282-8060

Department of Industry, Trade and Tourism

155 Carlton Street, 5th Floor
Winnipeg, MB   R3C 3Y8
204-945-7738

Ministry of Northern Affairs

250-500 Portage Avenue
Winnipeg, MB   R3C 3X1
204-945-8337

Aboriginal Organizations:

First Nations Confederacy
203-286 Smith Street
Winnipeg, MB   R3C 1K4
204-944-8245

Assembly of Manitoba Chiefs
400-286 Smith Street
Winnipeg, MB   R3C 1K4
204-956-0610

Manitoba Keewatinowi Okimakanak
23 Station Road
Thompson, MB   R8N 0N6
1-800-442-0488

Manitoba Métis Federation Inc.
408 McGregor Street
Winnipeg, MB   R4W 4X5
204-586-8474

5. Saskatchewan

Province of Saskatchewan
(Ministries with responsibility for First Nations)

Social Services
2240 Albert Street
Regina, SK   S4P 3V7
306-787-3700

Justice
1874 Scarth Street
Regina, SK   S4P 3V7
306-787-8971

Saskatchewan Indian and Métis Affairs (SIMAS)
2151 Scarth Street
Regina, SK   S4P 3V7
306-787-6250

Saskatchewan Environment and Resource Management
3211 Albert Street
Regina, SK   S4P 3V7
306-787-2700

Education
2220 College Street
Regina, SK   S4P 3V7
306-787-1885

Intergovernmental Affairs
1919 Saskatchewan Drive, 11th
Floor
Regina, SK   S4P 3V7
306-787-6355

Aboriginal Organizations:

Federation of Saskatchewan
Indian Nations (FSIN)

107 Hodsman Road
Regina, SK   S4N 5W5
306-721-2822

6. Alberta

Province of Alberta

Dept. of Family & Social
Services
Aboriginal Affairs
Commerce Place, 13th Floor
10155-102 Street
Edmonton, AB   T5J 4L4
403-422-9526

Aboriginal Justice Initiatives
Alberta Justice
J.E. Brownlee Building
10365-97 Street, 10th Floor
Edmonton, AB   T5J 3W7
403-422-2779

Native Employment
Initiatives
Human Resource Services
Alberta Justice
9833-109 Street, 1st Floor
Edmonton, AB   T5K 2E8
403-427-4978

Native Liaison Officer
Alberta Fish and Wildlife
Petroleum Plaza N
9945-108 Street, Main Floor
Edmonton, AB   T5K 2G6
403-297-6423

Aboriginal Organizations:

Indian Association of Alberta
P.O. Box 159
Hobbema, AB   T0C 1N0
403-421-4926

Métis Nation of Alberta
Association
13140 St. Albert Trail
Edmonton, AB   T5L 4R8
1-800-252-7553

Métis Settlements General
Council
Princeton Place
10339-124 Street, Suite 649
Edmonton, AB   T5N 3W1
403-488-6500

Confederacy of Treaty 6 First
Nations
10025-106 Street, Suite 601
Edmonton, AB   T5J 0B3
403-944-0334

Grand Council of Treaty 8
First Nations
Scotia Place Tower 1
2300-10060 Jasper Avenue
Edmonton, AB   T5J 3R8
403-424-8504

Treaty 7 Tribal Council
310-6940 Fisher Road SE
Calgary, AB   T2H 0W3
403-258-1775

7. British Columbia

With one of the country's largest and most diverse Aboriginal populations, British Columbia boasts a wide variety of government and Aboriginal organizations. The British Columbia government's Ministry of Aboriginal Affairs publishes two directories about Aboriginal people, the *Directory to B.C. Programs and Services for Aboriginal People* and the *Guide to Aboriginal Organizations and Services in British Columbia*. You may obtain either from the Ministry of Aboriginal Affairs (see below).

Province of British Columbia

Ministry of Aboriginal Affairs
Treaty Negotiation Division
908 Pandora Avenue
2nd Floor
Victoria, BC   V8V 1X4
250-356-9516

Ministry of Agriculture,
Fisheries and Food
First Nations Liaison Officer —
Fisheries
2500 Cliffe Avenue
Courtenay, BC   V9N 5M6
250-334-1459

Agriculture Policy Analyst
808 Douglas Street
Victoria, BC   V8W 2Z7
250-356-8177

Ministry of Attorney General
Corrections Branch
910 Government Street, 4th
Floor
Victoria, BC   V8V 1X4
250-387-5059

Aboriginal Justice Unit
Policy Planning, Legislation
and Communications Branch
910 Government Street, 4th
Floor
Victoria, BC   V8V 1X4
250-953-3645

Ministry of Education
Aboriginal Education Branch
634 Humboldt Street
Victoria, BC   V8V 2M4
250-387-1544

Ministry of Energy, Mines and Petroleum Resources

Aboriginal Affairs and Special Projects
1810 Blanshard Street, 4th Floor
Victoria, BC   V8V 1X4
250-952-0526

B.C. Hydro
Corporate and Aboriginal Affairs
333 Dunsmuir Street, 18th Floor
Burnaby, BC   V3N 4X8
604-623-3863

Ministry of Environment, Lands and Parks, Multiculturalism and Human Rights
Aboriginal Affairs Branch
B.C. Environment
737 Courtney Street, 4th Floor
Victoria, BC   V8V 1X4
250-387-9730

Ministry of Forests
Interim Measures and Aboriginal Programs
610 Johnson Street, 3rd Floor
Victoria, BC   V8V 3E7
250-356-0544

Ministry of Health and Ministry Responsible for Seniors
Provincial Coordinator
B.C. Aboriginal Health Council
c/o B.C. Association of Indian Friendship Centres
3-2475 Mount Newton Cross Road
Saanichton, BC   V0S 1M0
250-652-0210

Ministry of Skills, Training and Labour
College and Aboriginal Programs
838 Fort Street, 3rd Floor
Victoria, BC   V8V 1X4
250-387-6184

Ministry of Small Business, Tourism and Culture
Senior Advisor
Aboriginal Initiatives
1405 Douglas Street, 4th Floor
Victoria, BC   V8W 3C1
250-356-2035

Ministry of Social Services
Aboriginal Deputy Superintendent
Aboriginal Services
614 Humboldt Street
Victoria, BC   V8V 1X4
250-356-5378

Ministry of Transportation and Highways
Aboriginal Relations Branch
940 Blanshard Street, Plaza Level
Victoria, BC   V8W 3E6
250-387-5925

Aboriginal Organizations

Aboriginal Council of British Columbia
6822 Salish Drive
Vancouver, BC   V6N 2C6
604-264-1114

First Nations Summit
Plaza Towers
208-1999 Marine Drive
North Vancouver, BC   V7P 3J3
604-990-9939

Union of B.C. Chiefs
73 Water Street, 7th Floor
Vancouver, BC   V6B 1A1
604-684-0231

United Native Nations
736 Granville Street, 8th Floor
Vancouver, BC   V6Z 1G3
604-688-1821

8. North of 60: Yukon and Northwest Territories

The northern territories cover the largest land mass of any jurisdiction within Canada, spanning the continent from the Atlantic to the Pacific oceans and bordering on the Arctic Sea. The small northern population has a unique mix of Aboriginal people from the Inuit in the far north to the Dene in the southwest. The federal government has direct responsibility for the operation of the territorial governments. The regional offices of Indian and Northern Affairs Canada in Yellowknife and Whitehorse would be two main starting points for enquiries. The following list is of relevant territorial government offices and Aboriginal organizations that may be of assistance.

Government of the Northwest Territories

Minister of Economic Development and Tourism
Minister of Energy Mines and Petroleum Resources
P.O. Box 1320
Yellowknife, NT   X1A 2L9
403-669-2311

Minister of Justice
Minister of Renewable Resources
as above
403-669-2366

Minister Responsible for Aboriginal Affairs
as above
403-669-2333

General Enquiries
as above
403-873-0169

Aboriginal Organizations

Gwich'in Tribal Council
P.O. Box 86
Fort McPherson, NT   X0E 0J0
403-952-2330

Dogrib Treaty 11 Council
P.O. Box 1106
Yellowknife, NT   X1A 2N8
403-873-6680

NWT Treaty 8 Tribal Council
Fort Resolution, NT   X0E 0M0
403-394-3313

Deh Cho First Nations
P.O. Box 89
Fort Simpson, NT   X0E 0N0
403-695-2355

Sahtu Dene Council
P.O. Box 155
Deline, NT X0E 0G0
403-589-4719

Baffin Regional Inuit Assoc.
Box 219
Iqaluit, NT X0A 0H0
819-979-5391

Inuit Tapirisat of Canada
see above for national
organizations

Nunavut Tunngavik Inc.
(also offices in Ottawa, Rankin
Inlet and Cambridge Bay)
Box 638
Iqaluit, NT X0Z 0H0
819-979-3232

Nunavut Implementation
Commission
Box 1109
Iqaluit, NT X0A 0H0
819-979-4199

Yukon Government

Land Claims Secretariat
204 Main Street, 2nd Floor
Whitehorse, YT Y1A 2B2
403-668-4936

Minister of Land Claims
Yukon Government
Administration Building
2071 Second Avenue
Box 2703
Whitehorse, YT Y1A 2C6
403-667-5603

Minister of Justice
as above
403-667-5716

Minister of Economic
Development and
Minister of Renewable
Resources
as above
403-667-5376

General Enquiry
as above
403-667-5811
or 403-667-5812

Aboriginal Organizations
(contact the CYFN for information
on the 14 Yukon First Nations)

Council of Yukon First
Nations (CYFN)
11 Nisutlin Drive
Whitehorse, YT Y1A 3S4
403-667-7631

CONTRIBUTORS

Stephen Aronson is a lawyer and mediator in Ottawa who devotes his legal practice full time to Aboriginal legal issues.

Kevin Bell, a Mohawk from Kahnawake, was called to the Ontario bar in 1988. He practised commercial litigation in Toronto before joining the Ontario Native Affairs Secretariat. Mr. Bell offers legal advice to the Secretariat on issues of land claims and self-government.

Michael Coyle, co-editor of this book, is director of land claims at the Indian Commission of Ontario. Formerly the chair of the Canadian Bar Association (Ontario) Aboriginal Section, he has facilitated land claims negotiations at the Commission for seven years, including the first tripartite claim settlement in Ontario.

Carol Etkin is Senior Intergovernmental Relations Officer at Indian and Northern Affairs Canada, where she specializes in negotiations and intergovernmental relations. She earned a Master's Degree in Environmental Studies specializing in Native Canadian Community-Based Development in 1989.

Jerry Fontaine, an Ojibwa, has served four terms as chief of the Sagkeeng First Nation in Manitoba. He has been active in raising environmental concerns of the Sagkeeng through both the Winnipeg River Task Force and Winnipeg River Futures Round Table, of which he is chairperson.

Paul Frits is a lawyer with the Toronto firm of Morris/Rose/Ledgett. He currently practises Aboriginal law and business law, and has represented First Peoples across Canada in a wide variety of areas including gaming, energy, tourism, fisheries, government administration, and intergovernmental relations. He is the past chair of the Aboriginal Law Section of the Canadian Bar Association (Ontario).

Joseph Gilbert has served three elected terms on the Council of Three Fires and most recently was chief of the Walpole Island First Nation. Mr. Gilbert is an ordained minister, serving First Nations churches in Canada and the United States since 1964.

Philip Goulais is the commissioner of the Indian Commission of Ontario and was chief of the Nipissing First Nation for 14 years.

Derek T. Ground is a lawyer practising Aboriginal law in Toronto. His publications include "An Act of Self Determination" (The Native Canadian Centre of Toronto) and with William B. Henderson, "Survey of Aboriginal Claims" (Ottawa Law Review Vol. 26, No. 1, 1994). Mr. Ground acknowledges the support and resources of the Native Canadian Centre of Toronto.

Carol Hilling is counsel for the firm of Hutchins, Soroka & Dionne in Montréal. She is also a lecturer in pubic international law at the law faculty of the University of Montréal.

Peter W. Hutchins is the senior partner in the law firm of Hutchins, Soroka & Dionne in Montréal and a senior partner in the law firm of Hutchins, Soroka, Grant & Peterson in Vancouver, B.C. He is also a lecturer in Aboriginal law at McGill University's law faculty.

Ian Jackson is a director of Chreod Ltd., an Ottawa-based firm of consultants, and has carried out a number of environmental audits of First Nations.

Dean Jacobs, Ojibwa/Potawatomi, is executive director of Nin.Da.Waab.Jig., the Walpole Island Heritage Centre which serves as the research department of the Walpole Island First Nation. Mr. Jacobs sits on the editorial advisory board for Syracuse University Press and is also a member of the editorial advisory committee for the *Quarterly Journal of the Ontario Historical Society*.

Elizabeth Jordan, a third-year law student at the University of Toronto Law School, is a Mohawk from the Six Nations Reserve. She also works with the Aboriginal Banking Department of the Bank of Montreal in Toronto.

Manny Jules has been Chief of the Kamloops Indian Band since 1984. He is past co-chair of the National Chiefs Committee on Claims and of the AFN/Canada Joint Working Group on Specific Claims Policy.

Harry S. LaForme is a member of the Mississaugas of New Credit First Nation. In 1996, he was appointed as a judge to the Ontario Court, General Division. Formerly, Justice LaForme was Commissioner of both the Claims Commission and the Indian Commission of Ontario.

Tony Mandamin is an Anishnawbe member of Wikwemikong First Nation of Manitoulin Island, Ontario, now residing in Edmonton, Alberta. A lawyer since 1983, he has a general law practice and deals with a wide range of Aboriginal and treaty issues.

Hans Matthews, from the Chippewas of Rama First Nation, is president of the Canadian Aboriginal Minerals Association.

Anne B. McAllister is a lawyer with the Department of Justice, Government of Canada.

J. Stephen O'Neill is a partner in the Sudbury firm Miller, Maki and practises Aboriginal law exclusively. He has successfully negotiated and resolved a number of land claim settlements, including the Manitoulin Island Land Claim Settlement, Ontario's first settlement, and the Point Grondine Land Claim Settlement, one of the two largest claim settlements in Ontario history.

Stephen Smart, co-editor of this book, practices litigation as a partner at Osler, Hoskin & Harcourt, in Toronto. He is a past chairperson of the Aboriginal Law Section of the Canadian Bar Association (Ontario).

Roger Townshend is an associate lawyer at Morris/Rose/Ledgett, Toronto, Ontario. For a more technical treatment of the same issues discussed in this chapter, see his paper entitled "Some Highlights of the Interaction of Aboriginal Law and Municipal Law," given to a joint program of the Municipal Law and Aboriginal Law Sections of the Canadian Bar Association in Toronto on April 26, 1995.

Donald Wakefield is a partner with the law firm of Osler, Hoskin & Harcourt in Toronto, where he practises mining and resource development law.

INDEX

295

298

and Oka 81; and resource development 192, 195, 202-206; and self-government 125, 175; and the media 76; and the public 75-78; and treaties 9-10; assessing compensation for 66-67; background to 6; comprehensive claims 61-62, 63, 65, 67-68, 203-206, 239; costs 57-58; criteria 61-64; definition 54; effects on non-Aboriginals 240; extinguishment of rights 68; federal policy 39-40, 65, 69; imbalance of power 70-72; impasses 69-70; in eastern Canada 51; in the courts 57, 71; land compensation 67-68, 77; made illegal 1927-1951 69, 131; mediators 72-75; negotiation process 60-68, 72-78; negotiations vs. standoffs 82-82; specific claims 62-63, 65, 66, 239; statue of limitations 64. *See also under specific province or territory*

Land Titles Act 42

Leonard v. R. in the Right of British Columbia 161

loan circles 216

Long Lake No. 58 Indian Reserve 81

lotteries. *See* gaming

Lovelace 265, 268

Lubicon Band 265

Lysyk, Kenneth x

M

Métis 118, 124-125, 204-205, 235, 238, 246-247, 248, 252, 277; and the environment 168; hunting rights 29; organizations 122, 273, 279, 281, 284-285

Métis National Council 122

Mabo v. Queensland 261

Macdonald, John A. 118, 235

Mackenzie Valley pipeline 41

Makivik Corporation 207-208

Maliseet Indians 85

Mandamin, Tony 154

Manitoba 29, 235; Aboriginal issues 178; organizations 284; resource conflicts 175-181; self-government examples 135; treaties 26, 27-28, 36, 235

Manitoba Hydro 176, 179, 181

Manitoba Model Forest 181

Manitoulin Island treaty 22

Maritimes: treaties 35

marriage: traditional 15, 17-18

Marshall, Chief Justice 16, 257, 261

Matsqui Indian Band 102

Matsqui Indian Band v. Canadian Pacific Ltd. 102

McLachlin, Justice 95

McLeod Lake Indian Band 94-96

Meech Lake Accord 122

Mi'kmaq 20-21, 26, 82, 114, 260

Mickenberg, Neil H. x

Migratory Birds Convention Act 27-28

mining industry 194-208; and land claims 195. *See also* resource industry

Mississauga Northern Boundary Claim 58

Model Self-Government Agreement 248-249

Mohawk Bands of Kahmawake et al. v. Glenbow-Alberta Institute 91

Mohawks 79-80, 91, 122

Mulroney, Brian 80, 122

municipalities: and land title 149-150; and relationship with First Nations 138-153; bylaws' application to reservations 141-144; boundary issues 144-145; jurisdiction issues 144-148; powers 138-139

Muscowpetung Indian Band 106

Musqueam First Nation 19, 44-48, 85

N

Nacho Nyak Dun 241

Naskapi 42, 204

self-government 12-13, 97-98, 100-101, 107, 147-148, 162, 204, 236, 239, 248-255; Aboriginal perspective of 127-137; and economic self-sufficiency 210-211; and environmental issues 173, 188-189, 191; and gaming 220, 224, 228-230, 232-233; and international law 114-115, 139, 257; and land claims 240, 244-245, 247; and off-reserve members 249; and resource issues 173; and taxation 165; and the Constitution 249; and treaties 116; as racist system 136; different models of 125-126, 132-133; economic spin-offs from 134; effect on non-Aboriginal communities 133-134; examples of 135-136; foundation for xii; future of 136-137; history of 112-117; in practice 130; in southern Canada vs. northern 254, 255; legal basis for 112-126, 129; Nunavut 251-252; off reserve 124-125; recognized in Charlottetown Accord 123; termination of 121. *See also* Indian Act; taxation

Shaughnessy Golf Club 44

Shawanaga First Nation 86-87, 229

Shuswap 29

Sioui, Conrad 84-85

Sissons, Judge 18

Six Nations of the Grand River 59-60

Six Nations reserve 118

Skerryvore Ratepayers Association 86-87, 146-147

sovereignty. *See* self-government

Specific Claims Policy 55, 63-64; criteria 66

Squamish Indian Band 104

St. Catharine's Milling and Lumber Company v. The Queen x, 37; series of cases 149-150

Statement of Political Relationship 145, 148

Stoney Point First Nation 82

T

taxation 143, 154-167, 212-213: aboriginal tax exemption 155-158; drafting First Nation taxation bylaws 165-167; power to tax on reserve 102, 160-164

Teme-Augama First Nation 51, 90-91

temporary injunctions 89-96

Teslin Tlingit 241

tourism 192

"traditional lands" 145-146, 194

treaties 6-11, 116: Aboriginal treaties 19-20; Aboriginal view of 6, 11, 35, 114-115; and international law 114-115, 258-262; and land claims 61-62, 239; and land surrender 22, 24-25, 34, 37; and the Queen 128; as nation-to-nation agreements 116, 128-129, 140, 261-262; European treaties 20; examples of 24; extent of 50; in prairie provinces 26-28; international treaties 269; map of 23; modern treaties 10, 25, 41; peace and friendship treaties 20-22, 260; powers flowing from 139-140; purposes of 20-25, 36; under Royal Proclamation 22-24, 34; written vs. oral 22, 24, 28. *See also* numbered treaties; Royal Proclamation (1763); *and specific treaties by name*

Treaty of 1752 35

treaty rights 9-11, 14-31: and federal legislation 27-28; and law 20-22, 24, 25-31; origin of 14; and provincial legislation 25-28. *See also* treaties

Trudeau, Pierre Elliott viii, xi, 41

Tungavik Federation of Nunavut 204

U

unemployment 9, 135, 210

Union of B.C. Indian Chiefs 41

United Nations 262-264, 271; Commission on Human Rights 262-263, 272; Draft Declaration on the Rights of Indigenous Peoples 258; Educational, Scientific, and Cultural Organization (UNESCO) 264-265, 271, 272; Human Rights Committee 265-266, 268-271; Working Group on Indigenous Populations 263, 271

V

voting rights 69
Vuntut Gwichin 243

W

Walpole Island First Nation 170-175, 181-187
Walpole Island Heritage Centre 182
Western Arctic Agreement 155
Wet'suwet'en people 48-50, 261
White Bear reserve 230
White Paper (1969) viii, xii, 40-41, 119, 127
Whiteshell Laboratories 176, 181
Whittington, Michael 169

Williams 156
Williams treaties 39
Winnipeg River Task Force Report 176
women: loss of Indian status 265
Worcester v. State of Georgia 17, 261

Y

Yesno, Johnny ix
Yukon Agreement 25
Yukon Territory 25; Aboriginal organizations 289; creation of 235; demographics 237; government departments 288-289; government of 237; land claims 61, 237, 240, 241-244; land claims (map) 242-243; land claims settlements 203, 241; provincial status 255-256; self-government 237, 248-249